Introduction to Management of
Reverse Logistics
and Closed Loop
Supply Chain
Processes

The St. Lucie Series on Resource Management

Titles in the Series

Applying Manufacturing Execution Systems
by Michael McClellan

Back to Basics:
Your Guide to Manufacturing Excellence
by Steven A. Melnyk and
R.T. "Chris" Christensen

Basics of Supply Chain Management
by Lawrence D. Fredendall and Ed Hill

Collaborative Manufacturing:
Using Real-Time Information to Support
the Supply Chain
by Michael McClellan

Enterprise Resources Planning and Beyond:
Integrating Your Entire Organization
by Gary A. Langenwalter

ERP: Tools, Techniques, and Applications
for Integrating the Supply Chain
by Carol A. Ptak with Eli Schragenheim

Handbook of Supply Chain Management
by Jim Ayers

Integral Logistics Management:
Planning and Control of Comprehensive
Supply Chains, Second Edition
by Paul Schönsleben

Integrated Learning for ERP Success:
A Learning Requirements
Planning Approach
by Karl M. Kapp, with William F. Latham and
Hester N. Ford-Latham

Introduction to e-Supply Chain
Management: Engaging Technology to Build
Market-Winning Business Partnerships
by David C. Ross

Inventory Classification Innovation:
Paving the Way for Electronic Commerce
and Vendor Managed Inventory
by Russell G. Broeckelmann

Lean Manufacturing: Tools, Techniques,
and How To Use Them
by William M. Feld

Lean Performance ERP Project
Management: Implementing the Virtual
Supply Chain
by Brian J. Carroll

Macrologistics Management:
A Catalyst for Organizational Change
by Martin Stein and Frank Voehl

Restructuring the Manufacturing Process:
Applying the Matrix Method
by Gideon Halevi

Supply Chain Management:
The Basics and Beyond
by William C. Copacino

The Supply Chain Manager's
Problem-Solver: Maximizing the Value of
Collaberation and Technology
by Charles C. Poirier

Supply Chain Networks and Business
Process Orientation: Advanced Strategies
and Best Practices
by Kevin P. McCormack and William C. Johnson

Introduction to Management of
Reverse Logistics and Closed Loop Supply Chain Processes

Donald F. Blumberg

CRC PRESS

Boca Raton London New York Washington, D.C.

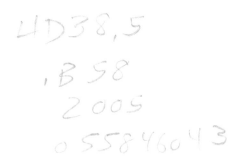

Library of Congress Cataloging-in-Publication Data

Blumberg, Donald F.
    Introduction to management of reverse logistics and closed loop supply chain processes / Donald F. Blumberg.
        p. cm.
    Includes index.
    ISBN 1-57444-360-7 (alk. paper)
    1. Business logistics. I. Title.

HD38.5.B58 2004
658.5'6—dc22   2004055107
                                                                              CIP

Visit the CRC Press Web site at www.crcpress.com

© 2005 by CRC Press

No claim to original U.S. Government works
International Standard Book Number 1-57444-360-7
Library of Congress Card Number 2004055107
Printed in the United States of America 1 2 3 4 5 6 7 8 9 0
Printed on acid-free paper

FOREWORD

The management of reverse logistics and closed loop supply chains is by far one of the most critical aspects of any business involved in the manufacture, distribution, and service and support of products of any type. The resources in terms of people, technology and processes to support these functions are enormous. It is obvious that the proliferation of manufactured goods will only magnify the amount of time, effort, and capital required to support the activities associated with reverse logistics and closed loop supply chains. Furthermore, in order to remain responsive to customer needs and behave as good global citizens, business enterprises, whether they are manufacturers, retailers, or independent service organizations, must become familiar and proficient in the processes and functions necessary to support a product from the moment it enters the distribution channel until it is disposed of at the end of its life.

The need to understand the reverse logistics and closed loop supply chain has become increasingly important in this age of commerce that we live in, defined in terms of shorter and shorter product lifecycles, liberal product return policies, rapid response times, and 24/7 customer service has placed a greater emphasis on the management of the return, refurbishment, and restocking of finished goods, including whole units, product subassemblies, and spare parts. In some sectors, particularly any industries concerned with the distribution and support of electro-mechanical, electrical, or electronic equipment, this responsibility extends beyond the distribution channel to the actual replacement of products on the customer premise. New governmental regulations and "green laws," with respect to the return and disposal of electronic and other hazardous waste materials, is also forcing managers and executives responsible for logistics and supply chain operations to take a closer look at the reverse logistics process.

Clearly, knowledge of the basic fundamentals of managing the reverse logistics and closed loop supply chain is essential to any manager or executive involved in a business enterprise that is engaged in this function. Knowledge of the basic fundamentals is a key to managing these functions on an efficient and productive basis and responding to structural changes in the industry brought about through economic, technological, market, and government regulatory trends. Equipped with the basic fundamentals, a manager can deploy more advanced concepts which will further help the optimization of reverse logistics and closed loop supply chain functions and processes leading to increased levels of productivity and efficiency for the business enterprise and increased levels of service quality for the consumer.

This book, written by the late Donald F. Blumberg, is designed to deal with both basic and advanced concepts involved in managing reverse logistics and closed loop supply chains. It is based on over 35 years of practical industry experience in the development and implementation of productive and efficient reverse logistics and closed loop supply chains on behalf of client organizations in a wide array of industries and markets. Don's clients included organizations representative of both industry and government, such as the U.S. Department of Defense, Square D, Siemens, IBM, General Electric, Albertsons, Eastman Kodak, AT & T, and Xerox.

Don was not only my father, friend, colleague and mentor, but a true expert and guru on this subject. He was also a pioneer in his field. The concepts and data contained in this book are simply more than a representation of the functions and processes employed by leading organizations. They are the result of rigorous research and analysis of industry trends and best practices, a life long dedication to the study of this topic and a never ending commitment to advance the body of knowledge on this subject.

Donald F. Blumberg died of heart failure on May 29, 2004. He had completed writing the final draft of this book a few months before he passed away and before it went into publication. This book is essentially one of his greatest and final accomplishments.

Michael R. Blumberg
President, D.F. Blumberg Associates, Inc.

ACKNOWLEDGMENTS

The concept and analytical framework, technology, and processes for managing closed loop supply chain and reverse logistics service in industrial, commercial, and consumer businesses and government, civilian, and military operations, as outlined in this book, is a result of more than 40 years of management consulting experience in the service field. I would like to credit the staff of D.F. Blumberg Associates, Inc., particularly Michael Blumberg, its chief operating officer (and my son), who helped in developing many of the concepts and directed much of the market research studies supporting the evaluations. Other members of the D.F. Blumberg & Associates staff, including Robert Snyder, Tony Mercogliano, and Gaby Shaw, all contributed to the research and development efforts. I also owe an extreme debt of gratitude to the many service executives with whom I have worked, including Tom Faughnan, Chief Executive Officer of TSI/Kodak; Russ Spencer, Senior Vice President of Service at Agfa; Peter vanVoorst, Managing Director at Getronics; Bob Williams, Vice President/General Manager at Kodak Service; John Schoenewald, Vice President at Imation and Chief Executive Officer at AFSMI; Ray Thurston, Senior Vice President at UPS; Paul Gettings, Vice President UPS; Bill Klein, Chairman of the Board of Cerplex Group; Lowell Peters of Sears; Joe Patton, Chief Executive Officer, Patton Consultants; and many others who provided real-world insight and rules of thumb.

My thanks also to the Council for Logistics Management (CLM), Reverse Logistics Trends, Inc. (RLTI), Association For Service Management International (AFSMI), the National Association of Service Managers (NASM), and Service Industry Association (SIA), for both their encouragement and the use of their platforms to present many of the views and concepts discussed in this book.

A sincere debt of gratitude goes to my wife, Judy Blumberg, Chief Financial Officer of D.F. Blumberg & Associates, and my children, and their children, who allowed me the time to do all the research. A final debt of gratitude goes to Pat Pilgermayer, my outstanding administrative assistant, for her personal support in the production of this work.

THE AUTHOR

Donald F. Blumberg, *friend and colleague of many, died from heart failure on May 29, 2004. Mr. Blumberg will be remembered and missed by the global high tech service industry, where he made a significant contribution and impact.*

Donald F. Blumberg became an internationally recognized authority on the service and support industry and market, and on the design, operation, service, and support of computer, telecommunications, process control and plant automation, and related high technology equipment and software service. Mr. Blumberg was the founder of D. F. Blumberg & Associates, and served as president and chief operating officer from 1969 to 2004.

Mr. Blumberg's education included a Bachelor of Science degree received in 1957 from the University of Pennsylvania in electrical engineering, majoring in computer sciences; a Master of Business Administration degree with a major in management and operations research, received in 1958 from the Wharton School of Business of the University of Pennsylvania. In 1963, he also completed all course work leading to a Ph.D. in applied economics with a major in microeconomics and business planning from the graduate school of the University of Pennsylvania.

Mr. Blumberg had more than 40 years of experience in strategic planning, market research, and management of service and logistics support. He also pioneered in the development of reverse logistics and closed loop supply chain business, with particular focus on transportation, distribution, warehousing, and depot repair. This included experience as a U.S. Army Corps of Engineer Officer, specializing in military combat logistics support and experience as acting principal deputy assistant secretary of defense (installation and logistics) for the U.S. Department of Defense. He served as a consultant to the U.S. Navy and NATO on global and regional logistics support operations and processes. In addition to extensive military logistics experience, he served as a consultant to many industrial and commercial logistics and reverse logistics support firms including FedEx, UPS, SonicAir, USCO, and Data Exchange.

CONTENTS

1 Introduction to Closed Loop Supply Chains and Reverse Logistics 1

Reverse Logistics and Closed Loop Supply Chain Service 6

Overview of Reverse Logistics and Closed Loop Supply Chain Models 12

General Market Definition 12

Reverse Logistics and Closed Loop Supply Chain Business Models 12

Product vs. Parts Returns 18

Strategic Issues in Closed Loop Supply Chains 19

Summary 21

2 The Business of Closed Loop Supply Chains and Reverse Logistics 23

Introduction 23

Introduction to Life Cycle Management 24

Trends and Opportunities 28

3 Overview of the Market for Closed Loop Supply Chains and Reverse Logistics Services 37

Introduction 37

Key Trends 39

Reasons for Using Reverse Logistics and Repair Services 40

General Characteristics of Closed Loop Supply Chains and Reverse Logistics Services 40

The Structure, Size, Dimensions, and Forecast of the Market 41

Depot Repair and Value-Added Services 43

Operating Dynamics of the Reverse Logistics and Closed Loop Supply Chain Markets 55

Competitive Evaluation 57

4 Managing High Tech Closed Loop Supply Chains and Service Parts Logistics 65

Introduction 65

Closed Loop Supply Chain Strategy 71
Factors Affecting Efficiency and Productivity of Closed Loop Supply
   Chain Management and Control 74
Advanced Forecasting Mechanisms for Closed Loop Supply Chain
   Management and Control 77
Control Mechanisms within the Logistics Pipeline 83
   Stock Control of Key SKU 83
   Use of Advanced Forecasting 84
   Bar Coding and RFID Methods for Identifying and Improving
     Accuracy of Inventory Counts 84
   Improved Just in Time Scheduling and Control of Depot
     Refurbishing and Repair Operations 84
   Other Mechanisms for Improving Logistics Management and
     Control 85
Closed Loop Supply Chain Management Systems 86
High Tech Closed Loop Supply Chains Metrics and Parameters 87
   Closed Loop Supply Chain and Reverse Logistics Benchmark
     Results 92
      Impact of Products and Technology Supported 92
      Impact of Using Closed Loop Supply Chains vs. Simple
        Reverse Logistics Processes 92
      Forecasting Impacts 92
      Return Velocity Rates for High Tech Products 98
High Tech Product Return Experience 98
Summary 105

5 Managing Consumer Goods Reverse Logistics **107**
Introduction 107
Manufacturer Consumer Goods Management Structure 107
Retailer/Distributor Consumer Goods Management Structure 108
Consumer Goods Return Rates 115
   Organization and Structure of Consumer Goods Reverse
     Logistics 117
   The Relationship between Consumer Product Life Cycles and
     Product and Parts Returns 120
   Consumer Good Return Rates and Life Cycle 120
   Effect of Branding on Consumer Goods Returns 122
   Consumer Goods Industry Return Rate Averages and Metrics 124
   Other Consumer Product Return Issues 127
   Consumer Goods Reverse Logistics Practices 132
Summary 137

**6 Depot Repair and Its Role in Closed Loop Supply Chains
and Reverse Logistics** **139**
Introduction 139
Structure of the Depot Repair Market 141
   Depot Repair Operating Models 144

Depot Repair Practices in Support of Closed Loop Systems 145
Depot Repair and Reduction Process in Simple Reverse
Logistics Operations 145

7 **Warranty Management, Return Process, and
Benchmarks**... 153
Introduction: Types of Warranties 153
Managing the Strategic Value of the Warranty Process 154
The Importance of Perceptions in Managing Warranty and
Postwarranty Service 158
Managing Warranty and Postwarranty Support in a Dealer
Environment 159
General Warranty Process Benchmark Analysis and
Evaluation 162

8 **Secondary Markets and Final Disposal of Returned
Products and Materials**.. 167
Introduction 167
Offshore Secondary Markets 168
Use of Third Party Service Providers 171

9 **Advanced Systems and Technology for Managing Closed
Loop Supply Chains and Reverse Logistics Processes** 175
Introduction 175
Systems and Technology for Consumer Goods Operations 176
High Tech Logistics System for Closed Loop Supply Chain
Management 177
Logistics Support Management Systems Functions and General
Specifications 180
Other Technology Supporting Reverse Logistics and Closed Loop
Systems 183
Bar Coding 183
Radio Frequency Identification System (RFID) 184
Repair Depot Applications of Bar Coding or RFID Scanning 185
Configuration Control 185
Logistics Management Systems Technology State-of-the-Art 186
Impact and Value of Advanced Logistics Management Systems 187

10 **Bringing It All Together: Managing Reverse Logistics and
Closed Loop Supply Chain Processes** 193
Introduction 193
Stage 1 — Establishment of Market Focus 194
Stage 2 — Collection of Data on Existing Processes and Structures 194
Stage 3 — Establish Strategic Direction and Business Plan 194
Stage 4 — Determine and Establish a Management Organization
and Operating Structure 195
Stage 5 — Development and Implementation of a Business
Model 195

Stage 6 — Full Operations 195
Use of Third Party Service Providers 198
Trend 1: New Software Focus 198
Trend 2: New Vendors, Advanced Tools 199
Trend 3: Move to Real-Time Control 199
Additional Factors 200
The Internet and E-Commerce 200
Application Service Providers 200
The Role of the Supplier in Obtaining Increased
Efficiency through Partnering 201
To Outsource, or not to Outsource? 202

**11 Summary and Conclusion: Management of Closed Loop
Supply Chain and Reverse Logistics Process Directions
and Trends**... **203**
Introduction 203
Long-Term Impact of Green Laws 205
Recommendations 207

**Appendix A Closed Loop Supply Chains and Reverse Logistics
Bibliography**.. **211**

**Appendix B Forecasting Methodology and Special Data Sources
Used to Develop Benchmark and Market Forecasts**............. **219**

**Appendix C Additional Data Sources on Reverse Logistics
and Closed Loop Supply Chain Operations and
Performance**.. **227**

Appendix D Firms Providing Reverse Logistics Services............. **231**

**Appendix E The Waste Electrical and Electronic Equipment
(WEEE) Directive of the European Union**............................. **245**

Index **263**

1

INTRODUCTION TO CLOSED LOOP SUPPLY CHAINS AND REVERSE LOGISTICS

Increasing attention has been given to reverse logistics (RL) and closed loop supply chain (CLSC) markets and business models over the last decade. This is due in part to the recognition of increasing value of the products and technology created in the field at the end of general direct supply chains and the impact of green laws, particularly in Europe. The problem and concerns of the ultimate disposal of junk, trash, and waste has always been an issue as a function of urbanization, and the increasing population density of metropolitan areas. With the industrial revolution, the problems were intensified as a result of the appearance of hazardous waste and materials, environmental impact, and the growing need for control and disposition of human and animal wastes to protect the health and safety of the population. These responsibilities were initially the focus of local and regional governments, and later supplemented by independent businesses providing trash removal and recycling services under contract to government organizations, or for a profit, based on the recoverable value of the trash and waste.

However, the last 20 to 30 years have resulted in the creation of an entirely new array of products and goods at the end of the traditional direct supply chain. This has included:

- Products that have failed, but can be repaired or reused
- Products that are obsolete, or at the end of leasing life, but still have value
- Unwanted and unsold products on retailer's shelves

- Products that have been recalled
- Parts and subassemblies created from "pull-and-replace" repair in the field, which still have value

These products, parts, subassemblies, and materials represent rapidly growing values and economic opportunities at the end of the direct supply chain. They are now the focus of business, industrial, government, commercial, and consumer organizations, looking at the RL process and/or CLSC as a basis for generating real economic value, as well as support of environmental concerns. This focus is increasing in all markets including industrial and high tech, commercial, and consumer product areas.

Based on in-depth consulting with various participants in the market, primary market research, and extensive analysis and evaluation, a quantitative representation of the RL and CLSC market has been developed and forecast. Different types of RL and CLSC operation models are presented along with quantitative estimates of market activity by segment. The dynamics and key processes found in both the general RL process and the related CLSC business management model are also described in depth, based on anecdotal and pragmatic experience, surveys, benchmarking, and historical industry-based rules of thumb.

The RL and CLSC fields have significant interest for a number of groups:

- Executives, managers, and operational personnel currently running RL and CLSC operations
- Executives and managers of third party logistics and depot repair support organizations concerned with potential market opportunities
- Executives and managers of high tech services organizations that must provide CLSC services as part of their business practices
- Executives, managers, and operational staff of consumer oriented manufacturers, wholesalers, dealers, and retailers are concerned with the growing cost and disposition of excess shelf and inventory stocks
- Executives, managers, operational personnel, and government organizations in the European Union directly concerned with green laws in general, and specific new directives, such as the Waste Electrical and Electronic Equipment (WEEE) directive, which directly impact their business operations
- North American, and other, regional executives and managers who are faced with compliance with European Union green laws, or who will soon be impacted by environmental legislation and rules in their own countries

- Logisticians, students, and researchers interested in new logistics and supply chain processes
- Vendors and developers of technology, infrastructure, and software for managing RL and CLSC operations

In summary, the combination of economic pressure to recover and make use of valuable products and technology in the field, and the requirements of new and emerging green laws and environmental concerns require an in-depth focus and consideration of the RL and CLSC management and operational processes, dynamic markets, and technology covered in this book.

This overall subject of RL and CLSC as a separate topic or area of focus distinct from the general direct supply chain management is still relatively new, with the original investigation and documentation outside of the limited area of waste and trash disposal only occurring in the early 1990s. Much of the original interest in this subject was in extremely narrow applications areas, such as computer technology, advanced office automation, and military and weapon systems logistics support. This came about as a result of the growing recognition of life cycle support costs in product management. Extensive studies, particularly in military weapon systems and computer electronic products, in the 1960s and 1970s, began to recognize that the full cost of service and support of equipment in the field could easily exceed 150% of the initial product or systems acquisition costs. In other words, the commitment to procure $10 billion worth of airplanes was in reality a longer-term commitment to expend $25 billion of which $10 billion was the initial weapons systems cost and the remainder (or $15 billion) was the continuing support cost over the life cycle of the weapon system or product. These continuing costs were driven by a combination of labor costs, parts, assemblies, and subsystems and modification and repair and overhaul of the whole unit.

Further research into this area of life cycle costing began to indicate that the typical practice of disposing of parts and assemblies, which had either failed, or appeared to have failed in the field as trash or junk, was a major cost contributor. In addition, moves to introduce modularization and open architecture interfaces as part of the overall technical trend towards large scale and very large scale chip integration, created new possibilities for retrofit change, modification, and upgrade of whole units, products, and systems, rather than disposing of a product or system simply because it was becoming obsolete or at the end of its original design life. In effect, the growing costs and complexities of military weapon systems and data processing technology, and the switch from special purpose designed analog devices to standard digital technology and integrated circuits, created a real product design change. Specific functional applications through digital software, as opposed to analog hardware, created not only a change in thinking about management of the product life cycle, but a growing awareness of the value of the technology found in the field at the end of the direct supply chain. These insights drawn from the military experience and related development in data processing technology were rapidly transferred into industrial and commercial product management.

This basic concept — that real values were to be found at the end of the direct supply chain and that processes to manage and control returns from the field or from the end of the direct supply chain could result in a significant reduction in life cycle support costs and an increase in value — was also independently discovered and developed in the consumer goods area. However, the drivers in the consumer goods field were different. In the consumer goods market, the focus on values in the field were driven more by the need to deal with higher rates of returns of nondefective goods and products rather than by product failures in the field, per se. In essence, in the consumer goods market the critical existence of wholesale and retail distribution channels separating the end user from the original manufacturer introduces another area of complexity and the potential for build up of values in the field. The wholesaler/retailer's move to acquire products and goods for sale to the end user may result in excess inventories of perfectly satisfactory goods and products on the retailer's shelves. This could be caused by a number of factors including a lack of demand, an excess of supply, or change in fashion and style, or a short life cycle.

While there are, therefore, differences in the dynamics and structure of the need to manage and coordinate RL flows and processes in the industrial, commercial, and military markets as opposed to the consumer goods markets, the basic management issues and processes are pretty much the same.

Unfortunately, it has not been recognized that the management systems processes, dynamics, and infrastructure technology applicable in the high tech industrial, commercial, and military market could also be applied in the consumer market and vice versa. A critical objective in this book is to try to bring both processes and sets of experience to the table in order to take advantage of new workable techniques, technology, systems, and infrastructure.

A second major objective is to attempt to bring some degree of quantification to the size and dimensions of the RL and CLSC process, based upon in-depth surveys and market research rather than anecdotal experiences or broad "rule of thumb" estimates alone. In this regard, we have carried out very extensive surveys and research over a 5-year period of the economics and values associated with RL and CLSC in all major markets. While the primary objective of this quantitative survey and research was to produce proprietary recommendations for our consulting clients, we also recognize that the nonproprietary portion of this research could provide a needed dimension in the study, analysis, and management of these processes on a global, regional, and local basis by market segment. This extensive array of surveys carried out over a 5-year period are described in summary form in Appendix B and Appendix C, and provide a source for many of the data tables and benchmarking evaluations provided in this discussion. The results of these extensive studies carried out on both a time sequential and cross sectional analysis basis provide the ability to separate the anomalies from steady state characteristics and to identify key trends, directions, and workable solutions affecting the management process. We suggest readers interested in the details of these surveys and data collection processes review Appendix B and Appendix C to gain a full understanding of the survey mechanisms and time frames involved.

Another factor or issue of importance is to recognize the importance of the CLSC processes and the management, coordination, control, and delivery of field service, particularly in high tech environments. As described above, new technologies involving very large-scale integration, modular design, and pull-and-replace repair philosophies developed in military weapon systems and information technology fields have created the demand for more effective management of the RL process in order to effectively control life cycle costs and maximize values found in the field. This subject is discussed in considerable detail in a companion book titled *Managing High-Tech Services Using a CRM Strategy*, also published by Auerbach, CRC Press. Readers interested in high tech field service and support environment will find this other reference of particular value.

In summary, this book has been developed as an introduction to the management, coordination, and control of RL and CLSC, taking a very broad look at such processes in a high tech industrial and commercial practice, and in consumer goods practice.

We have organized our presentation into a top down discussion covering, in sequential order:

- Concept, definition, and operational structure of CLSC and RL processes
- Size and direction of market demand and expenditures for CLSC and RL
- Specific issues and processes for:
    - Consumer goods reverse logistics
    - High tech product and parts closed loop supply chains

- New and advanced technology for managing RL and CLSC processes
- Further direction of RL and CLSC and the impact of green laws
- Recommendations for management action and business strategy development

The reader should also recognize that this field is growing and evolving very rapidly. This book has been designed to introduce the reader to processes, dynamics, market size and dimensions, and general trends. We have also provided insight into the variety of organizations on the cutting edge of this field in both North America and Europe in Appendix D, as well as both an extended bibliography and special data sources. We recognize that this is a work in progress with new insights and management disciplines developed every day. We hope that you will find this subject as exciting and challenging as we have. We welcome your suggestions and comments concerning the future direction of this field.

REVERSE LOGISTICS AND CLOSED LOOP SUPPLY CHAIN SERVICE

The service market in general is going through a rapid, almost revolutionary change as increasing focus is being placed on the need for more efficient, real time, and optimized control of service and logistics support as a line of business. This is especially true in the area of supply chain management, which deals with the full management and control of material and supplies to the ultimate users. Traditionally, supply chain management was built on the underlying premise of the existence of a product to be manufactured, sold, delivered, and supported. The supply chain business process, therefore, was focused on such functions as sales; order entry and processing; inventory management and control; physical transportation and distribution; and warehouse management control, including picking, packing and shipping, pricing, and, finally, delivery and receiving. This process is generally forward moving and is focused on getting products and materials to the user or buyer.

However, as discussed previously in this process, relatively little attention was given to the question of what happens to the material and goods at the end of the direct supply chain (i.e., after final delivery to the ultimate user or purchaser at the end of the direct supply chain). The predominant view in the earlier literature (see Appendix A) was that the final delivery to the end user customer represented the "end of the supply chain line." Conventional wisdom holds that one only gets into questions of final disposal of trash and waste after that point.

The growing complexity of servicing and supporting high tech equipment and products in the field, particularly with the introduction of digital computer technology in data processing, office automation, medical technology led to the need for management and control of whole units, parts and subassemblies, down to the field and back again to central facilities for disposition, repair and potential return to the field.

In this high tech field, pull-and-replace, rather than fix and repair in the field and the related new approach to modular design became accepted, resulting in an increasing volume of valuable material to be returned for processing. In addition, there has been increasing recognition of complex disposal issues from hazardous materials, toxic waste, and industrial waste, which could be recycled. Over the last decade, particularly in the European community, the passage of green laws requires the manufacturer to be responsible for the ultimate disposal of certain products. In addition, the growing recognition on the part of many high tech product and service organizations that material in the field has real value — at the same time environmental impact legislation required specific focus on return and disposal of material in accordance with standard rules and regulations — have led to increased interest in RL process.

There are a number of reasons why attention needs to be placed on the processes, dynamics, and structure involved in the return of goods, material, parts from the field at the end of the direct supply chain. In addition to the normal situation, where the products and goods at the end of the supply chain are no longer wanted or needed, or have little value because they are obsolete or not operating, there is, of course, a requirement for disposal, which deals with specific questions involving solid waste, liquid waste, and hazardous materials.* Furthermore, many other products and materials in the field have value that could be recovered through repair, disposition, and recycling, such that it may not be efficient to simply throw them away. These could include the following types of goods and products:

- Products in the field that have failed and need to be repaired or properly disposed
- Parts and subassemblies of products that can be reused, either because they are perfectly good (no trouble found), or that can be repaired or reworked

---

* RL for solid, liquid, and hazardous waste materials has been covered in some depth elsewhere (see Appendix A) including the path breaking book, *Reuse and Recycling* by the Council of Logistics Management (CLM), and will not be covered in this analysis.

- Products that are perfectly good but have, nevertheless, been returned by the purchaser, as well as products sitting on retailer's shelves that have not been sold
- Products and materials that have been recalled or are obsolete, but still have a useful life
- Products, materials, and goods that have been thrown away, but can be recycled and reused
- Products at end of lease, but not at the end of life

In these situations, and others, RL is important from an economic recovery standpoint, and because of the reduction or elimination of trash and junk. In addition, it has been increasingly linked to the general *direct* supply chain since in many cases the original supplier is in the best position to control the return process as well. This full process of shipment out and back by the *same* organization, found particularly in high tech service and support roles, is defined as a *closed loop supply chain* (CLSC). Both CLSC and RL will be discussed in more depth in subsequent chapters.

Before we explore this issue further, we should define more precisely the dynamics of returns. Products are returned by end users or purchasers to the outlet from which they were purchased, or to other disposal chains in the consumer, commercial, and industrial markets.

- In the case of the *consumer market*, the product may be returned by the consumer to a retailer, and then to a distributor for transport to the manufacturer or to waste or trash dealers and recyclers. Depending on the product, this cycle may be further complicated by the presence of an independent or third party organization that specializes in refurbishment/repair of a returned good, reselling them into other or secondary markets at a discount rate.
- In the case of commercial goods, the return cycle will be almost the same except that the names of the organization will change. Products are returned by the end user to a reseller, and then to a manufacturer or a third party repair/wholesale agent.
- For industrial or high tech products, the returns are usually coordinated, controlled, or both by a field service organization supplied by the buyer or the seller.

The reasons why products are returned also may vary in a typical consumer or retail vs. commercial and industrial environment.

- Commercial and industrial product returns deal a lot more with performance issues or the current technical or economic need for the item; in general, these returns require some type of processing, repair, or both. The fact that commercial and industrial products usually need a detailed cost justification to be completed before a purchase tends to eliminate many of the impulse issues seen in consumer buying/returns.

■ Consumer returns are often based on impulsive buying, trying out a product, or how a product fits into existing environments (color, size, etc.); thus, a significant portion of these returns may be perfectly good.

Returns within some segments of the supply chain are not caused by any consumer end user behavior. These include stock balancing issues (i.e., products sit too long on retailer shelves), and internal product recalls.

Thus, when addressing the topic of product returns, it is important to define the context of the question, such as:

■ Retail consumer to retailer
■ Commercial or industrial end user to reseller
■ Distributor to manufacturer

A brief look at anecdotal examples in these categories provides a framework for formulating a focus on this emerging market.

■ High tech products, parts, and subassemblies — Normally, products and their embedded parts and subassemblies flow from the manufacturer to the end user. This process can be more complex, particularly in high tech markets dealing with complete products including process controls, voice and data networks, medical technology, office automation, computers, and so on. For these products, field service and support organizations — owned by the manufacturer, the end user, or independent service organizations (ISO)* — travel to the field to install or fix (maintain and repair) the product. In the course of this process, parts and subassemblies and even whole units may be removed by the service engineer and fixed or replaced. Since this process is increasingly carried out on a pull-and-replace basis, rather than by fixing units in the field, a good deal of valuable material is created and is generally returned to a central or regional repair

---

* For a more detailed discussion of high tech services, see *Managing High-Tech Services Using a CRM Strategy*, by Donald F. Blumberg, 1999, CRC Press.

depot for evaluation and processing. Typically, about 30 to 35% of these returns are "no trouble found" (i.e., perfectly good). This is due to the fact that many field service engineers increasingly use parts and subassemblies as test equipment upon arriving at a customer's site, based on a request for service and/or product failure. They try a new part in the product, pulling out an old one; if the unit now works, the old part is assumed to be bad and returned. However, if the new part, as replaced, does not fix the problem, the old part is not replaced with the new part returned to a central inventory. The old part is returned. The field engineer then tries another new part until the product is back in operation. This pull-and-replace process creates a return flow of both good and bad parts and materials, which are initially all assumed to be bad. As more and more field engineers or service techs use parts as test equipment through the pull-and-replace approach, the RL process becomes larger and increasingly important.

■ Consumer products — Consumer goods, such as TVs, washers, dryers, refrigerators, toys, and clothing, may no longer be wanted by the original purchaser, or may have failed from the viewpoint of the purchaser, but still have a useful life as is or after repair or refurbishment. Since the original manufacturer is often separated from the buyer through indirect distribution and retail channels, the return process and the responsibilities and economics of return are somewhat different from the high tech situation discussed above.

■ Unwanted, unsold, and unused products — Large retail chains and stores usually have an agreement with their consumer goods suppliers that allows them to return goods. While this practice was originally designed to deal with the case of customer returns for failure, it has been expanded to cover the general practice of returns. Retailers often return perfectly good products simply because they have not moved off of store shelves. Sometimes a buyer purchases a product, makes very limited use of it or simply decides not to keep it and returns it, sometimes in the same box with the original tags. These goods may also be perfectly good, without defect or failure and have value, but they may have to be returned because the goods are no longer fresh, or the retailer wants to clear his shelves.

■ Recalls or obsolete products — Products that have been made obsolete due to new product development and products that have been recalled by the manufacturer or dealer due to change in portfolios or product manufacturing error are another category that creates a return flow of material that has more than scrap or waste value.

■ Green goods control — Another category of goods, now emerging in Europe and other countries as a result of legislation, are products covered by green laws, or environmental impact, legislation and direction. In these areas, the original manufacturer or dealer is ultimately responsible for the final disposal of the product. If a buyer fails to properly dispose of the unwanted product, the manufacturer is considered at fault if the disposed product becomes a hazard. In other words, there is a real cost to the manufacturer from the failure to control and manage the full return process from the end user purchasers. Newer legislation also requires the end user to formally dispose of the product according to regulations, if the manufacturer refuses, thus penalizing the buyer for dealing with a manufacturer or product that is not fully covered by formal return processes.

In summary, as indicated above, material and products in the field that are no longer wanted by or used by the purchasers need to be returned if they have value, or if they represent a hazard or a threat to the environment or population. Much of this is not just junk, but has a real product (as opposed to scrap) value, and the disposal, refurbishment, and resale or reuse of this returned material represents a real economic opportunity and base of business.

Over the last 15 to 20 years, a combination of existing supply chain firms and new vendors who focus on third party logistics providers and fourth party depot repair providers* have emerged. In addition, new technology and software for RL management and high tech CLSC control has also been developed. This combination of growing needs and requirements on the part of the general marketplace, the increasing availability of vendors interested in and focusing on the issues of RL and CLSC management services, and new RL management systems and technology are all serving to create new markets and opportunities for RL and CLSC processes.

This book discusses the RL and CLSC businesses from the perspective of economic size and activity, processes, competition, systems and technology, and future direction. A primary emphasis is placed on managing these processes as a line of business.

---

* Fourth party repair firms, such as Data Exchange, DecisionOne, etc., operate specifically in high tech markets, where they process returned parts and subassemblies for reuse or sale.

OVERVIEW OF REVERSE LOGISTICS AND CLOSED LOOP SUPPLY CHAIN MODELS

General Market Definition

The full CLSC includes:

- Forward logistics and direct supply chain management — This includes the overall management and coordination and control of the full direct service logistics pipeline, including the flow of the original material, parts, and the final products to the central warehouse and distribution system, as well as the initial physical flow down to regional and local supply points to the end user or purchaser.
- Reverse logistics — This process is found either as a subset of closed loop systems or standing alone. This includes full coordination and control, physical pickup and delivery of the material, parts, and products from the field to processing and recycling or disposition, and subsequent returns back to the field where appropriate.
- Depot repair, processing, diagnostics, and disposal — This includes the services related to receiving the returns from the field, via the RL process, and then the processes required to diagnose, evaluate, repair, and/or dispose of the returned units, products, parts, subassemblies, and material, either back to the direct/forward supply chain or into secondary markets or full disposal.

Reverse Logistics and Closed Loop Supply Chain Business Models

The typical processes addressing RL and CLSC can be readily classified depending on the characteristics of the manufacturers and sellers, the buyers, the distribution channels used, the use of third and fourth party logistics providers, the degree of interest, and the value of the material in the process. Four models currently exist:

- Basic RL model — The basic RL business model simply deals with the return of unwanted materials and products to a central location for processing and disposal (Figure 1.1). It operates *independently* of the direct supply chain, which originally delivered it. This basic model describes the activities of the traditional waste and junk dealer or service organization. In this model, which can be run as a business or as a governmental service, usually at the city, municipality, or local level, the emphasis is on the economic disposal

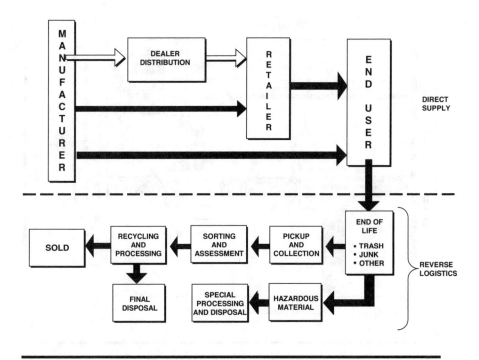

Figure 1.1   Independent reverse logistics processes.

or waste or trash through land or sea dumping or recycling. Much of the earliest literature research has been focused on this model.

■ CLSC, involving integrated direct and RL and repair service cycle for high tech products — In this business model (Figure 1.2), generally found in a high tech product environment, the original equipment manufacturer (OEM) supports its own product line sold to its customers in the field, and takes responsibility directly for the RL process. The products, as well as any subassemblies, parts, and components that are in the field after delivery, are returned and recovered by an OEM through indirect (dealer) channels representing the OEM, or the OEMs own field service force. The primary differentiator is that in this model the entire direct and RL flow can be and usually is controlled by the OEM. The RL flow to depot repair will either put the material back into inventory for resupply directly to the field or into a qualification and reconfiguration process, which leads to either reuse at the manufacturing level or full disposal into secondary markets.

■ CLSC, involving independent direct and RL and repair service cycle for standard low tech products — In this business model (Figure 1.3), the end user or purchaser uses its own internal plant and

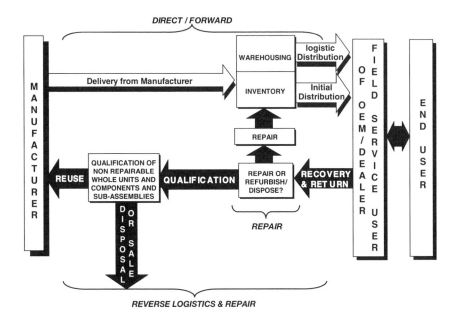

Figure 1.2 Typical high tech closed loop supply chain.

building maintenance service force or its own supply chain processes rather than relying on the outside OEM or indirect dealer channels. In this model, the buyer or user is typically a large organization with a number of smaller dealers or OEMs supporting it. In this situation, the buyer tends to pick up more of the responsibilities for RL or repair, using its own forces or third party logistics (3PL) organizations. In essence, this process looks very similar to the high tech process discussed above except for the issue of who is specifically responsible for which actions. In this model, the direct and RL supply chains are independent of each other; the OEM does not control the full process.

■ Consumer-oriented CLSC — The fourth business model (Figure 1.4) is typically found in the consumer market. In this business model, the primary interaction is between the retailer and the OEM. Some of the returns from the purchaser back to the retailer are failed units or products that were simply purchased and returned. A portion of returns are unsold products returned to clear the retailer's shelves, or products returned by the retailer's customer.*

---

* A rule of thumb used in many consumer businesses is that 3 to 5% of products sold to retail chains by the OEM are returned by the retailer.

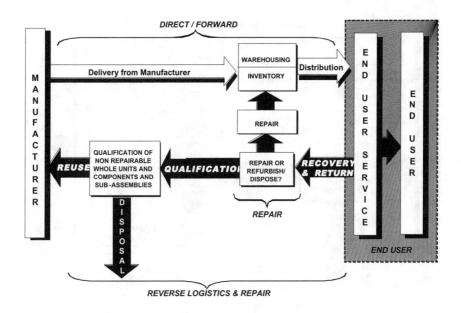

Figure 1.3   Alternative high tech closed loop supply chain.

This process is also very typical of the consumer goods and material recall process. In this model there are two RL linkages, consumer to retailer and retailer to OEM.

As indicated in the general description above, and in Figure 1.1 to Figure 1.4, real differences exist in the RL and CLSC processes under different business models. In the pure independent RL process, identified in Figure 1.1, the process starts with the end user or purchaser's decision that the product is at the end of its life for the purposes of the original buyer and needs to dispose of the materials. The whole RL process is carried out *independently* of the direct supply chain. As indicated above, pickup and collection for residential consumers is usually done by local government agencies directly or under subcontract. Hazardous materials are usually picked up separately and processed and disposed based upon specific green law type regulation. Other materials, after pickup and collection, are then sorted and assessed leading to recycling and processing and sold for the value of the recycled materials or sent for final disposal. This is a relatively simple business that is carried out by a government services organization or by an independent business organization and is compensated by local government contracts, by providing the pickup and collection service and through the value generated from recycling or

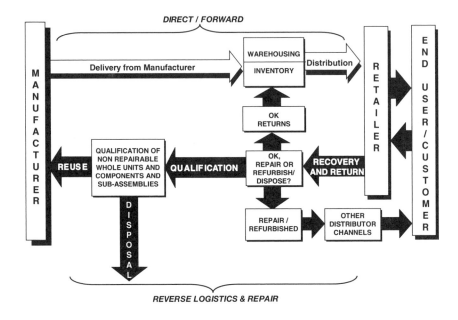

Figure 1.4 Closed loop supply chain in consumer goods.

processing of the trash and waste into materials that can be sold to third parties.

The more complex RL processes, described in Figure 1.2, Figure 1.3, and Figure 1.4, typically introduce the concept of a CLSC, which is management handling both the direct supply to the end user and the reverse supply chain from the end user. While the processes may seem similar, definite differences exist in the process flows, as shown in Figure 1.2, Figure 1.3, and Figure 1.4. In the typical high tech CLSC, in which the manufacturer also provides his own distribution and field service and support capabilities, a true closed loop process is at work. The material flows out from the manufacturer through warehouses and inventory to organizations owned or contracted by the manufacturer for installation, and these high tech situation products are generally treated and tracked by serial number or at least by type, as part of the initial installation. Continuing service and support of the equipment under warranty, extended warranty, or after warranty support on a service contract or time and materials basis is usually done by a field service organization as part of the OEM or under direct contract to the OEM. Thus, as shown in Figure 1.2, the return flows are also tracked and controlled by the *same organization* that supported the direct forward supply chain operations. The primary reasons for this full closed loop control are as follows:

- Tracking of the whole unit and experience in terms of failure and repair provides considerable insight in how to most cost effectively service and support equipment in the field.
- Value of the parts, subassemblies, and whole units is high and through close control and rapid recovery the amount of inventory required to support the field can be minimized.

As noted in Figure 1.2, returns from the field under a CLSC process can generally result in parts and material immediately sent back into the field inventory or returned for full qualification and subsequent reuse in the manufacturing operation or sales organization or for final disposal to secondary markets, or to trash or recycling organizations using the processed outlined in Figure 1.1.

The alternative CLSC process, outlined in Figure 1.3, occurs in situations in which the manufacturer does not also control the installation, field service, and support directly to the end user. In many markets, the end user operates its own internal plant and building maintenance service forces, which take the responsibility for delivery from the manufacturer, dealer, or distributor, and provides service for the equipment. These organizations normally acquire both the whole unit and appropriate parts and subassemblies in order to support the unit over its life cycle. Another option is for the end user to make use of a third party service provider rather than its own internal service force. In either case, the problem of full closed loop control becomes more difficult because the manufacturer does not directly control the service organization, except for those situations in which the whole units, parts, or subassemblies are under warranty or extended warranty. Thus, the alternative high tech CLSC process (described in Figure 1.3) operates in a fashion similar to the process shown in Figure 1.2, but with a much more difficult tracking and control problem. Since the service organization is under the control of the end user, as opposed to the manufacturer, the process can be managed and controlled by the end user. The manufacturer does not have access to information about failure rates and parts demand since the owner carries out the process rather than the manufacturer.

The final business model, shown in Figure 1.4, involves RL operation in a consumer goods environment. This represents a further modification of the alternative high tech CLSC, outlined in Figure 1.3, in that a full separation exits between the manufacturer and the end user through separate and independent retailer or distributor organizations, which may or may not supply full service and support. The existence of the separate and independent retailer not only creates increasing problems for the control of the entire logistics support pipeline (direct and return), as outlined in Figure 1.3, but also introduces other important dynamic factors.

In the first place, under the processes outlined in Figure 1.2 and Figure 1.3, the primary return dynamics are generated from the prospective of the end users experience and use of the products. In the consumer goods business model, outlined in Figure 1.4, the retailer may also be returning material and goods independently of the end users purchases, due to the distribution or retailer requirement to clear shelves, obsolescence, and recalls. These will be discussed in more detail in Chapter 5, but in broad terms the return rates to the manufacturer in a consumer goods CLSC is internally much higher than in the supply chain situations outlined in Figure 1.2 and Figure 1.3. Another additional feature of the consumer goods CLSC, as described in Figure 1.4, is the fact that the return process, as controlled by the manufacturer, can lead to a resale of goods returned from the retailer as perfectly good through discount sales and through other distribution channels in the secondary markets. Since some of the large mass retailers have return agreements or policies with individual manufacturers that prohibit the manufacture from resale of the returned goods into directly competitive markets, it is essential for the manufacturer in these cases to use noncompetitive distribution channels for resale, including, but not limited to offshore foreign sales.

In summary, our top level process flow charts, as outlined in Figure 1.1 through Figure 1.4, articulate different paths, dynamics, and structures that need to be effectively managed, coordinated, and controlled. In essence, the simple RL process, as shown in Figure 1.1, becomes much more complex and sophisticated as one moves to apply these concepts in both high tech and consumer goods markets, where various factors, constraints, and technology systems for tracking, coordination, and control vary substantially.

PRODUCT VS. PARTS RETURNS

The process description outlined above also can vary as a function of the type of material in the closed loop or RL pipeline. The difference in flow can be observed more clearly in terms of:

- Parts and subassemblies — The return of parts and subassemblies generated by field level pull-and-replace or module repair by technicians lead very well to CLSC management and control. This process is usually found in high tech markets in which the parts and subassemblies are continuously reused, after repair and processing in the field.
- Consumables and materials — These include chemicals, paper, glass, and other consumables that cannot be reused directly but must be recycled and fully processed before they can be reused

in the manufacturing process as material input or sold to third parties.

■ Whole unit equipment and products — Whole unit returns usually include technology coming off lease, or trade-ins on new product sales, obsolete products, or whole units requiring major repair that cannot be done in the field. These products can be returned through the primary supply chain as part of a closed loop system or sold into secondary markets.

STRATEGIC ISSUES IN CLOSED LOOP SUPPLY CHAINS

A new concept is that CLSC have become a strategic issue, particularly for global manufacturers that serve multiple markets, including those that require product technology on the cutting edge, as well as other markets into which less advanced technology can be sold. The concept also has great strategic value for organizations involved in service and support of either their own products and technology or other manufacturers, products, and technology in situations in which product sales revenue growth is stagnated and product margins are eroded. In these situations, in particular, a customer asset management strategy focusing on generating revenues and profitability from the service and support of the customer base can create a major turnaround. In essence, the CLSC process introduces a differentiated service offering to an existing customer base in which service sales are used to grow revenues and increase profitability through expanding the full service offering of the firm to provide comprehensive customer support.

In essence, this strategic value of CLSC and RL management operations will have a very positive effect in terms of:

■ Reducing cost of returns
■ Increasing the value of the salvage merchandise
■ Capturing vital information and reliability, maintainability, and dependability of products supported
■ Reducing transportation and warehousing expenses and time including the partial or full elimination of small package shipments
■ Automate and fully control the total returns process

General experience dictates that the introduction of CLSC management can result in the bottom line direct savings of 1 to 3% or more of total revenues, particularly for organizations in a mature or stagnating market as well as those that have elected to move to customer service–oriented business strategy.

These strategic values are accomplished through the primary goals of CLSC RL strategies, which include the maximization of inventory value through:

■ Rapid returns to the manufacturer for reuse
■ Ability to liquate products, parts, and subassemblies with value in secondary markets
■ Controlled recycling or disposition within environmental and other legal requirements
■ Ability to efficiently process returns back into the original direct supply chain

The primary goal of maximizing inventory use in CLSC, including the embedded RL process, often produce significant additional efficiencies and results to the firm as well as to its distribution channels, including:

■ Simplifying processes of retail and wholesale return, reducing labor cost
■ Reducing undesirable shrinkage and damage from returns
■ Increasing recovery of value from secondary suppliers and dealers
■ Improving the database and visibility of products throughout their life cycle
■ Reducing disposition cycle times, thereby, increasing cash flow

In addition to these overall impacts, the full implementation of CLSC has the major advantage of pushing the resolution of the returns "upstream" through centralization and overall control of the full returns process. By centralizing the management of the returns process decisions, with respect to repair, refurbishment, disposition, and secondary market, sales can be made more efficiently. This reduces transportation and time costs through multiple touch points and eliminates long cycle times in resupply, thus reducing the levels of service inventory investment requirements. Return cycle times under a typical RL process, as compared to a high tech closed loop supply system, demonstrate the real operational value in terms of reduced time and cost of moving to a full CLSC system.

SUMMARY

In summary, our initial analysis and evaluation has focused on

- General return and RL
- Returns and RL as part of CLSC operations to minimize life cycle costs

We have also identified the need to differentiate the RL process as a function of the type and kind of:

- Whole unit products and equipment
- Parts and subassemblies of products and equipment
- Consumables and items of supply

The return flows for consumables and items of supply tend to follow the basic RL cycle, as shown in Figure 1.1. The more important and complex processes are the product and parts/subassembly returns, which generally follow the same process, and in high tech, are often connected in a closed loop, as shown in Figure 1.2, Figure 1.3, and Figure 1.4.

Using this analytical framework, we will build up our understanding of the processes, metrics, infrastructure technology, and economics of the RL and CLSC. We will examine the similarities and differences in these processes, driven by issues of:

- Kind of product (consumables vs. products)
- Type of product (industrial, commercial, consumer)
- Management/distribution channel focus (OEM, retailer, end user)
- Services involved (direct, returns, repair, etc.)

This framework, summarized in Table 1.1 will describe and explain the various elements determining the CLSC and RL processes. We will demonstrate and describe the size, dimensions, and future growth of the market for these services. We will also build up strategic management approaches to management of these processes in different market environments, as well as provide key metrics and parameters. We will discuss the current state of the art in systems and infrastructure for management of these operations. Finally, we will deal with the future direction and key trends in this new business form.

Table 1.1 Closed Loop Supply Chains and Reverse Logistics Market Segments

Segment Description		Services					Market Opportunities
Business	Products	Forward Ordering Inventory/ Warehouse and Distribution	Field Services/ Outward Bound	Pickup and Collection Return	Depot Repair and Return	Return to End User	
Manufacturer (OEM)	High tech industrial and commercial	✓	✓	✓	✓	✓	High
Dealers and distributors	High tech industrial and commercial		Potential	✓	✓	Dealers	Low
Retailers	Consumer goods		Potential	✓	✓	Secondary markets	Medium
End users	Industrial and commercial		Potential	✓	✓		Low to medium

2

THE BUSINESS OF CLOSED LOOP SUPPLY CHAINS AND REVERSE LOGISTICS

INTRODUCTION

The idea of reverse logistics (RL) businesses has been around at least since the early industrial age when merchants recognized that old clothing and rags, linens, and so forth, could be reproduced and used to produce new textile products. The business gained significant momentum, gaining visibility in the 1980s when environmental issues became emotionally charged sensitive topics. This led to the emergence of waste (general and hazardous) processing and recycling business.

The closed loop supply chain (CLSC) concept, embedding RL principles, developed in the early 1980s as a direct result of microminiaturization, large-scale integration, and modularization design; it was first implemented in the electronics industry (computing, office automation, telecommunications process, control and plant automation, etc.).

Until this time, the typical process for repair of a product or piece of equipment was to make the corrections in the field (i.e., fix in place). However, the use of large-scale integrated digital circuits and circuit boards, with built in diagnostics and defined test points, led to two changes:

- Increased reliability of the subsystems and components
- Reduced repair time through pull-and-replacement of modules rather than field repair

The increased sophistication and complexity of the circuit boards and pull-and-replace modules in turn increased the value of these components, which, in turn, increased the economic value of returning the material for repair and reallocation. This trend has now been extended from electronics into other technologies, including mechanical and electromechanical equipment. In addition, sensors and control mechanisms originally provided in analog mechanical form are increasingly converted to digital functions to increase reliability and reduce size, weight, and power requirements. This has, in turn, created the business need to apply RL and CLSC processes in the high tech market.

Using RL as a business strategy to explore new markets or improve a company's bottom line emerged in the early 1990s; for example:

- RL strategy used by Genco Distribution System increased its RL revenue from $300,000 in 1991 to an estimated $40 million in 1994.
- RL saved AT&T's Network Services Division $90 million between March 1993 and October 1994 — this at a cost of only $1.6 million, and with a staff of only seven people; it was carried out by Burnham's Tel Trans Division.

What are the basic underpinnings of RL process as a business? The key is to understand the concept of life cycle management and support — viewing a product or technology over its entire life cycle of use.

INTRODUCTION TO LIFE CYCLE MANAGEMENT

The general view of a product life cycle and its service and logistics support requirements is shown in Figure 2.1. As indicated, the service and support needs change as a function of the life cycle. Historically, new technology and product concepts were developed by private inventors and brought to users for development and funding. For industrial and commercial usage, the user would generally turn to the initial developer or a consortium for development and production. For military technology development, production and roll-out was generally handled by the purchaser (Department of Defense, etc.), although some specialized civilian contractors could be involved.

In any case, the life cycle support, after initial production, including the full logistics support process, was considered to be the responsibility of the end user since they were often involved in the product design concept. Commercial and industrial firms often used internal plant and building maintenance forces for this purpose, augmented by the original equipment manufacturer (OEM). In the military, life cycle support and logistics support was developed and expanded internally in terms of naval bases and facilities, air stations, and army ordinance centers. In essence, the military built a high and broad logistics support establishment to support the life cycle of their products and technology.

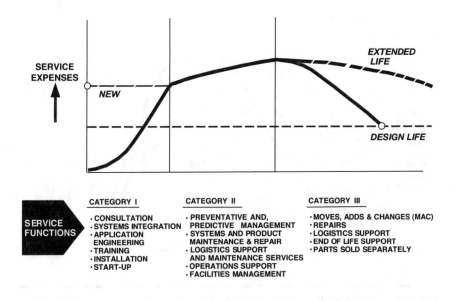

Figure 2.1 Defined service categories as a function of product/systems life cycle.

Major consumer products (white and brown goods) were treated somewhat differently in that product development was done by the manufacturer in anticipation of future demand and some items were developed with planned obsolescence in mind (electronics), while others (white goods) were designed to have a relatively long life. As a result, a great deal of attention was given in commercial, industrial, and military technology and products to managing life cycle support. This included the development of modular and subsystem replacement through pull-and-replace design, onboard diagnostics and testing as discussed earlier.

The use of these "new" life cycle support design concepts, different roles and functions of the service provider, and component design for pull-and-replace rather than fix in the field, has changed the duration of life cycles as well as the manner in which products are maintained, repaired, and supported. The rapid development of small, inexpensive, and powerful computer chips has reduced the life cycles of these products; this is especially true in the area of high tech electronic products. However, it is clear that regardless of the length of the product life cycle (3 years, 10 years, 20 years, or more), there is a correlation between the product life cycle and the need for service and support. As shown in Figure 2.2, service costs and revenues tend to rise more slowly than the size of the product installed base. As the base grows, the economics of service grows even more rapidly, until service and support exceeds the annual sales of

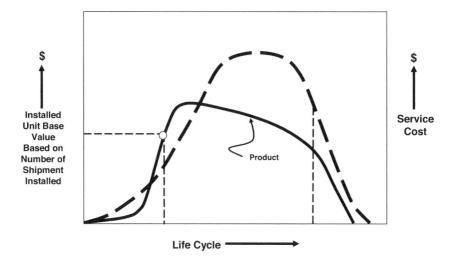

Figure 2.2 Relationship between product installed base and service costs (annually) as a function of life cycle.

the product. As the product cycle continues, service expenditures remain high, even as the installed base decreases. The difference between the product life cycle and its associated service and support cycle is driven by several factors, including:

- Greater attention and focus of the early product adapters and their willingness to commit to the new technology
- Changing nature of product, subproduct, and parts failures over the life cycling in which early failures are often identified leading to design or field changes and improve reliability and subsequent erosion or failure rates, as the product reaches its end of life and no longer fully supported (see Figure 2.3)
- Design on the part of certain users to extend product life through continued end of life support and in field upgrades

The overall impact is that the typical total life cycle support cost can easily rise to 150% or more of the installed product base cost. Alternatively, a good rule of thumb is that total life cycle costs of a product is in the range of 2.5 to 2.8 times present segment costs. This important relationship between the product life cycle and the service and support life cycle has an important effect on the entire RL and CLSC process.

The cited development of plug and play technology and use of more reliable material in consumer goods has severely reduced the time and effort needed to maintain consumer goods, and has changed the life cycle

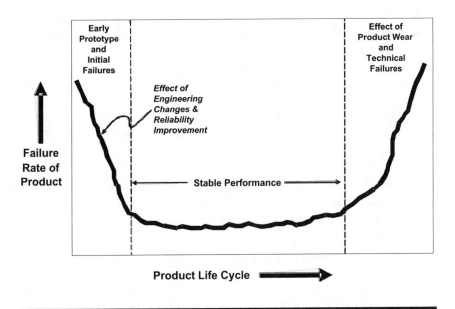

Figure 2.3 Typical product failure rate pattern as a function of life cycle.

support process. In the commercial industrial world, many of the new technologies available in the 1960s and beyond (computers, communications, process control, etc.) required skill sets not in the hands of the internal maintenance organizations. In these cases, the manufacturer or contractors generally supplied the support at added costs, creating the high tech service industry.

The military began to realize the impact of these changes by the end of the 1960s, as study after study began to show that full life cycle costs of weapons systems were running at over 300 to 350% of initial purchase cost. In essence, the cost of life cycle support was out of control. A number of initiatives, including life cycle cost management and design to cost, were initiated to place more emphasis on the total cost of support.

In the industrial and commercial markets, the effect of this recognition of the service revenue (and profit) potential (and profit) for life cycle support cost management resulted in creating new service and support organizations run initially as cost or profit centers, and now, increasingly, as strategic lines of business. This, in turn, created a broad new array of technology and products aimed specifically at managing and delivering life cycle support service efficiently. This included:

- Integrated field service management systems
- Remote diagnostics
- Call avoidance

- Full closed loop logistics management systems and technology
- Advanced depot repair and disposal technology systems and infrastructure

It also led to changes in product design to reduce support costs, including:

- Open system architecture
- Standard module and interface specifications (plug and play)
- Software standards

An overall comparison of different life cycle support patterns in different markets is shown in Table 2.1. The major difference in support in the direct supply chain vs. the RL supply chain is outlined in Table 2.2.

TRENDS AND OPPORTUNITIES

A number of forces are driving the increased interest in business providing RL and CLSC services activities and markets. They include:

- Heightened consumer awareness due to the legislation imposed by government and environmentally friendly products designed by competitors
- Increasing customer demands for improved customer service satisfaction
- Cost reduction by sellers to reduce working capital requirements through full product control and reverse processes
- Emergence of various new types of return options, including return goods for credit, warranty returns, short- and long-term rental and lease returns, and product recalls
- Shift in consumer buying behavior from in-store shopping to non-store purchasing
- Increase in products and units sent to an outside organization for repairs, remanufacturing, upgrades or recalibrations, as internal plant and building maintenance forces were downsized or outsourced
- Increase in the rate of product obsolescence
- Increase in use of reuseable containers
- Changes in retail distribution market strategies allowing retailers to clear shelves of unsold merchandise

A large number of distribution centers and warehouses prefer to keep the RL processes in-house due to the following concerns:

- Products usually turn around in 2 to 3 days, compared to typical 2 to 4 weeks for some of the earlier third party RL companies

Table 2.1 Comparison of Consumer, Industrial, and Commercial off-the-Shelf (ICOTS) and Milspec Life Cycle Support Practices

Factors	Technology Type		
	Consumer	Icots	Milspec
OEM or prime contractor supplies support	• Through distribution channels support role	Broader support role	Primarily engineering and technical support
Role of government establishments in support	• Nonexistent	Secondary	Major
Subcontractor support	• Limited role • Generally depot repair and parts	Support of COTS product technology	Dictated by prime — generally limited
Configuration control	• Not required	Sometimes required	Required
Documentation support	• Required, but at very limited level	Required	Required — but supported by DOD
Field service	• Provided by OEM prime or distributors	Provided through OEM or prime contractor	Generally supported by DOD
Technology insertion	• Rarely used • Occurs as a new model or product line	Increasingly used — critically important	Not used
Depot repair	• Supplied by distributor	Supplied by prime or sub	Supplied by DOD and prime
Help desk/TAC	• Through OEM or distributor	Through prime or sub	Through DOD
Other support (training, etc.)	• Supplied by OEM	Supplied by contractor	Supplied by DOD

Table 2.2   Direct vs. Reverse Logistics Comparison

Direct Logistics	Reverse Logistics
Product quality uniform	Product quality not uniform
Disposition options clear	Disposition not clear
Routing of product unambiguous	Routing of product ambiguous
Forward distribution costs more easily understandable	Reverse costs less understandable
Pricing of product uniform	Pricing of product not uniform
Inventory management consistent	Inventory management not consistent
Product life cycle manageable	Product lifecycle less manageable
Financial management issues clearer	Financial management issues unclear
Negotiation between parties more straightforward	Negotiation less straightforward
Type of customer easy to identify and market to	Type of customer difficult to identify and market to
Visibility of process more transparent	Visibility of process less transparent

- Customer contact can be maintained
- Confidential customer, client or product data remains out of the hands of a third party
- Significant investment in RL equipment such as shredders, and balers

However, as new independent service logistics businesses grow and expand their portfolio and offering, comparative advantages emerge for manufacturers, wholesalers, and retailers to outsource RL functions due to:

- RL provided by specialized logistics and transportation companies can reduce cost of shipment
- Firms with efficient RL processes and secondary markets can put value back into goods that are otherwise considered worthless
- Third party providers usually have advanced software and information systems that can be configured to satisfy the organization's needs
- In-house operations often lack internal expertise or available personnel to carry out RL operations effectively

It is estimated that approximately 70% of RL service is still presently performed in-house. However, significant market potential exists for third party RL specialists to explore in terms of outsource and support of all or part of a firm's RL functions. This is particularly true in the following market segments:

- Electronic components and equipment — Including semiconductors and related devices (memory ICs, microcomponent ICs, etc.), electron tubes, printed circuit boards (PCB), passive components, semiconductor manufacturing equipment, and superconductive devices
- Industrial control and analytical instruments — Including laboratory instruments, measuring and controlling instruments, and instruments to measure electricity
- Photographic and printing equipment and supplies — Including photographic equipment, accessories and parts, photo finishing equipment, photocopy and microfilm equipment, press and pre-press equipment, etc.
- Computer equipment — Including supercomputers, mainframes, midrange computers, workstations, PCs, multimedia products, disk storage, and software
- Communications equipment — Including network equipment, customer premises equipment (CPE), cellular telephone systems, wireless personal communication systems, microwave radio systems, fiber optics, search and navigation equipment
- Medical equipment and supplies — Including surgical and medical instruments, surgical appliances and supplies, dental equipment and supplies, x-ray apparatus and tubes, electromedical equipment
- Other consumer and commercial materials — Including:
  - Auto and other parts
  - Electrical goods
  - Hardware, plumbing, and heating materials
- Validation of "green" product claims
  - A small, but growing number of organizations now offer services to green marketers by providing independent verification of environmental claims via methods including life cycle analysis and comparisons of products that make environmental claims with others in their class
  - Companies interested in producing, purchasing, or selling green products must overcome consumer skepticism about their motives, contradictory labeling laws, and differences of opinion as to preferred environmental attributes
  - This area traditionally offered relatively little opportunity to third party providers because there has been no commonly accepted definition of "green products" in the U.S.; this has been changing over time with increased interest of environmental issues.
- Independent management of reusable packaging and pallet pools
  - The expense of purchasing and disposing of single-use packaging has created increasing interest in reusable containers and dunnage
  - Within the grocery industry, a self-administered pallet pool has resulted in substantial savings, while independent companies that

own pallets and other shipping containers and rent them to manufacturers and distributors across many industries are having increasing success at maintaining quality and profitability.

■ Reclamation of personal consumer (end user) products
  – These services involve the retrieval of personal consumer products that are distributed by wholesale and retail distributors, and catalog, and online sellers. They generally include contract warehousing, distribution, and return center services. Some vendors have the ability to repair or refurbish returned goods.

■ RL service market for reclamation of personal consumer products — segmented into the following categories:
  – Manufacturing level — Products returned to manufacturers from wholesalers or retailers
    · Food and kindred products — Primarily specialty items, non-perishables, and packaged foods
    · Apparel and other textile products
    · Pharmaceuticals
    · Cleaning preparations and cosmetics — Including soaps and detergents, cosmetics, polices and sanitation goods, surface active agents and toilet preparations; but excluding aerosols and other hazardous material items
    · Automotive and transportation equipment — Including automotive parts reclamation and remanufacturing
    · Instruments and related products — Including following types of instruments, when delivered to end users: laboratory instruments and apparatus, medical and dental instruments and supplies, industrial and analytical instruments, measuring and controlling instruments
  – Wholesale level — Including products returned to wholesalers from retailers
    · Auto and other parts
    · Electrical appliances
    · Paper and related products
    · Miscellaneous durable goods
    · Apparel and piece goods
  – Retail level — Includes items returned to retail or wholesale distributors from end users or customers
    · General merchandise
    · Food
    · Apparel
    · Pharmaceuticals
    · Consumer durables

■ Commercial wastes collection, sorting, and marketing.

- Many waste hauling companies now provide collection, storing, and marketing services for common commercial recyclables such as corrugated, office paper, and beverage containers
- National waste management companies are also beginning to merge with scrap dealers and offer more customized services such as on-site processing to large facilities
- Margins for pure waste collection are very low and in some cases must be subsidized by municipalities and others, while full channel vertical integration offers increased profit margins since profit margins in this area are very volume sensitive
■ Specialized commercial waste collection, processing, and marketing
- Vendors offering these services tend to specialize in managing large volumes of homogeneous wastes or problem wastes (e.g., used oil, batteries, and tires) from small businesses and industry
- They tend to be dedicated to a particular material type, such as used oil, metal scrap, or paper
■ Hazardous materials collection, processing, and remanufacturing.
- Environmental concerns and EPA regulations are leading to more stringent packaging, labeling, and shipping regulations.
- Many industries have made serious efforts to develop programs to handle hazardous materials (e.g., toxic chemicals used in semiconductor manufacturing, solvents, insulating fluid) in a systematic way to fully comply with regulations and to avoid liability exposure due to environmental damage or personal injury for discarded materials.

The RL market for containerized hazardous materials includes the following segments:

■ Chemicals and allied products
■ Cleaning and related products
■ Bulk pharmaceuticals
■ Biological and medical wastes (biohazards)
■ Radiological wastes (radioactive products)

To summarize, we can group the overall business of RL and related CLSC into five major segments:

■ Industrial, technical, and commercial products
■ Consumer goods reclamation, return, and disposal
■ Green product legislative-based returns
■ Packing and pallet recycling
■ Waste collection return and processing

This broad view of the general business market is summarized in Table 2.3 and Table 2.4.

Table 2.3 General Segments of Reverse Logistics Service Business

Service Market Focus/Segment	Examples	Competitors
Industrial, technical product and parts collection, consolidation, and return	• Deinstall and remove computer, office equipment, medical equipment, copying equipment, etc. • Consolidate and ship and dissemble, repair and/or disposal point	• High value product OEMS • Major long haul transportation and distribution firms
Consumer goods reclamation or disposal	• Warranty processing • Product recalls • Return management	• 3PLs • Package shipping companies • Trucking and freight companies
Green product validation and control	• Validate material defined by legal requirements	• Green specialists
Packing and pallet recycling	• Reusable packaging systems • Exchange and rent pallets • Recycle dunnage	• Packaging and shipping goods manufacturers • Specialized recycling concerns
Commercial and industrial waste collection, processing sorting, marketing • General • Specialized • Hazardous materials	• Recover and pickup • Separate, identify and sort • Salvage and recovery • Market and sell	• Waste management companies • Trucking and freight companies

Table 2.4   Key Characteristics of Major Reverse Logistics Segments

Segments	Major Activity in Segment	"Typical" Third Party Logistics Providers in Segment	Third Party Penetration*	Special Requirements
High value technical products	Return of used or broken equipment and parts for repair, refurbish, reclaim or disposal	Asset-based logistics providers and logistics operations within repair depots	• Manufacturer level: 33 to 35% • Wholesale level: 24 to 25%	Providers must address depot repair issues in some way and interface with broader service operations of OEMs, ISOs, VARs, etc.
Consumer products	Return of goods due to damage, expiration, seasonality or similar reason for disposal or disposition	Asset- or nonasset-based providers; widest pool of 3PRL types	• Manufacturer level: 26 to 29% • Wholesale level: 22 to 24% • Retail level: 32 to 35%	Individual segments have regulatory requirements or other subsegment characteristics
Green products	Validation of environmental regulatory compliance, recycling, etc.	Niche specialists and waste specialists; not a clear "typical" provider here	40 to 42%	Requires depth of understanding of environmental regulations
Packing, pallets and containers	Management of parts of containers and packing for shipment	Owner/mergers of container and pallet parts, trucking or rail companies	35 to 40%	Strong links to other providers; usually requires ownership of shipping assets, but opportunity may be becoming much broader
Waste disposal and remediation	Disposal of wastes from commercial/industrial operations	Asset-based 3PRLs; most specialize in waste disposal and related activities, rather than hauling of goods	• General: 70% • Specialized: 80 to 82% • HAZMAT: 85%	Heavily regulated and, in hazmat area, requires special assets and capabilities

*Average penetration ranges

3

OVERVIEW OF THE MARKET FOR CLOSED LOOP SUPPLY CHAINS AND REVERSE LOGISTICS SERVICES

INTRODUCTION

Based upon the general structure and definitions described above, we can now look at the major segments of the closed loop supply chain (CLSC) market (Table 3.1). This includes the following major segments:

- Technical and industrial products (high tech)
- Consumer products
- "Green" products
- Packing, pallets, and containers
- Waste and trash

Since the general subject of waste disposal and recycling has been covered in some depth elsewhere,* we will primarily focus this discussion on the first two (high tech products and consumer products), which represent areas of high growth business potential. The basic business model for these segments can be identified generically in terms of the business process flow shown in Figure 3.1. In general, products and material in the field move through reverse logistics (RL) and repair services either back to the original buyer and user, or to other users, or to final

---

* See Appendix A.

Table 3.1 Major Reverse Logistics and Closed Loop Supply Chain Market Segments

Segments	Underlying Market Characteristics	Implications for Third Party Logistics
High tech products	One of the strongest reverse logistics markets with wide range of service content making demand stable on trend	High growth subsegments are generally due to shift from in-house to outsourced reverse logistics operations
Consumer products	Demand trends positively, but is also strongly influenced by business cycles	Dynamics are largely segment-specific, but third party logistics portion driven mostly by changing attitudes toward outsourcing
Green products	Key determinants of underlying demand are consumer attitudes toward environmental issues and government regulation	Nature of market and growth characteristics tend to be very unstable
Packing, pallets and containers	Entirely dependent on the transportation and logistics industries for demand base; new shipping technologies and need for cost savings among customers drive growth	Third party growth comes from attempts by in-house organizations to reduce loss of shipping materials; customer base includes other third party logistics services and third party RL services

Source: From Blumberg Associates, Inc. surveys.

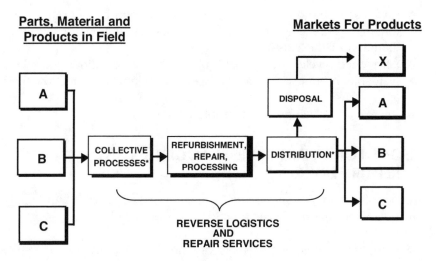

Parts, Material and Products in Field

Markets For Products

* May be through third party logistic firms.

Figure 3.1 The reverse logistics and repair services general business model. (From Blumberg Associates, Inc. surveys and forecasting methodology [Appendix B and Appendix C].)

disposal. From this fairly simplistic view, we will explore more specific market issues in terms of dynamics and segmentation.

KEY TRENDS

A number of forces are driving the CLSC and RL markets to be examined. These include:

- Heightened consumer awareness and legally imposed constraints ("green laws") by governments, leading to the requirement for safe return of products from the field, as well as for the design of environmentally friendly products
- Increasing customer demands for improved customer service and satisfaction
- Desire for cost reductions by the seller to lower working capital levels
- Existence of many types of return options for the buyer, including return goods for credit, warranty returns, short- and long-term rental returns, and product recalls
- Shift in consumer buying behavior from in-store shopping to non-store and e-commerce purchasing

- Increase in the demand for service and support by the purchasing organization, including repairs, remanufacturing, upgrades, or recalibration of the existing product base
- Shortened cycles of product obsolescence, creating potentially valuable products that are viewed as lacking in value by their current user
- Increased utilization of reuseable containers

REASONS FOR USING REVERSE LOGISTICS AND REPAIR SERVICES

A number of advantages encourage manufacturers, wholesalers, and retailers to outsource RL and repair functions. These include:

- Specialized third party logistics and fourth party depot repair companies can reduce the overall cost of supply chain operations resulting in reductions in the cost of return and repair compared to original equipment manufacturer (OEM) operations.
- Reasonable prices and efficient processes for RL and repair services can put value back into goods that would be otherwise considered worthless.
- Third party RL and fourth party repair service providers usually are able to make greater investments in advanced logistics management systems hardware and software than OEMs, and these systems can be configured to fully satisfy individual client needs, due to economics of scale.

GENERAL CHARACTERISTICS OF CLOSED LOOP SUPPLY CHAINS AND REVERSE LOGISTICS SERVICES

The processes described above contain a number of important characteristics that need to be managed, coordinated, and controlled if the operation is to be economically viable. These include:

- Uncertain flow of materials — Usually firms do not know when an item will be coming back, nor do they know its condition.
- Customer specific — The return flow is quite diverse and depends on the end user or customer, which requires in-depth knowledge and understanding of the specific customers using the service.
- Time criticality — A critically important element of RL and repair services is the need to process the asset as quickly as possible to make it available for reuse or disposal.

- Value improvement — RL and repair service requires the vendor to maximize the value of the assets being returned.
- Flexibility — The RL process needs to support flexible capacity in terms of the facility, transportation, and other related services to achieve goals for returned materials where demands fluctuate.
- Multiparty coordination — In general, RL and repair processes require several parties to be involved. It is therefore essential to establish a communications network that can facilitate efficient, rapid, real time communication between the parties to avoid slow-downs or inefficiencies.

THE STRUCTURE, SIZE, DIMENSIONS, AND FORECAST OF THE MARKET

In order to get a full understanding of the dimensions, structure, dynamics, and forecast of the CLSC RL services market, a set of large scale market surveys were conducted using a stratified random sample, double-blind telephonic approach. Respondents included executives in decision making capacities involved in CLSC management in both high tech and consumer markets covering general supply chain operations, field service, and logistics support operations, and operation of third party and fourth party firms. The surveys were designed to examine the following:

- Needs and requirements for RL and repair services in the context of CLSC
- Current expenditures for RL and repair
- Use of outside third party and fourth party service providers
- Key factors and influences in the selection of outside vendors
- Importance of having a single source for services

These market research surveys and studies,* which were directed towards senior service and logistics executives representing a broad range of market segments, indicated that total expenditures for CLSC, including RL and repair services, were divided up into:

- Shipment/transportation
- Depot repair**

---

* Initial research results were reported in "Strategic Evaluation of Reverse Logistics and Repair Service Requirements, Needs, Market Size, & Opportunities," Donald F. Blumberg, *Journal of Business Logistics,* Vol. 20, No. 2. The actual methodology and survey data base is described in Appendix B and Appendix C.

** Depot repair by an independent provider is generally referred to as fourth party services as contrasted with the third party logistics (transportation, distribution and warehousing service[s]).

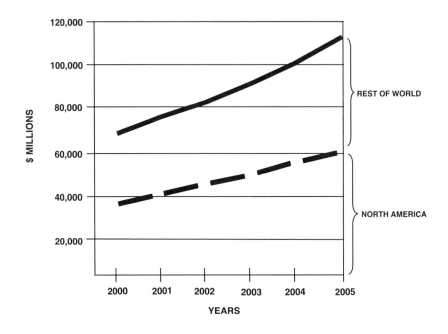

Figure 3.2   World reverse logistics and repair services market (forward portion of the supply chain not included). (From Blumberg Associates, Inc. surveys and forecasting methodology [Appendix B and Appendix C].)

- Warehousing
- Parts management and forecasting
- Inventory management
- Other services

As has been indicated above, the overall markets for RL and repair services have been growing rapidly due to a number of factors and trends. Based on extensive survey data and our forecasting methodology, we estimate total 2005 expenditures for RL and repair services in the world market at approximately $80 billion, with approximately 56% in North America (Figure 3.2). Using the same data and process, we estimated the North American market, as shown in Figure 3.3, growing primarily through increasing participation of third and fourth party service organizations. A detailed view of the total North American closed loop logistics market, combining both the RL services and the direct supply chain related services activities for 2003, shown in Table 3.2, provides an understanding of the economic activity by function and service category. A further analysis,

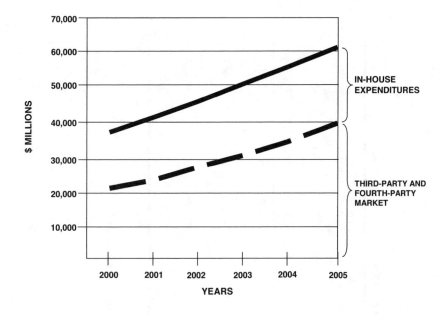

Figure 3.3 Total North American reverse logistics and repair services market (forward portion of the supply chain not included). (From Blumberg Associates, Inc. surveys and forecasting methodology [Appendix B and Appendix C].)

shown in Table 3.3 identifies that portion of the total closed loop market that is carried out by third and fourth party service logistics organizations.

In summary, it is very clear that the market demand for RL and related repair services, either stand-alone or as part of CLSC, is large and growing in both the high tech sector (defined in Table 3.4) and the consumer sector (defined in Table 3.5). This is shown in Table 3.6. The repair portion of this process, defined in Table 3.7, is in the range of about $23 billion, as shown in Table 3.8. It should be noted that there are also value-added services associated with depot repair, as summarized in Table 3.9, which represent an additional market demand.

The actual allocation of these services in total CLSC management is found in Figure 3.4.

DEPOT REPAIR AND VALUE-ADDED SERVICES

In general, the depot repair market includes both actual repair services and related value added services. Including value-added services, (in addition to depot repair), the total repair services market is larger by an

Table 3.2 Total Closed Loop Supply Chain Market in North America (2003)

Functions	Major Service Categories		Total by Segment
	Basic Services (Transportation, Warehousing and Repair)	Value-Added Services (Planning, Inventory Control, Scheduling, Etc.)	
Forward logistics related to total service logistics pipeline	8,454*	2,452	10,906
Reverse logistics related to total service logistics pipeline	7,595	3,370	10,965
Depot repair and associated value-added services	23,447	12,169	35,616
Total market	39,496	17,991	57,487

*$ = Millions

Source: From Blumberg Associates, Inc. surveys and forecasting methodology (Appendix B and Appendix C).

Table 3.3 Estimates of Total Available* Third Party and Fourth Party Closed Loop Service Logistics Market in North America (2003)

Functions	Basic Services (Transportation, Warehousing, and Repair)	Value-Added Services (Planning, Inventory Control, Scheduling, Etc.)	Total by Segment
		Major Service Categories	
Forward logistics related to total service logistics pipeline	2,460**	1,167	3,627
Reverse logistics related to total service logistics pipeline	2,426	1,250	3,676
Depot repair and associated value-added services	14,336	3,083	17,419
Total market	19,222	5,500	24,722

*Available market to external vendors, rather than internal logistics and repair organizations.

**$ = millions.

Source: From Blumberg Associates, Inc. surveys and forecasting methodology (Appendix B and Appendix C).

Table 3.4 Key Characteristics of Reverse Logistics Subsegments within the High Value Technical Products Market

Subsegments	"Typical" Third Party Logistics Providers in Segment	Third Party Penetration	Special Requirements	Revenue Drivers for Third Parties
Computers, peripherals and communications equipment	Most are repair depots or independent service providers who carry out RL as part of their overall service portfolio or solution	About 34% in both segments and approaching 42% over 5 years	Strong need for turnkey logistics/parts/repair solution in this segment, but need not be under one roof	Increased outsourcing, as a number of large OEM repair operations are now being outsourced
Industrial equipment (includes building systems)	Logistics in these segments is provided by third party logistics or third party RL services some depots and sales channel participants	31 to 33% now, with penetration in instruments falling to 30% and in machinery to 25% over 5 years	Here, the link to depots is not as strong as in some other segments, but ability to link with optimized service parts processes is a major issue	Market is retrenching with greater OEM focus on service; works against outsourcing in the immediate future
Medical equipment (includes scientific equipment)	Independent service providers, third party logistics providers, and third party RL providers	Stable in 33 to 36% range over forecast period	Ability to handle high criticality situations is very important; repair capabilities not an issue as OEMS generally do repair/refurb work	Although total share is stable, focus in shifting away from ISOs and depots toward OEMs for service in general

Electronics	Repair depots, third party logistics providers, and third party RL providers	Stable in 33 to 36% range over forecast period	Repair capabilities critical here; similar to computer and communications segments	Probably would see more growth if component markets were healthier; may take off in the long run
Electrical equipment	Repair depots, third party logistics providers, and third party RL providers	32% currently, falling off to 25 to 26% over 5 years	"Plan vanilla" segment well served by depots	Lack of clear outsourcing incentive for OEMs, relative third party positions slowly deteriorating
Photo/printing	Third party logistics providers, and third party RL providers	32% currently, falling to 27% over 5 years	Hazardous wastes are a key issue here	Increased emphasis on disposability is pushing third party RL opportunity into waste and "green" categories
Wholesale channels	Package shipper or independent service provider	Average 23 to 25%; most segments growing slightly over 5 years	May require multilevel approach serving both wholesale and OEM layers	Third party logistics and third party RL growth here is stunted by the fact that wholesale level is often either the service provider channel also, or is simply a pass-through to the OEMs

Table 3.5 Key Characteristics of Reverse Logistics Subsegments within the Consumer Goods Market

Subsegments	"Typical" Third Party Logistics Provider in Segment	Third Party Penetration	Requirements	Revenue Drivers for Third Parties
Food and kindred products	Asset-based third party logistics at manufacturer level, asset or nonasset based at others	Holding in 26 to 28% range at manufacturer level, growing slightly to 38% range at retail level	Heavily skewed toward disposal of expired, damaged, spoiled articles, but some reclamation activities	Growth at retail level comes from increased outsourcing in response to cost cutting/thinning margins and competition
Apparel/textiles	Mixed market at all levels, depends on type of apparel and retailer	Growing dramatically to 38% at manufacturer level and 43% at retail level	Need to handle both bulk and single-package returns; helps to have processing capabilities and other value-added services	Segment most affected by online/catalog buying, which comes with high return rates with deeper penetration
Appliances/ electronics and other durables	Mixed market at all levels, skewed toward asset-based at wholesale level	Holding steady around 21 to 22% at wholesale level; growing moderately 37 to 38% at retail level	Similar to apparel in mixed nature of market with less seasonality but also preference driven; helps to have value-added capabilities such as warranty processing and claim services	Increasing demand at retail level driven by increased outsourcing

Pharmaceuticals	Mostly nonasset based, except bulk waste disposal	Holding in 28 to 29% range at manufacturer level and 30 to 32% retail level	Requires regulatory knowledge and enhanced opportunity comes with hazmat/waste disposal capabilities	Growing with underlying product market and some moves to outsource additional services
General merchandise/ grocery	Strong area for nonasset-based providers, but asset-based third party logistics play here too	Rising slightly from 35 to 37% range	Most generic of all categories, requiring a solid base of basic RL capabilities	Rise in third party penetration comes as retail level sheds some capacity to save costs
Transportation/ automotive	Mixed market space, significant presence for package shippers	Holding in 21 to 22% range for wholesale level, growing to 32% in manufacturer level	Interface with parts depots and a variety of end users, as well as providing rapid delivery for refurbish and repair	Third party RL is trending with market in this segment, for the most part
Instruments, building equipment, etc.	Asset-based players are stronger force here than nonasset based	Some growth in third party share, to 31% by 5 year horizon	Works more like a technical goods market, with need to interface with or act as repair depot	Third party RL is trending with market in this segment, for the most part
Chemicals (cleaning, cosmetics, etc.)	Mixed base of providers, dependent on exact product types	Holding in the 28 to 29% range	Disposal and hazmat issues come into play here, along with accompanying regulatory knowledge	Third party RL is trending with market in this segment, for the most part

Table 3.6 Estimated Total North American Reverse Logistics Market (By Major Segment Category)

Major Service Category	Years						CAGR
	2000	2001	2002	2003	2004	2005	
Specialized high-value technical products	4,314.3	4,718.0	5,168.6	5,672.1	6,235.0	6,865.2	9.6%
Consumer goods	4,396.8	4,679.7	4,973.4	5,292.9	5,638.2	6,011.3	6.4%
Green product validation	903.1	948.0	997.0	1,048.7	1,103.3	1,160.9	5.1%
Packing, pallets, and containers	2,668.3	2,885.2	3,120.0	3,374.1	3,649.0	3,946.4	8.1%
Waste disposal and remediation							
General	6,302.9	6,922.0	7,622.1	8,415.2	9,315.4	10,339.0	10.3%
Specialized	5,236.9	6,098.1	7,159.2	8,473.5	10,110.1	12,159.5	17.9%
Hazmat	3,149.8	3,484.6	3,875.2	4,332.2	4,868.4	5,499.3	11.5%
Waste subtotal	14,689.6	16,504.6	18,656.5	21,220.9	24,293.9	27,997.9	13.4%
Total	26,972.1	29,735.5	32,915.5	36,608.7	40,919.4	45,981.8	11.0%

$ = million.

Source: From Blumberg Associates, Inc. surveys and forecasting methodology (Appendix B and Appendix C).

Table 3.7 Major Segments of the Depot Repair Market

Segment	Description	Assessment of Opportunity
Computers and EDP components and peripherals	• Large and growing • Highly competitive • Saturated with suppliers • Many very large suppliers	• Major opportunity in selected submarket segments (i.e., medical electronics, government)
Process control, plant and building automation	• High growth opportunity • Specialized suppliers • Relatively few firms • Good revenue and profit growth	• Large market; requires demonstrated reputation and validated capability in field for longer-term growth opportunity
Military and aerospace	• Highly fragmented • Generally stagnant growth • Declining margins overall	• In general, aerospace and defense segments presents several niche opportunities • New opportunities with DOD outsourcing initiatives
Telecommunications, terminals, and CPE	• Dominated by very large and/or specialized suppliers	• Strong growth opportunity for established firms, but hard to enter
Office products and office automation	• Many suppliers and distributors • Primarily involves electro-mechanical technology (as opposed to high tech) • Relatively low returns on investment	• Limited opportunity; requires expansion into office products distribution
Medical electronics	• Small but growing rapidly • Relatively high margins • Specialized suppliers	• Potential growth opportunity • Strong competition from resurgent large OEM/TPMs

Table 3.7 Major Segments of the Depot Repair Market (continued)

Segment	Description	Assessment of Opportunity
Electronic test and measurement equipment	• Small market compared to other major opportunities • Slow growth • Numerous small local and regional suppliers	• Limited growth potential in direct market • Good synergy with other market segments
ATE software and fixturing	• Small market size • Low growth expectations • May involve supplying potential competitors	• Limited opportunity
Other electronics	• Miscellaneous equipment and instrumentation • Generally many small, local service providers	• Limited market • Should be evaluated on a case-by-case basis

Source: From Blumberg Associates, Inc. surveys and forecasting methodology (Appendix B and Appendix C).

Table 3.8 Total Depot Repair and Related Logistics Support Market (By Major Segments)

Services	Year		
	2001	*2002*	*2003*
Computer/EDP	3,063*	3,191	3,325
Process and environmental controls/plant building and automation	4,029	4,319	4,631
Military/aerospace	2,825	2,979	3,138
Communications/networks	5,390	5,826	6,311
Analytic/test and measuring instruments	1,885	2,001	2,123
Office products/office automation	883	893	904
Medical electronics	935	987	1,042
ATE software/fixturing	224	236	248
Other electronics	1,070	1,201	1,350
Total	20,304	21,633	23,073

* $ = millions.

Source: From Blumberg Associates, Inc. surveys and forecasting methodology (Appendix B and Appendix C).

Table 3.9 Total Market for Selected Value-Added Services Related to Depot Repair Service (By Type of Service)

Services	Years			CAGR
	2001	2002	2003	
End-of-life management	2,082*	2,191	2,305	8.8%
Contract manufacturing	2,128	2,449	2,820	12.6%
Advanced logistics and inventory support	1,061	1,215	1,391	12.1%
Extended warranty support	471	532	601	11.0%
Spare parts sales	2,145	2,321	2,511	7.3%
Technical support	1,067	1,266	1,501	15.1%
Equipment leasing	1,108	1,252	1,414	11.0%
Total	10,063	11,227	12,543	10.8%

*$ = millions.

Source: From Blumberg Associates, Inc. surveys and forecasting methodology (Appendix B and Appendix C).

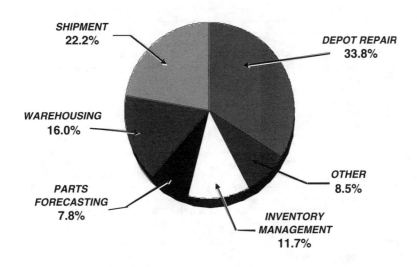

Figure 3.4   Allocation of repair services/reverse logistics including expenditure by function. (From Blumberg Associates, Inc. surveys and forecasting methodology [Appendix B and Appendix C].)

additional 21% overall throughout the projection period. In total, the repair, related logistics, and value-added market available is projected to grow from $11.7 billion in 1999 to $21.6 billion in 2004 (see Figure 3.5). This represents compound annual growth in the outsourced market of 13%, as compared to 3.4% in the captive segment. As a result, the share of outsourced services available to fourth party providers is expected to rise from 45.2% in 1999 to 56.2% in 2004 (see Figure 3.6). Clearly, outsourcing and other key market trends are working in favor of fourth party repair depots in a number of market segments.

OPERATING DYNAMICS OF THE REVERSE LOGISTICS AND CLOSED LOOP SUPPLY CHAIN MARKETS

In addition to measuring the size of these markets, surveys have been used to evaluate competitive market dynamics and trends. Approximately two-thirds of the market use outside vendors for some or all RL and repair service support activities. In the high tech market, it is quite clear that logistics managers see a critical need for interaction, coordination, and integration of their (field) service activities with RL and depot repair

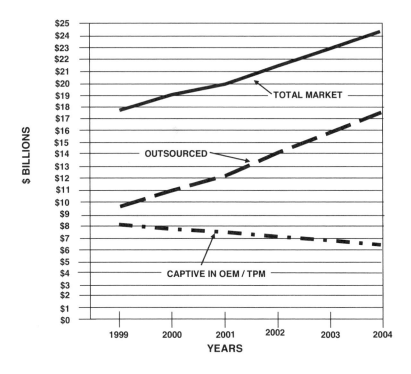

Figure 3.5 Depot repair and logistics market opportunity: captive vs. out-sourced. (From Blumberg Associates, Inc. surveys and forecasting methodology [Appendix B and Appendix C].)

functions in day-to-day operations. A survey conducted in 2002 indicated that approximately 72% of respondents saw this interaction as being critical. The surveys also identified the growing importance of having a single outside provider capable of providing the full range of CLSC support service. These surveys also show that both high tech– and consumer-oriented organizations are looking to receive a very broad array of services as part of CLSC management portfolio, as shown in Table 3.10.

The surveys also looked at the current processes and dynamics of the CLSC process as practiced, identifying the methods of shipment as a function of the type of part shipment, as shown in Table 3.11. This investigation also indicated that, particularly in the high tech market, requests for new parts resupply and control of refurbished parts in the field are usually made 46% of the time through a laptop, handheld or other wireless device, as opposed to 51% telephone call, and 5% using fax, or standard mail.

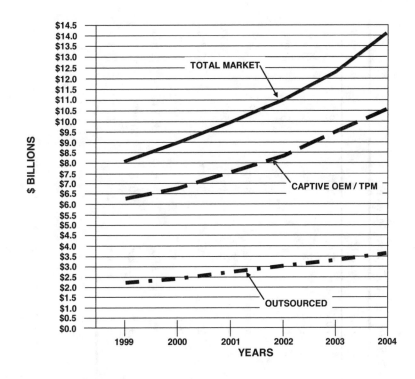

Figure 3.6   Value-added services market related to depot repair: captive vs. outsourced. (From Blumberg Associates, Inc. surveys and forecasting methodology [Appendix B and Appendix C].)

COMPETITIVE EVALUATION

The surveys used to identify the size and trends in the market were also used to identify competitive players and participants. As shown in Figure 3.7, the market identifies:

- Service arms of OEM organizations
- Full repair and return logistics providers
- Logistics/distribution providers with repair and RL capability or alliance
- Logistics suppliers with RL capabilities
- RL specialists and consultants
- Fourth party maintainers (depot repair facilities)
- Commercial waste collection and processing companies
- Public warehouse companies

Table 3.10 Depot Repair Value-Added Service Opportunity (Outsourced vs. Captive Services)

Services	1999	2000	2001	2002	2003	2004	CAGR
End-of-life management	583*	643	703	770	841	917	9.5%
Contract manufacturing	400	460	529	608	698	803	14.9%
Advanced logistics and inventory support	201	230	262	300	342	391	14.2%
Extended warranty support	77	89	104	121	140	162	16.1%
Spare parts sales	417	468	527	592	663	743	12.25%
Technical support	187	220	259	305	359	423	17.7%
Equipment leasing	198	227	260	289	322	352	12.2%
Subtotal: outsourced	2,063	2,338	2,644	2,984	3,366	3,791	12.9%
Subtotal: captive**	6,063	6,698	7,419	8,206	9,098	10,088	10.7%
Total	8,126	9,036	10,063	11,190	12,464	13,879	11.3%

*$ = milllions.

**Captive in OEM or TPM operations.

Source: From Blumberg Associates, Inc. surveys and forecasting methodology (Appendix B and Appendix C).

Table 3.11 Logistics Service Currently Purchased from Outside Providers

Logistics Service Offerings	Percentage That Currently Purchase from an Outside Provider	Mean Rating of Importance	Mean Rating of Impact
Call handling and dispatch	32.5%	6.38	5.77
Entitlement	30.0%	7.08	5.75
Order management	82.5%	7.33	6.55
Real time order tracking and shipment visibility	62.5%	8.04	7.40
RMA coordination	35.0%	7.00	5.36
Call avoidance and technical assistance	10.0%	6.75	6.50
Service parts management	12.5%	6.40	5.60
Repair and refurbishment	50.0%	7.10	6.15
Strategic stocking locations	17.5%	7.14	6.43
Central distribution	37.5%	7.60	5.60
Replenishment	37.5%	7.13	6.07
Reverse logistics and returns capability	55.0%	7.09	5.73
Service parts planning and forecasting	22.5%	6.89	4.67
Service parts inventory visibility	20.0%	7.50	5.50
Transportation and shipping	92.5%	7.68	7.32
Optimization of parts shipments	30.0%	7.67	5.50
Warranty management	17.5%	7.29	5.29

Table 3.11 Logistics Service Currently Purchased from Outside Providers (continued)

Logistics Service Offerings	Percentage That Currently Purchase from an Outside Provider	Mean Rating of Importance	Mean Rating of Impact
On-site parts/components swaps	12.5%	7.60	7.00
Whole unit swaps	7.5%	7.00	7.00
Screening and testing	20.0%	7.13	5.88
Disposition and end-of-life management	12.5%	7.40	6.20

Source: From Blumberg Associates, Inc. surveys and forecasting methodology (Appendix B and Appendix C).

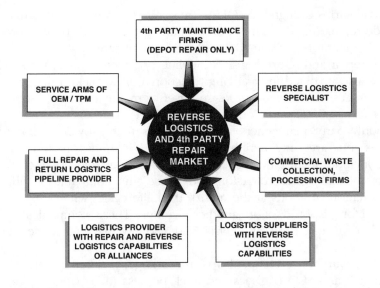

Figure 3.7   Competition in the closed loop supply chains and reverse logistics and repair service market. (From Blumberg Associates, Inc. surveys and forecasting methodology [Appendix B and Appendix C].)

Logistics suppliers with RL capabilities include companies such as:

- Yellow Freight Systems
- U.S. Freightways
- Consolidated Freightways

These competitors began operations in the logistics market and have created divisions or subsidiaries that capitalize on the growing market for RL.

RL specialists like Genco have completely organized their companies with a focus on the market for return management and RL. Another category of competition includes logistics companies that have widened their focus to include RL services. In addition, some of these companies have developed repair capabilities in-house or have made strategic alliances with repair specialists in order to offer this service to customers. At an initial glance, key competitors in this category include:

- Airborne Express
- Federal Express
- UPS Logistics

Service arms of high tech OEMs are competition in the sense that they provide repair services; an important part of the overall returns process. These competitors include IBM and GE, among others.

Full repair and return logistics pipeline providers offer repair services, but are also involved in arranging transportation to pickup materials and return processed materials to the end user or manufacturer. These include firms such as CDTI and Genco.

Fourth party maintainers are companies that provide depot repair services, but are only peripherally involved in transportation services. These include organizations such as Data Exchange and Datatech Depot.

Commercial waste collection and processing companies handle the transportation of goods at the end of their life cycle, when they may be recycled or disposed of in another manner. These companies include Brooklyn Salvage, Browning-Ferris, and Waste Management, Inc., among others.

Public warehouse companies — these large, national or international firms, such as USCO Logistics and Exel, possess RL capabilities. Because storage of wastes, recyclables, and returns must occur at some point in the RL channel, all participants can be viewed as potential competitors or partners to these firms.

The market analysis, surveys and competitive evaluation clearly demonstrate the increasing importance of the full CLSC, including RL and depot repair support, in a variety of important market segments. End users, retailers, and OEMs are also increasingly outsourcing their RL and repair requirements. Consolidation is important in the RL and repair and fourth party repair service supply market through mergers and acquisitions.* This trend will continue.**

In summary, key market trends and market potential, as identified above, will force RL and repair service outsourcing vendors, operating in a pure RL capacity or as part of the overall CLSC process, will continuously improve the efficiency and productivity of their operations. It is also necessary to be cost and time competitive, as market demands for CLSC management services continue to grow. This will also result in increasing the number of strategic alliances and partnerships between various vendors and their customers.

Finally, the surveys and forecasts show a significant increase in the amount of money being spent on CLSC and RL process improvements in both high tech and consumer goods markets. This is driven by the

---

* See recent merger and acquisition activities of third and fourth party logistics firms by UPS, Genco, USCO, DecisionOne, etc.

** For example, the acquisition of Airborne by DHL, in mid-2003.

recognition of the growing value of goods (whole units, parts, subassemblies, etc.) created in the field. By speeding up the RL and repair process, the effect is to reduce the amount of inventory required to meet a given level of future purchases and end user demand.

4

MANAGING HIGH TECH CLOSED LOOP SUPPLY CHAINS AND SERVICE PARTS LOGISTICS

INTRODUCTION

The very significant changes that have been taking place in the high tech service and logistics support industry over the last 10 to 15 years have led to dramatic improvements in the strategic management, control, and direction of field reverse logistics (RL) support for whole units, subassemblies, and spare parts control using a closed loop system. In order to understand and make use of these improvements, it is essential to see, in a broader perspective, the almost revolutionary changes, which have taken place in the typical field and logistics support service organization. In general, in the 1950s through the 1980s, in almost all equipment manufacturing sectors, but particularly in high tech areas (data processing, office automation, telecommunications, medical electronics, etc.), field service, including the provision of whole unit installation, maintenance, and repair services, was operated as a cost center.

Typically, these service organizations were highly decentralized, focusing primarily on the issues of getting the service engineer to the site to support installation tasks for whole units in the event of failure observed by the customer after installation, to repair the equipment, and for preventative and/or predictive maintenance tasks. Service management, as it existed, was primarily concerned with the supervisory questions associated with field control of service personnel, and logistics delivery with a heavy emphasis placed on general customer satisfaction along with an adherence to the agreed upon budget or cost allocation. Manufacturers and distributors provided these services in the high tech industries; in other industries, internal building or plant maintenance service organizations performed these tasks.

At this time, logistics and parts support generally came from the "factory" manufacturing function. Complete products (whole units), subassemblies, and parts were usually obtained from the manufacturing inventory, or in crisis situations, directly from the production line. From the perspective of the service organization supporting manufacturing or distribution, parts were "free." Even for the end user with its own internal maintenance and service forces, parts were acquired by the user at the time of installation or by a purchasing office. Here again, for the service personnel, parts were considered as free, or as part of the initial purchase.

The starting point for this service was the result of a product sale; this set up an order request to the service organization for product delivery and installation. Typically, the product delivery and installation was accompanied by an installation service engineer who provided the setup, test and check out, training and documentation, and orientation of the end user to the equipment and technology. In general, the presumption was that this equipment, once installed, would be permanently utilized by the purchaser until the end of its life. In general, depending upon the business distribution model used, the actual service after installation would be provided either by the original equipment manufacturer (OEM) or dealer service organization as part of a full closed loop supply chain (CLSC) system, or by the purchaser's own internal plant and/or building services organization involving self-maintenance and repair. The whole product was rarely, if ever, returned as a full unit unless major catastrophic failure or failure to perform occurred. In general, if the full unit failed, individual components, subassemblies, or parts were pulled and replaced by either the assigned service personnel from the manufacturer or distributor or available service personnel from internal plant and building maintenance service forces. The ultimate disposal of the product was at the discretion of the purchaser. In some cases, a manufacturer would accept the old, used unit as a trade-in, providing limited credit against the new purchase price. In most cases, however, the product was sold to a broker or junk dealer who then disposed of the product, or simply paid for the product removal. In certain limited markets, such as office furniture, small secondary market dealers developed selling both new and used products.

This highly decentralized, fragmented cost center approach to field service in the high tech sector changed dramatically in the 1980s and 1990s and has continued to change into the twenty-first century. Service is now being managed typically as a profit center or independent line of business; it is generally run centrally with its own physical distribution, logistics support, parts management, and control functions. In the modern service organization,* a service call from the customer is not viewed as a call for an automatic on-site dispatch, but rather as a basis for determining what actions are to be taken in order to resolve the customer's problems in the most timely and cost-effective manner possible.

In-depth technical analysis, remote diagnostics and call avoidance mechanisms are now being increasingly used as an online part of the call handling process (see Figure 4.1) to attempt to avoid altogether the need for physical on-site dispatch (through advising the customer to take his own corrective action or through the dispatch and shipment of whole units, parts, supplies, corrective software, etc., directly to the end user). In addition, many of the internal plant and building maintenance organizations have been outsourced to third party or OEM service organizations, requiring dispatch and assignment of independent service engineers from outside the plant or facility.

In the modern call management process, discussed in Figure 4.1, the initial request for service could involve:

- Initial purchase ordering process and request to deliver/install the product
- Product problem on requirement for service assistance
- Need for change, modification, or retrofit of the product
- Product removal

The first process step involves a diagnostic analysis to determine what actions to take, what resources are required (service, personnel, parts, whole units, etc.) and the timing of the service requirement. The next step is to schedule, assign, and dispatch the appropriate resources (service on installation, engineer, product shipment, etc.) and to initiate the service call task. The third step is to modify the field service organization through:

- Paper request
- Beeper/pager
- Laptop or PDA

The final stages involve the management of the service process, leading to a completion of the service request, and "close out" of the call, and this would in turn, provide complete data on:

- What was done (installation, repair, preventative maintenance, etc.)

---

* This entire process is described in detail in Managing High Tech Service Using a CRM Strategy, by Donald F. Blumberg, CRC Press, 1999.

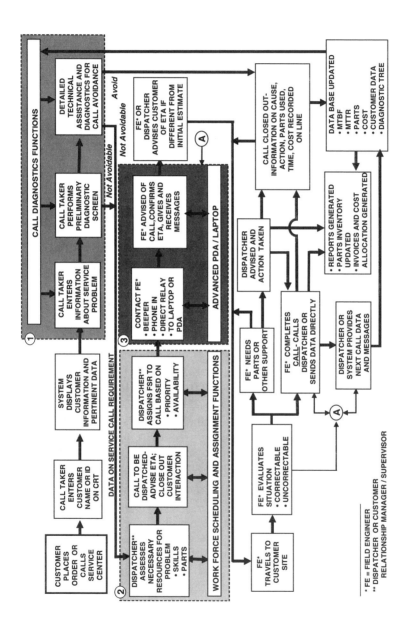

Figure 4.1 Overview of call management process. (From Blumberg, D. [2002], *Managing High-Tech Services Using a CRM Strategy*, New York: St. Lucie Press.)

- Time and cost data
- Updated, customer tasks and requirements, including configuration status
- Parts and materials used
- Other information about service calls

In those cases in which an actual on-site call is required after such "call avoidance" diagnostics is completed, the analysis as part of the call handling process can provide specific recommendations to the service engineer as to which parts should be taken with him on the service call, thus, reducing the percentage of "broken" calls, or calls in which the service effort must be halted until a subsequent time when parts or technical assistance is available. An alternative approach is to dispatch another service engineer or "courier" to get the part or subassembly to the service engineer in the field. In effect, by looking at the full timeline of a service call request (Figure 4.2), it is possible to see the impact of parts, knowledge and data, and real parts availability and resupply on overall service efficiency and elapsed time. Parts and subassemblies management impacts the service timeline in the following areas: call handling and diagnostics and the service call on site.

- Call handling and diagnostics — An analysis of the customer call request can often be used to determine the cause of the service problem, the parts required to fix it, and other actions. If these actions are simple, and can be carried out by the user, the call

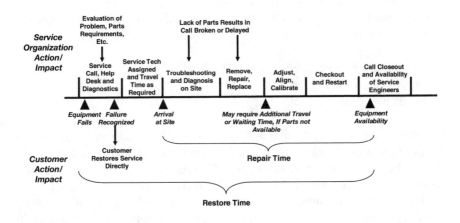

Figure 4.2 Field service timeline.

handling process could result in providing instructions and guidance to the user-operator and/or shipping a part, item of software, or supply to the user, thus closing out the call. If the problem can not be corrected centrally or through the user himself, then diagnostics can be used to determine who should be dispatched, and with what parts. Since 60 to 75% of all service calls require one or more parts, this step is very important. In essence, through the use of call diagnosis, based on past data about parts failure and relationship or equipment failure to parts failure, the problem can be resolved by the user directly, or the service dispatch can be much more efficient through insuring that both the right skill sets and parts are dispatched and assigned.

■ Service call on site — Upon arrival at the site, as shown in the timeline in Figure 4.2, the service engineer begins his troubleshooting and diagnostics, typically using a pull-and-replace process, requiring one or more parts or subassemblies. If the parts are available, the process can be completed rapidly; if the parts are not available in the hands of the service engineer, in his trunk, or at the site, the service engineer has one of three options:
  - Break off the call altogether and request a new dispatch
  - Leave the site to pick up a part at some location and return
  - Await the delivery of the part by another service engineer or courier

In any case, the lack of the right part or subassembly at the right place and at the right time leads to either a short delay or long delay (broken call) in the same timeline. This analysis and evaluation of the service timeline shows that parts, subassemblies, and even whole unit availability (for full swap out) can directly affect service efficiency and cost effectiveness in terms of:

■ Overall restore time
■ Service repair time
■ Travel time

The most effective way to manage and control this situation is to optimize the field engineer trunk stock fill rate and reduce broken or delayed calls. This is best accomplished through a CLSC to control the logistics flow down to the field level and back to the repair depot.

As a result, substantial changes have, and are taking place with respect to the management, direction, and control of the full logistics pipeline in the high tech field. While much is being currently done in the area of improvements in call handling, diagnostics, and dispatch, it is in the area of closed loop control of service parts, subassemblies, and whole unit logistics management where some of the most innovative and productive improvements have been made.

As indicated above, service operations usually require a combination of service personnel skills and parts in order to successfully complete the process of installation, maintenance, and repair in the field. Depending upon the product technology involved, for between 60 to 70% of all service calls on average, a part or parts, subassemblies or whole units are required in order to complete a "fix" or repair. As a result of this important requirement for parts in the field, there is a great tendency for proliferation and distribution of parts locally, often found in the trunks of the service engineer's cars or vans on sites, and in some cases, squirreled away in service engineer's homes or lockers, or at the installation site itself.

Given the general structure of the logistics and distribution pipeline, it is very important to recognize that perhaps the most important element of the pipeline is to insure an optimum fill rate at the service engineer trunk or site level. Service engineers fill rate is computed by dividing the number of times a demand for the part is made, divided by the number of times that the part is available at the particular stock location.

CLOSED LOOP SUPPLY CHAIN STRATEGY

The key to understanding the effective management of logistics and control in high tech service rests on a strategic conceptual approach to the total flow of parts, subassemblies, whole units, and so forth, in the field. In the typical field service environment, a closed logistics pipeline exists, as shown in Figure 4.3, which involves the continuing flow of parts, subassemblies, and whole unit/loaners, as well as test equipment to and from the field. At the central warehouse facility, material flows in from the organization's manufacturing centers (to the extent they exist), as well as from external vendor purchases. They also flow to the central warehouse through a return loop from the field for depot refurbishing and rehabilitation operations. The parts (stock-keeping units; SKU), subassemblies, and whole units then flow downward to district or branch warehouses/depots, and ultimately to service engineers, installers in the field, or both. This material is then used in the installation, maintenance, and repair tasks associated with servicing the installed customer base.

In general, and typically in the maintenance/repair actions, some SKU are pulled out of customer equipment and replaced to fix the unit. These could include low value or cost, or nonrepairable items that are often disposed of, and high value or cost, repairable items that are sent back for rehabilitation and refurbishment. It should be noted that the current philosophy of pull-and-replace rather than repair in the field usually leads to perfectly good parts and units also being returned. The final link in

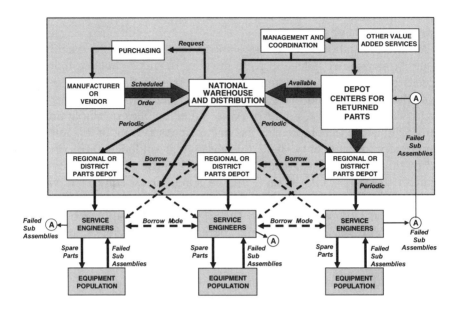

Figure 4.3   High tech closed loop chain.

this integrated, closed loop pipeline is the refurbishment/depot repair function which returns the units "pulled" and replaced in the field, back to the central warehouse or the district and/or branch local depots, and from there back to the field.

Given this concept of an integrated logistics "closed loop" pipeline, which describes the flow of the material within the service environment, it is of interest to note some key operational parameters. These include:

- Approximately 50% of the total value of the inventory within the pipeline is generally found below the manned warehouses or depots, either being transported to or from the field in the trunks or hands of the service engineers, or in some cases, stored at customer sites, or flowing from the service engineers themselves back to a central location for processing and dispatching. In addition, of course, is the installed base of the product, which will also flow back as it is "built" and/or replaced.
- Approximately 80% of the value of the service inventory flows from service engineers and the installed base in the field, back into the return pipeline through the refurbishment and rehabilitation depots.
- Approximately 30 to 35% of the material returned by the service engineer from the field to the repair depot is, in fact, good or "no

trouble found" units. This particular parameter is increasing as more and more service engineers use pull-and-replace as part of their diagnostic test activities in emergency maintenance and repair in the field.

These critical and key parameters all support a general strategic philosophy that the logistics pipeline in field service should be managed as a total integrated closed loop process on an "end-to-end" basis. In addition, one of the most critical points in the pipeline process is reporting on the status and use of parts and the related cause at the service engineer field level. Finally the most effective means for resupply of the pipeline back to the field service engineers is through effective control of the depot refurbishment and rehabilitation return loop operations.

In essence, the key to efficient and profitable management and control of service operations in the field is heavily dependent on the ability to provide an extremely high fill rate (the rate determined by dividing the number of requests for a SKU into the number of times that the request can be filled at a given stock location), at the field service engineer trunk level, in order to minimize the percentage of broken off or aborted calls due to lack of parts, subassemblies, or whole units. This is, of course, not the only parameter of field service, but it is certainly an important one. The other component of the logistics objective function in the field service CLSC would be to minimize the investment in inventory and operating costs of the logistics pipeline. Investment optimization becomes more critical as the cost of individual SKU increases. Since the level of integration on individual circuit boards, components, and modules is rising daily, thus, increasing the inventory carrying value of the individual SKU, it makes closely controlled logistics investment management of the pipeline more important than ever. In essence, the closed loop logistics supply chain must be managed such that the cost-effective service engineer trunk level fill rate objective is met at minimum or at least optimum investment in inventory and logistics support operating costs.

A typical trunk level fill rate ranges from about 85 to 95% depending upon target levels of customer satisfaction (i.e., response and repair time objectives) and willingness to accept investment risk. Unfortunately, many service organizations still do not operate utilizing the integrated CLSC concept as described. Many service organizations fail to recognize the need to achieve total control of the full pipeline with particular focus on tracking of all parts and SKUs used down to, at, and returned from the field. This can be best done through reporting of parts used and changes in installed base at the time of service call close-out for installation service and repair or removal services. Other organizations fail to recognize the vital importance of the depot refurbishment and rehabilitation and repair return loop. In point of fact, through utilizing a "just in time" approach to field depot repair, it is actually possible to significantly reduce the total logistics inventory investment in a closed loop system.

Finally, many logistics organizations are still utilizing inventory control systems and processes developed in a manufacturing environment, which is not a closed loop. They fail to recognize the much more complex parts demand patterns that exist in the service environment due to the existence of a return cycle and long run product life cycle which can materially affect demand patterns over time.

In the manufacturing process, demand patterns are usually forecastable on the basis of production requirements forecasting and material resource planning (MRP) scheduling. In addition, the parts used in the manufacturing process do not, in effect, "return." In the production environment, the logistics inventory flows only outward to the customer. The complexities produced by the return loop cycle in the typical field service inventory generally invalidate the normal inventory forecast models and mechanisms used in the manufacturing environment for inventory control.

FACTORS AFFECTING EFFICIENCY AND PRODUCTIVITY OF CLOSED LOOP SUPPLY CHAIN MANAGEMENT AND CONTROL

For logistics managers of CLSC, it is vitally important to recognize several key factors that will influence the ability to successfully manage and control the SKU pipeline and optimize service engineer fill rate at minimum investment and logistics operations costs. These factors include installed base density impact, key inventory control mechanisms, and the efficient use of depot refurbishment, rehabilitation, and repair.

■ Installed base density impact
– The density of the installed base has a significant impact on the bottom-line profitability of the service operation. The key factor is that the higher the density, the easier it is to stock, control, and deliver spare parts, subassemblies, and whole units, and to avoid broken calls. Density also, of course, influences service engineer travel time and, therefore, response time. However, as shown in Figure 4.4, bottom-line profitability significantly improves as the density of the installed base increases. Thus, the denser the base of equipment served, the easier becomes the job of determining how much, and at what locations in the CLSC the inventory should be allocated and stored. Again, as the level of component and board integration rises, parts replacement at

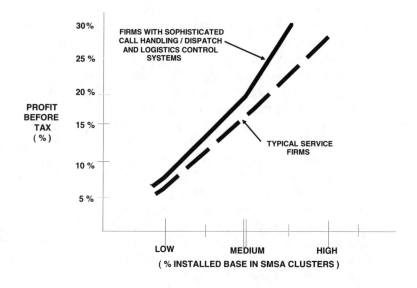

Figure 4.4   Impact of density and infrastructure on service profitability. (From Blumberg Associates, Inc. [Appendix B and Appendix C].)

the board level, rather than repair on site, becomes more prevalent. The cost of carrying inventory in the field increases significantly and density becomes even more a factor in achieving profitable performance. Where parts are a significant element of cost, an increase in number of customers without retaining or improving density levels can result in less profit rather than more. Unfortunately, the installed based density is typically not under the control of the logistics manager, but rather the product managers or (in the case of third party maintenance/independent service organizations) under the control of the service marketing managers. In point of fact, the introduction of third party maintenance service in a product-based service organization can provide a mechanism to significantly improve installed base densities, and therefore improve the effectiveness of CLSC logistics management and control.

■ Key inventory control mechanisms
   – An important factor affecting the efficiency of the logistics management is the level and specificity of control of the pipeline. Parts can be controlled at the individual SKU level, or in kits, or through a combination of parts and kit control for a specific product. Both kit control and SKU control have value in logistics management, but it is critical to understand where kitting strat-

egies work and do not work. Kits are best employed in situations involving very limited installed base density or during product roll-in or roll-out. Kits are not effective as SKU control during the general midterm life cycle of a product, particularly if the densities are reasonably high. Generally, service organizations should be using a combination of parts and SKU control down to and including the service engineer trunk level.

■ Efficient use of depot refurbishment, rehabilitation, and repair
   – Another mechanism that can be used to fine tune the performance of the CLSC pipeline is the detailed scheduling and control of repair, refurbishment, rehabilitation, or depot operations. By introducing a quality assurance check at the arrival of parts and subassemblies from the field, and tracking those subassemblies back to the service engineer who initiated the field pull-and-replacement, it is possible to identify those service engineers who are, in essence, utilizing the SKU pipeline as a test and diagnostic mechanism. This data can be utilized to retrain service engineers in the field to improve the effective use of the service engineer trunk stock, as well as to introduce more formal diagnostic procedures at the field level. Perhaps most important is the concept of detailed scheduling of resupply to the field through very rapid turn around of the depot repair operation.*
   – Some service organizations, such as Texas Instruments, have utilized artificial intelligence mechanisms in their depot repair and refurbished lines to significantly improve the ability to refurbish/repair any type of circuit board (from Texas Instruments or other manufacturers), as well as to significantly reduce the amount of time required to diagnose and ultimately repair the circuit board or unit. Using advanced test diagnostics, using conveyer systems to move the diagnosed SKU to the appropriate work stations for refurbishment and repair (R&R), it is possible to bring the total elapsed time from the initiation of a scheduled request for a SKU or board repair from a work in process (WIP) holding inventory to shipment to the field within approximately 2 to 4 hours. With this type of elapsed R&R time, a significant percentage of all parts requests can be filled from the just in time repair depot, rather than from central stocks or placed on back order for manufacturing or external vendor shipments.

In summary, there are a number of mechanisms, including changing the installed base density, through focused, proactive third party mainte-

---

* The depot repair process is discussed in more detail in Chapter 6.

nance marketing, improved stock control by stock keeping unit down to and including the service engineer trunk level, improved forecasting mechanisms and systems, and use of increasingly efficient depot refurbishment and rehabilitation operations that can all be utilized to significantly improve the efficiency and effectiveness of the CLSC in the high tech markets pipeline.

ADVANCED FORECASTING MECHANISMS FOR CLOSED LOOP SUPPLY CHAIN MANAGEMENT AND CONTROL

Of the various tools and techniques available to the logistics manager, one of the most important and yet least understood is the use of advanced forecasting to determine stock demand in a closed loop system. Typically most field service logistics organizations utilize simple linear or exponential smoothing forecasting models based upon inventory control systems developed in the manufacturing environment. Unfortunately, such simplistic techniques do not account for the more complex demand patterns found in a field service environment involving CLSC. In broad terms, parts demand is primarily affected by the multiple effect of both the product life cycle and the installed base density. Once a product has been rolled in and before phase out, and assuming a very large density of base, it is relatively easy to forecast demand using standard statistical models.

The problem in forecasting parts demand in field service primarily occurs in the situations involving:

- Product roll-in (i.e., early life cycle stage)
- Product roll-out (end of life cycle stage)
- Low density

For these situations in general, and in specific combinations (i.e., low density, early product roll-in) parts failure patterns occur sporadically in the form of a spiked demand (See Figure 4.5). In these cases, averaging forecasting techniques, based on a presumption of a Possion, Gaussion, or normal distribution of demand is essentially doomed to failure.

Examples of SKU parts demand patterns, during a product phase in/phase out period, or normal product midlife is shown in Figure 4.5. One approach to treating these differences is to recognize that cumulative demand pattern is much more stable than the actual demand pattern per unit of time (Figure 4.6). In essence, the generic shape of the cumulative demand pattern can be used as a general predictor at various stages of product life cycle. Examples of cumulative demand for a specific SKU in the early roll-in stage, late roll-out stage, or during the general life cycle are shown in Figure 4.7. Inspection of these cumulative curves show fairly

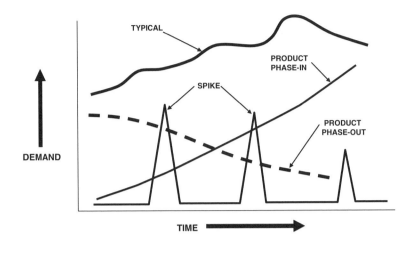

Figure 4.5 SKU demand pattern for stages of product life cycle. (From Blumberg Associates, Inc. [Appendix B and Appendix C].)

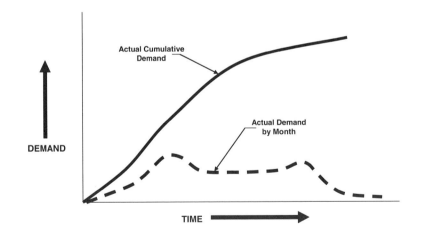

Figure 4.6 General parts demand pattern — comparing incrementally and cumulatively. (From Blumberg Associates, Inc. [Appendix B and Appendix C].)

stabilized demand. A combination of exponential or log normal forecasting mechanism, modified by the life cycle characteristics, could then be used to accurately predict future demand based upon actual real time failure, use, and demand data.

A powerful demand forecasting mechanism that can be useful in the field service CLSC, is the application of Bayesian inference for forecasting

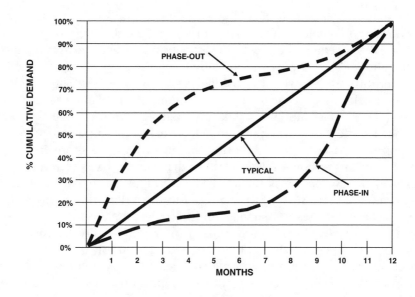

Figure 4.7   Rest of world UPS service market potential — by end user application. (From Blumberg Associates, Inc. [Appendix B and Appendix C].)

of spiked demand situations. Bayesian inference is predicated upon the assumption that the environment of demand may, in fact, not be normally distributed but is rather biased to the left or right or involves some other unusual demand characteristic. In essence, Bayesian inference is based upon a concept of establishing incremental time periods and to their use in at least two separate and differentiated formal forecasting mechanisms (for example, exponential smoothing and linear extrapolation). In Bayesian inference in time period t, historical demand data from approximately two to three previous time periods (t − 1, t − 2, and t − 3) are utilized to forecast future demand in the next time period (t + 1) utilizing the two separate forecasting mechanisms. For the time period t + 1, the actual forecast is simply a weighted average of the results of the two forecasting models. However, once the experience of the actual demand in t − 1 is gained, it is then possible to compare the actual experience at t − 1 with the weighted forecast made in time period t for the period t − 1. This data (the ratio of the t − 1 actual to forecast demand) index, which compares the actual demand to the forecast demand at t − 1, becomes the start of a new data time series that can also be forecasted. In essence, in forecasting for t − 2, the previous actual demands for t - 1, t, and t + 1 are then used to forecast. The forecast is then made for t + 2, utilizing the two individual basic forecasting methods.

In summary, it is critical to the effective control of the closed loop logistics supply chain that accurate forecasting mechanisms provide the basis for both setting the stock levels to be maintained at the manned central and regional depots and stocking locations, as well as at the service engineer trunk stock level. It is also necessary to have the ability to adjust these stock levels in terms of both minimum and maximum levels over time as the product life cycles that drive parts demand change.

The first step in developing an effective forecasting approach is to recognize that data must be collected on an accurate basis, driven by the use of parts at the time of repair, rather than on the basis of requests or issuances. In essence, it is essential to determine the actual mean time between failure (MTBF) by SKUs in order to drive demand estimates. The use of data that relates to issuance tends to reflect the tendency of service engineers to stockpile or hoard parts. It may not be directly related to the product life cycle which drives demand, the MTBF of the SKUs, or the effects of the actual logistics management strategy employed.

Given that accurate data can be developed on demand (MTBF) by SKUs, the next major step, prior to actual forecasting, is to recognize that the form of the data can be analyzed on the basis of either demand in unit time, or cumulative demand. The problem of looking at demand patterns in unit or sequential time is that the demands can be masked or affected by change in product life cycle demand. The general characteristic cumulative demand curve profile is significantly different than the average demand over time. In essence, converting the unit time demands to cumulative demand not only smooths out the demand patterns, but allows the framework for an analytical consideration of the effects of the product life cycle on parts demand.

Given the demand data and the consideration of product life cycle stage, six broad types of analytical forecasting methods can be, and are used, in CLSC control. These include:

- Simple average — The typical approach used by many unsophisticated logistics managers is the use of simple averaging. This includes computing the average of all past demand data in order to get a future demand forecast.
- Moving average — The moving average method selects data from the last few time periods. This provides a somewhat more accurate method in response to recent changes and trends.
- Weighted moving average — The weighted moving average method places different weights on the previous time frame data, for different time periods. This approach will, in general, improve on either the simple moving average or the basic averaging technique, but does require the introduction of judgments for the weighting mechanisms.

- Exponential smoothing — The exponential smoothing method is a variation of the weighted moving average. It utilizes an exponential weighting curve to develop the weighting mechanism. Thus, the weights are applied systematically eliminating the need for judgmental views. The exponential smoothing method is probably the most widely used amongst sophisticated logistics managers.
- Holt's method — Holt's method is a more sophisticated variation of the exponential smoothing forecasting approach in that it adds additional factors or historical trend mechanisms. In general, Holt's method will improve on exponential smoothing forecasting accuracy if the general changes in demand are gradual.
- Bayesian inference — A more powerful analytical forecasting method is the use of Bayesian Inference. This provides the ability to adjust forecasting methodology and techniques based upon the probability of state change of individual SKU. Bayesian inference is particularly valid and valuable in the typical case in an electronic environment for slow moving parts, in which the demands are spiked or the changes are not gradual.

A summary of the available analytical forecasting methods used in closed loop logistics control is presented in Table 4.1. Of the above methods, exponential smoothing and Bayesian inference represent the most useful tools in closed loop logistics management and control.

While it has been pointed out above that accurate forecasting of demand is critical, there is another option. Since the driver in forecasting is the accuracy and timeliness of the forecast, we can also consider the concept of real-time coordination and control.

If a service organization is prepared to make an investment in wireless PDA or laptop technology to equip each service/installation engineer in the field with the ability to report both actual use and new parts demands as it occurs, and if we can accelerate the rate of movement of the RL return chain to include physical movement and depot repair (using just in time) technology as described in Chapter 6, it is possible to reduce the need for accurate short-term forecasts. In other words, real-time control and coordination of the full CLSC (Figure 4.3) offers the ability to meet field demands in the short run from expediting the return to the field of SKUs within the timeframe required by the service engineer (i.e., 2 to 6 hours). It should be noted that this real-time control and coordination can reduce the need for highly accurate short-term forecasting (by replacing the forecast with real-time data). It does not resolve the need for accurate mid- and long-range forecasts to insure flexibility response and changing market demands over time.

Table 4.1 Basic Analytical Forecasting Methods Used in Closed Loop Supply Chain Logistics

Type	Methodology	Advantages and Limitations
Simple average	Averages all past data	Assumes no trends or systematic fluctuations
Moving average	Averages data from last few periods	Responds to recent changes in trends
Weighted moving average	Averages data from previous periods with different weights from different periods	Improves simple moving average, but requires judgment for weights
Exponential smoothing	Same as weighted moving average, but uses exponential weighting curve	Weights are applied systemically; requires only small computational effort
Holt's method	Exponential smoothing with added factor or historical trends	Improves on exponential smoothing if changes are gradual
Bayesian inference	Adjusts forecast methodology based on probability of state change	Improves on exponential smoothing if changes are not gradual

CONTROL MECHANISMS WITHIN THE LOGISTICS PIPELINE

Given the general structure within the closed loop logistics supply chain pipeline, it is quite clear that there are certain control "pressure points" that can be used to optimize the closed loop pipeline effectiveness and the service engineer fill rate efficiency. Clearly the fact that 50% of the logistics inventory is below the manned stock levels indicates the need for highly accurate and dynamic reporting on parts usage at the time of call close-out at the service engineer level. This can be best done through the introduction of formal reporting on parts use through an online call handling, dispatch and call close-out system. This, in turn, suggests the need for reliable and cost-effective means for the field engineer to also report stock status in real time through mobile, wireless laptops, PDA, digital cell phones, or special purpose field communications devices.

The service logistics management team must understand the critical importance of optimizing the full CLSC or logistics pipeline in achieving overall service profitability. The first step is in recognizing the vital need for improving forecasting accuracy and capability in logistics management and control, and providing for accurate data reporting and real time reporting on parts, subassemblies, and whole unit status in the field.

Key factors and control mechanisms used in CLSC include stock control of key SKUs, use of advanced forecasting, bar coding and RFID methods for identifying and improving the accuracy of inventory counts, improved just in time scheduling and control of depot refurbishing and repair operations, and other mechanisms.

Stock Control of Key SKU

Typically, a service organization controls possibly 20,000 to 40,000 SKUs of which approximately 10% (i.e., 2000 to 4000) are active. In addition, the most critical SKU used in day-to-day maintenance and repair actions are typically only 10% of the active items, in the range of 200 to 400. Thus, the primary focus of inventory control should be on the active and most critical items and transactions concerning the storage, movement, and receipt of the active SKUs in terms of both the effective and defective stocks should be maintained. This involves online updating of the inventory status at each location including field engineer use.

A critically important measure that should be continuously computed is the fill rate at each level of the closed loop system. As indicated above, fill rate is measured by dividing the number of times an SKU is required, into the number of times the SKU is available within the timeframe required. Thus, for example, if a typical field engineer turns to his trunk stock 100 times in a week, and finds that in only 75% of the cases are the parts available in the trunk, this would be calculated as a 0.75

instantaneous fill rate. It should be noted that this fill rate is different at each level in the closed loop system. In general, fill rate at each echelon or level of logistics support and control, particularly the instantaneous trunk stock fill rate at the field engineer level, are critically important parameters to measure, manage, and control to improve productivity. Typically, the central stock should have a 99.99% fill rate, regional or local stocks should have a 95 to 98% fill rate, and the service engineer trunk stocks should have fill rates in the range of 80 to 85%.

Use of Advanced Forecasting

As indicated above, planning of future inventory demands should be done, employing advanced forecasting methodology. This involves initially segmenting SKUs into various classes or groups. In general, experience indicates that the cumulative stock demands will vary as a function of stage in the product life cycle. Thus, for example, the demand will be considerably higher and nonlinear in terms of SKUs used in support of a product in the phase-in state, as opposed to the normal life. Similarly, the demand would also be nonlinear in the event of a product phase-out.

Bar Coding and RFID Methods for Identifying and Improving Accuracy of Inventory Counts

Typically, in many organizations, the transposition of SKU numbers or misreading of these numbers can lead to significant variation between the inventory levels and status as reported and physical counts made. These types of errors can be significantly reduced by introducing a bar code on each SKU and utilizing scanning devices at the manned stock levels, depots, and in the field, to reporting actual SKU information, rather than relying on "eyeball" reporting. Newer technologies, such as radio frequency identification devices (RFID), have been recently developed as an alternative to bar code scanners. RFID allows for electronic data rather than visual scanning of identification to provide accurate tracking data.

Improved Just in Time Scheduling and Control of Depot Refurbishing and Repair Operations

As indicated above (see also Chapter 6), one of the most efficient mechanisms for refilling the logistics pipeline is to significantly speed up the schedule and assignment of work within the R&R depot.

Other Mechanisms for Improving Logistics Management and Control

In addition to the use of an integrated closed loop logistics supply chain approach to total management of the services inventory to include (1) control over parts used by the service engineer at the trunk stock level through parts reporting at the time of call close-out, and (2) the application of advanced analytical forecasting, there are other sophisticated tools and techniques that can be used to effectively control the closed loop pipeline. These new approaches are based upon improvements in technology through rapid deployment of parts. Until recently it was presumed that the most efficient way to manage parts was to stockpile them at the point of use. However, significant improvements in distribution have led to the recognition that parts can be stored centrally or regionally, with a lower inventory level at the service engineer trunk stock level or site level, and still maintain high field fill rate. This can be achieved through the use of rapid local transportation and courier mechanisms for resupply. This could be achieved through the use of same day courier express, such as UPS/Sonic Air, or next day express service, such as provided by Federal Express.

An even more sophisticated approach is the use of a roving van based in each major metropolitan area, which can be dispatched to the individual service engineer during the day as a result of arriving customer calls for assistance. Under this concept, each call is initially analyzed through a problem diagnostics and call avoidance mechanism, as shown in Figure 4.1, in order to identify the needed parts or SKUs for the individual service call. Computerized systems are then used to determine whether or not the parts are available in the trunk stock of the service engineer to be assigned. If the stock is not available, a van, which is usually stocked at the 95% level or better, is then dispatched on a dynamically assigned basis and schedule to provide the service engineers requiring parts with the parts required at the time of his arrival, or immediately after his arrival on site. The effect of this dynamic use of a roving van or courier (see Figure 4.8) with higher stock levels, combined with a midrange investment in trunk stocks, can generate an extremely high service engineer fill rate capability at the service engineer trunk level, without imposing unacceptably high investment requirements in stocking each service engineer trunk. In essence, in high density areas, the roving van with augmented stocks, in conjunction with trunk stock levels at a lower (service engineer) inventory fill rate (say 50 to 60%), can produce a significantly higher fill rate in the field without incurring the normal cost of distribution and deployment of individual parts stock to each individual service engineer trunk stock. The combination of same day or next day courier service, allowing the rapid deployment of parts from central (or regional) depots

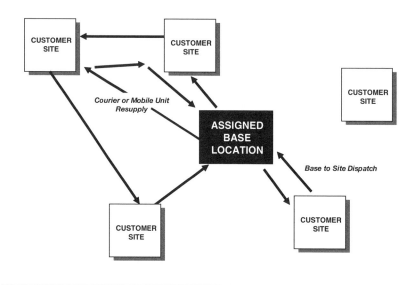

Figure 4.8 Alternative travel options; service engineers and couriers — in closed loop systems.

to local branches or direct to service engineers, and the use of a roving truck or van to deploy the parts down to the service engineer trunk level can achieve a significantly higher fill rate with lower overall logistics inventory levels.

CLOSED LOOP SUPPLY CHAIN MANAGEMENT SYSTEMS

The overall process structure outlined above can be supported through a computerized systems infrastructure* consisting of:

◼ End-to-end planning
◼ End-to-end delivery and distribution
◼ Procurement source management

The general system design provides the ability to control the full logistics pipeline through integrated consideration or all key logistical functions.

A variety of new tools and techniques are now being successfully implemented by sophisticated high tech service organizations to significantly improve the efficiency and effectiveness of their CLSC management and control in the field. The use of advanced forecasting methods and techniques discussed earlier, combined with new tools and technology to

---

* See Chapter 9 and Figure 9.1 for a more detailed discussion on systems.

rapidly deliver and deploy central, regional, or local stocks to the field service engineer, are leading to significant improvements in the profitability of field service operations.

In summary, it is very clear that the strategic approach utilizing a CLSC on an end-to-end basis for high tech industrial and commercial product service, and supported by a computerized infrastructure with real-time warehousing, depot, and field reporting, will have a significant effect on both operational productivity and efficiency of a service organization, as well as its bottom-line profitability. Improvement of the fill rate of the service engineering trunk level through a closed loop system can significantly reduce the number of broken calls and increase overall service performance. At the same time, logistics strategies which make use of modern technology for integrated management and control based on forecasting and depot R&R would generally generate a higher number of asset and spares turns and higher field fill rates then alternative strategic approaches.

HIGH TECH CLOSED LOOP SUPPLY CHAINS METRICS AND PARAMETERS

While the general RL flow and impact of life cycle on returns can be broadly described, the specifics of the RL process can be much more fully defined in the high tech industrial and commercial area. This is due to the fact that in these markets and industries, a full CLSC, which tracks product and parts flow out to the field and back, is usually in place in at least some organizations. By benchmarking, it is possible to more accurately quantify the process in the industrial and commercial markets, to examine CLSC processes, and to compare and evaluate the impact of closed loop vs. low tech or simple RL approaches.

The high-tech service industry, in general, and independent and multivendor equipment service organizations in the field specifically, have become more sophisticated and much more focused on improving service and life cycle support productivity and efficiency in recent years. The issue of strategic and tactical benchmarking has, therefore, gained increased attention and criticality. For example, both the ISO 900x processes for quality management and control, and the Baldrige Award approach emphasized the importance and use of benchmarking as a key to the comparative measurement of service operations.

In the high tech CLSC supporting the field service industry, relatively few accepted or published benchmark parameters and targets can be used by the service organization or manager in both establishing an effective logistics support service strategy and in assessing and evaluating performance relative to industry standards and norms. This type of data, properly

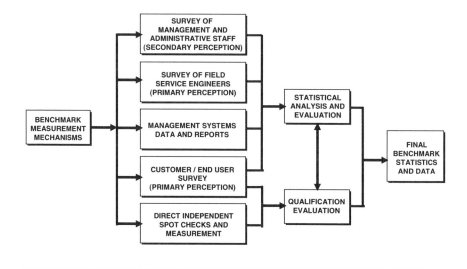

Figure 4.9   Data sources used in developing service logistics benchmark.

evaluated to determine key driving parameters and critical targets, can be extremely useful in improving CLSC service productivity and efficiency.

Given this broad objective, with specific emphasis on those CSLC and RL within field service logistics support, an extensive base of benchmark information and data parameters, by class, technology of products serviced, by type and size of service organization, and by geographic region serviced was constructed using the process shown in Figure 4.9. This information has been based, in part, upon extensive in-depth Service Market Audits* in studies of more than 230 small, medium, and large high tech service organizations, including OEMs, dealers, distributors, and independent third and fourth party maintainers and multivendor equipment service organizations (MVES) operating in the U.S., Europe, and globally (Table 4.2).

These organizations were involved in the service and support of a broad array of technology, identified in Table 4.3, including:

■ Computers
■ Office automation and office products
■ Telecommunications and network products
■ Medical electronics and technology
■ Process control, plant, and building automation
■ Retail, financial, and point-of-sale (POS) technology
■ Home appliances and white goods

---

* Trademark of Blumberg and Associates, Inc. (BAI).

Table 4.2   Service Organizations Represented in High Tech Logistics Benchmark Database (2002 Data)

Technology Serviced	Type service Organization		
	OEM	TPM	Total
Information technology	20	25	45
Office products and office automation	17	26	43
Retail financial automation and POS	10	4	14
Telecommunications and networks	17	12	29
Medical electronics	19	6	25
Consumer appliances/electronics (white and brown goods)	14	13	27
Building and plant automation/process control	32	16	48
Total	129	102	231

Source: From Blumberg Associates, Inc. (Appendix B and Appendix C).

Table 4.3 Major Benchmark Segment (Products and Technology)

Technology	Type of Products Serviced	Types of Firms	Typical Size of Firms (# of fes)
Information technology	• Mainframes • Minicomputers • Micro/PC/work stations • EDP peripherals	• OEMs • ISO/TPMs	• Medium to very large • Service firms with 500–20,000 field engineers
Office automation and products	• Office automation, PCs and workstations • Copying machines • Document management/imaging • Work processors • Micrographics • Office equipment	• OEMs • TPM/ISOs • Dealer/distributors	• Small to medium; 200–2,000
Retail financial, POS	• POS terminals • Cash registers (ECR) • Bank automation such as ATMS • Special equipment	• OEMs • TPM/ISOs • Dealer/distributors	• Small to large; 50–5,000
Building and plant automation/process control	• Instrumentation • Process control • HVAC controls • Switch gear • Plant robotics • Other automation systems	• OEMs • ISOs (limited) • Dealer/distributors	• Small to medium; 100–2,000

Telecommunications	• Data networks • Voice networks • PBX/key sets • Network switches • Bridges and routers • Modems	• OEMs • Utilities • Private bypass operations • TPM	• Small to large; 25–15,000
Medical electronics and technology	• Medical instrumentation and analyzers • Diagnostic imaging and analyzers • Diagnostic imaging system • Surgical suite • Anesthesiology • Sterilizers • Other medical technology	• OEMs • Hospital-biomedical groups • ISOs/TPMs	• Small to medium; 15–500
Consumer appliances/electronics (white and brown goods)	• Washers/dryers • Dishwasher • Ovens • Televisions/VCRS • Stereos	• OEMs • Dealers/distributors • ISOs (limited)	• Small to medium; 25–2,000

Closed Loop Supply Chain and Reverse Logistics Benchmark Results

The results of the benchmarking of high tech closed loop and RL supply chain operations can be seen in the terms of the following impacts and factors.

Impact of Products and Technology Supported

Key CLSC parameters, such as investment in parts as a function of total service revenue, field engineer trunk stock fill rate, service calls broken due to lack of parts, and so forth have been developed as a function of products and technology as shown in Table 4.4. This shows that some benchmark metrics are affected by the size, weight, use of the products and technology, installed base, and density, and others are not.

Impact of Using Closed Loop Supply Chains vs. Simple Reverse Logistics Processes

The benchmark data was also analyzed in order to separate results into two segments:

- Those who use a full CLSC process (high tech)
- Those using simple RL returns methods (low tech)

The results show clear differences in the impact of a full high tech closed loop management approach compared to the low tech approach. As shown in Table 4.5, the closed loop process significantly reduces the number of calls broken off due to lack of parts or due to the service engineer leaving the site. In the closed loop system, service engineers have a clear idea of how long they have to wait and thus tend to stay on the service site. The benchmark analysis also shows the impact of the CLSC logistics management process compared to simple low tech RL practices on operating effectiveness (Table 4.6).

Forecasting Impacts

The mechanisms used for forecasting and stock control, and the systems for communication to and from the field are quite different in the low tech simple RL process vs. the high tech closed loop process (Table 4.7). In the closed loop systems advanced forecasting, tools, and techniques are used to optimize stock provisioning levels based on accurate real-time data on parts status and use. In the low tech situations, the service engineers depend only on linear or, at best, exponential extrapolation of historical data. More often, in the typical simple RL process, much of the

Table 4.4 Benchmark Data for Logistics Parameters in Closed Loop Supply Chains (Mean)*

Parameters	Technology								
	Information Technology	Office Automation and Products	Tele-Comm	Retail, Financial, POS	Medical Electronics	Building Auto.	Industrial Plant Control	Home and Consumer Goods	General Industry
Investment at acquisition costs in parts as a percent of total hardware service revenue	46%	33%	25%	22%	28%	30%	32%	38%	31%
Logistics operating costs as a percent of total costs	10%	11%	9%	13%	12%	10%	12%	15%	11%
PI-priority orders shipped same day	96%	85%	89%	86%	94%	79%	80%	90%	88%
DOA in field from logistics	1%	2%	1%	2%	1%	2%	2%	2%	2%
Percent of service calls requiring parts	55%	39%	30%	65%	59%	34%	30%	71%	49%
Percent of call orders causing "broken" (closed incomplete or extended) due to lack of parts	16%	21%	11%	10%	32%	15%(SL)	12%	10%	17%

Table 4.4 Benchmark Data for Logistics Parameters in Closed Loop Supply Chains (Mean)* (continued)

Parameters	Information Technology	Office Automation and Products	Tele-Comm	Retail, Financial, POS	Medical Electronics	Building Auto.	Industrial Plant Control	Home and Consumer Goods	General Industry
					Technology				
Field engineer trunk stock fill rate	42%	36%	72%	66%	27%(B)	31%(SL)	32%(SL)	72%	50%
Parts delivery source									
Outside (UPS, FEDEX, SONICAIR)	85%	70%	83%	79%	94%	78%	80%	75%	81%
Internal (company van, other FE)	12%	25%	13%	18%	2%	8%	6%	21%	14%
Other	3%	5%	4%	3%	4%	14%	14%	4%	5%

*Note: E = Extrapolated, based on internal and internal data, B = Binomial distribution, SL = Skewed left.

Source: From Blumberg Associates, Inc. (Appendix B and Appendix C).

Table 4.5 Key Logistics Benchmark Parameters in High Tech Services

Key Logistics FACTORS	Type of service		Type of service		Type of service		Average	
	All OEM or ganizations		All TPMs/ISOs		ALL OEMs and ISOs supporting OA/PCs			
	Integrated closed loop pipeline	Typical	Integrated closed loop pipeline	Typical	Integrated closed loop pipeline	Typical	Integrated closed loop pipeline	Typical
Spares per field engineer ($1000s)	$71	$85	$36	$43	$34	$41	$40	$45
Field engineer stock fill rate (instantaneous trunk stock)	84%	76%	80%	77%	85%	80%	82%	74%
Broken calls due to lack of parts (all calls = 100%)	12%	15%	22%	28%	8%	13%	13%	18%
Spares inventory turns	5.4	4.5	4.5	4.0	7.1	6.2	5.6	5.2

Source: From Blumberg Associates, Inc. (Appendix B and Appendix C).

Table 4.6 Survey Findings — Logistics Support Benchmark Comparisons

Issue	Low Tech	Closed Loop High Tech
Percentage of calls extended due to lack of parts	27%	17%
Action when parts aren't available on van/truck/trunk (left to pick-up/terminate calls)	83%	(28%)
How many times do techs return to dealership for parts (at least daily or 2 or 3 times a week)	91%	(42%)
Desire for more sophisticated IT tools for parts support	78%	61%
Frequency of parts reorder (one or more times a day)	78%	66%
Potential for service parts improvement	51%	58%
Use of historic data to set trunk stock levels	69%	(41%)
Average van/truck stock	$6135	($2130)

◯ = Significantly better performance.

Source: From Blumberg Associates, Inc. (Appendix B and Appendix C).

Table 4.7 Survey Findings — Methods For Determining Van/Truck/Trunk Stock Inventory

Method	Low Tech	Closed Loop High Tech	Effect on Optimized Trunk Stock Fill Rate
Historic installed base and order data	64%	(11%)	Low
Fastest moving parts	18%	16%	Medium
Broad range of products — estimated by product	15%	11%	Medium
Advanced forecasts models and MTBF of each stock keeping unit	< 1%	(46%)	Very high
Troubleshooting and diagnostics at time of service call	6%	(16%)	High

◯ = Significantly better performance.

Source: From Blumberg Associates, Inc. (Appendix B and Appendix C).

demand forecasting is done by the service engineer in the field based on their own experience and without regard to product life cycles.

As shown in Table 4.8, the CLSC makes more use of real time wireless technology to track parts and subassemblies received and returned, parts used at time of call completion, and to place orders in real time.

By looking at best practices organizations using CLSC approaches vs. average performance, as shown in Table 4.9, these benchmark metrics clearly show the impact of CLSC performance on service operations.

Return Velocity Rates for High Tech Products

An analysis and evaluation of return time and velocity rate of tech products and parts also demonstrate improvements due to a closed loop approach. The typical return process is shown in Figure 4.10. Based on the benchmark data, an analysis of transit time and accuracy of the data reported, as shown in Table 4.10, demonstrates this improvement.

This evaluation was made using a standard or typical RL process in which products, parts, and subassemblies are returned on a purely sequential and uncontrolled or unmanaged step by step basis, as opposed to a CLSC in which the movement of material is managed and controlled in real time down to the service engineer trunk stock site level, and back to the central warehouse. The benchmark analysis measured both elapsed time (in days) and data accuracy based on the process flow. As indicated, the CLSC produces a significant reduction in elapsed time, along with a significant increase in data accuracy.

HIGH TECH PRODUCT RETURN EXPERIENCE

Using a combination of market and economic data, developed through the methodology outlined in Appendix C, and discussed in Chapter 3, and the results of benchmark evaluations, discussed in this chapter, it was also possible to make estimates of product return experience for high tech products in selected market segments. The starting point was to develop estimates of actual return rates by cause based on benchmarking survey results for 2003 and projected for 2004. These estimates are shown in Table 4.11. The value of the high tech returns are then computed by using historical experience and installed based values to estimate return values (as shown in Table 4.12). While preliminary, these estimates provide for the first time, a quantitative examination of the returns and values for high tech products.

Table 4.8 Survey Findings — Devices Used to Communicate with Field Service Person

Technology	Low Tech	Closed Loop High Tech	Rate of Decrease or Increase in High Tech Sector
Two-way radios	58%	18%	Decrease
Laptop or vehicle mounted computer	24%	38%	Slight increase
Pagers	67%	58%	Slight decrease
Cellular phones	81%	88%	Increase — moving to digital
Handheld computers/PDAs	4%	29%	Increase
PDA/laptop with GPS	< 1%	2%	Potential increase
Fax machines	5%	<1%	Decrease

◯ = Significantly higher use.

Source: From Blumberg Associates, Inc. (Appendix B and Appendix C).

Table 4.9 Key Operating Parameters Associated with Service Logistics Parts Planning and Forecasting (Mean)

Parameter Measurement	Best Practice Service*	Typical Service Organization	Percent Improvement
Total calls per repair completion	1.1	1.4	21%
% of calls "broken" due to lack of parts	14%	26%	46%
Field fill rate	92%	52%	77%
Resupply rate in days	180	300	40%
Repair turnaround (in days)	3.2	5.8	45%
Field dead on arrival (DOA)	1%	2%	50%
Transportation costs as a percent of total costs	8%	11%	27%
Logistics operating costs at a % of total costs	10%	13%	23%

*Based on cross representative sample evaluation of firms in IT/telecomm/medical with 250 or more FEs, using advanced closed loop supply chain.

Source: From Blumberg Associates, Inc. (Appendix B and Appendix C).

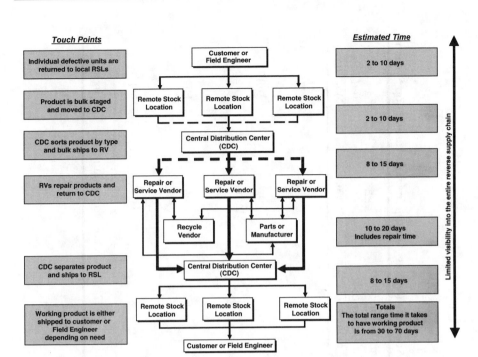

Figure 4.10   Typical high-tech return process for parts.

Table 4.10 Comparison of Return Velocity Cycle Times and Data Accuracy (Average vs. Optimized Closed Loop Systems)

Parts/Material Touch Points	Returning Organization Examples	Typical Holding and Transit Time		Accuracy of Data	
		Average (Days)	Closed Loop System (Days)	Average	Closed Loop System
Individual defective unit or part	User or field engineer	4–6	1–2	Low	High
Remote stocking	Field stock locations	5–8	3–5	Low	High
Central distribution and repair	Centralized collection center	7–14	4–5	Medium	High
Shipments to field	Repair and centralized warehouse supporting collection center	10–20	3–6	High	High
Shipped to the user	Field stocking or sales locations	15–30	2–4	Low	High
Totals		41–78	13–22	Low to medium	High

Source: From Blumberg Associates, Inc. (Appendix B and Appendix C).

Table 4.11 Return Rates Used to Estimate the Value of High Tech Products in the Reverse Logistics Pipeline (By Technology and Reason for Return)

Technology	Defective	Damaged	Errors/Stocking
Computer/office equipment	3.76%	2.30%	4.40%
Enterprise networking	2.50%	3.50%	4.40%
Medical equipment	4.75%	1.80%	2.20%
Retail/banking equipment	3.25%	4.25%	3.25%
Printing and publishing	2.25%	1.50%	1.25%
Imaging and document management	3.50%	3.25%	3.25%

Source: From Benchmarking study, Blumberg Associates, Inc. (Appendix B and Appendix C).

Table 4.12 Estimated Value of High Tech Products in the Reverse Logistics Pipeline: 2004 (By Technology and Reason for Return)

Technology	Defective	Damaged	Errors/ Stocking	End of Life Returns	Total
Computer/office equipment	4.7	2.9	5.5	9.4	22.5
Enterprise networking	3.5	4.9	6.2	10.5	25.1
Medical equipment	1.5	0.6	0.7	2.3	5.0
Retail/banking equipment	0.3	0.4	0.3	0.6	1.6
Printing and publishing	0.5	0.3	0.3	1.7	2.9
Imaging and document management	0.5	0.4	0.4	1.0	2.4
Total	10.9	9.5	13.4	25.6	59.4

Source: From Blumberg Associates, Inc. (Appendix B and Appendix C).

SUMMARY

The discussion, analysis, evaluation, and benchmark results all serve to identify the great value of using a full CLSC strategy, infrastructure, system, and processes, in a high tech market environment. A summary of the impact of moving to the closed loop approach, shown in Table 4.13, outlines these efficiencies.

Table 4.13 Key Logistics Productivity Improvement Strategies and Tactics

Action	Impact
Use of integrated logistics control system	Total online real-time control can improve logistics performance and/or reduce costs by 5–10% or more
Tracking of parts use down to and including service engineer trunk stock	Can improve fill rate and significantly reduce field stock out rate
Use of same day delivery, courier, and mobile vans	Can cut inventory investment by up to 25% and still maintain service levels
Just in time depot scheduling and control — production-oriented depot operations	Depot can become best source for spares replacement
Bar coding on parts and whole units	• Reduced probability of lost parts • Administrative and clerical input time reduced
Advanced forecasting models	• Can reduce total inventory investment by 10–20% or more • Can improve fill rate on slow moving items by 20–30%
Use of integrated field service management systems – Database maintenance – Report generation	Can reduce clerical and administrative work load by 10–20% or more

Source: From Benchmark Surveys.

5

MANAGING CONSUMER GOODS REVERSE LOGISTICS

INTRODUCTION

As indicated in previous chapters, the significant difference in the general reverse logistics (RL) process between industrial and commercial products on the one hand, and consumer goods products on the other, is the position of the distribution/retailer in the overall supply chain, and the ease or difficulty of applying closed loop supply chain (CLSC) processes and technology. In essence, in the consumer goods area, the customer usually deals directly with the retailers, or in some cases the distributor, if Internet or e-commerce processes are utilized. In general, the direct supply chain flows from the manufacturer to the dealer/distributor, the retailer, or both. Both returns and service and support to the customer are coordinated through the retail chain; thus, the closed loop structure found in industrial and commercial products is either not applicable, or is much more difficult to manage and control, since the entire process is not the responsibility of one organization.

MANUFACTURER CONSUMER GOODS MANAGEMENT STRUCTURE

The typical manufacturer-based management and control to the consumer goods market, described in Figure 5.1, involves various divisions of the manufacturer, including:

- Corporate strategy and business development
- Research and development
- Financial management
- Market and product design

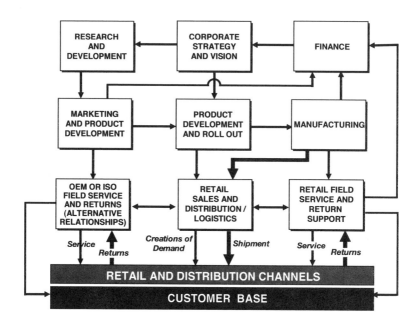

Figure 5.1 Operating relationships between manufacturing base and company functions, departments, and distribution channels in a retail environment.

- Product development and roll out
- Manufacturing

These manufacturing organizational units and functions interact with the distribution/retailer in several fragmented ways, making it difficult, if not impossible, to effect full CLSC control.

Typically, sales and distribution, logistics and customer service, and field support and returns are coordinated separately through the retail and distribution channels. They may, in special cases, be provided by the original equipment manufacturer (OEM) service organizations, or independent service organizations (ISOs). The various participants in this process are described and outlined in Table 5.1.

RETAILER/DISTRIBUTOR CONSUMER GOODS MANAGEMENT STRUCTURE

While the manufacturer organization in the consumer goods market is heavily concerned with new product development and introduction, as well as the manufacture and production of saleable goods, the general underlying assumption is that the responsibilities for sales and support to

Table 5.1 Manufacturer Participants in Retail Consumer Goods Reverse Logistics and Closed Loop Supply Chain Process

Organizations and Operating Units	Role and Mission	Importance and Criticality	Comments
Corporate	• Establishing strategy and vision • Establish service and support policies	• Depends on corporate focus on services	• Must keep abreast of market needs/desires responding to same
Market and product management	• Establish market fees and direction • Establish product portfolio	• Develops the "message" which is delivered	• Must use innovative technologies to identify and meet customer needs
Product research development and rollout	• Establish product configuration, costs and pricing • Establish support process and procedures	• Very critical — direct effect on returns	• Must "marry" marketing and manufacturing mission
Manufacturing	• Set product quality establishing manufacturing and assessing processes	• Issue of quality is of prime importance	• Must balance cost and quality issue carefully
Sales and distribution/logistics	• Develops sales channels and partner (retailer) in process	• Footprint will effect returns	• Must be tailored to target market
Financial and accounting	• Tracks life cycle and return costs • Evaluates profitability	• Critical to measuring product returns and life cycle costs	• May not focus on product life cycle and return costs

Table 5.1 Manufacturer Participants in Retail Consumer Goods Reverse Logistics and Closed Loop Supply Chain Process (continued)

Organizations and Operating Units	Role and Mission	Importance and Criticality	Comments
Customer and field service	• Provides maintenance and support to end user as necessary, through retailer • Provides return coordination	• After sales person and retailer customer service is the most important point of contact in continuing relationship with customer	• Field service may report to sales distribution or retailer • May also be supplied by stand alone (ISO)
Retail distribution	• Point of contact for repair	• Little contact after initial sale	• Retailers must have product when desired

the ultimate customer are the responsibility of the distributor/retailer. In broad terms, there are three major types of retail distribution channels. These include: mass/discount merchandisers, major retail chains with service capabilities, and small local retailers.

- ■ Mass/Discount merchandisers — These organizations primarily sell on the basis of high volume with heavy discounting and give very little attention to specific customer service and support after the sale. The general policies of these stores tend to be to accept all returns from the customer in terms of broad categories. The mass merchandisers also make liberal use of the general return policy to the manufacturer, often utilizing the returns process to clear shelves or reallocate inventory. In essence, the mass merchandisers generally place much of the responsibility and economic costs for RL on the original manufacturer/vendor, with primary objectives of very high volume sales through discount pricing.
- ■ Major retail chains with service capabilities — The second class of retailer, as typified by firms such as Sears, Circuit City, Best Buy, Albertsons, and so on, places much more focus on customer service and support as part of their overall selling and marketing equation. Since they are not selling on the basis of price alone, returns reflect an important issue that needs to be managed. In these types of stores, the ability of the sales person in individual store categories, and the customer service organization, serves a very important role in terms of controlling and managing the return process, as well as managing customer satisfaction or dissatisfaction, as reflected by both complaints with respect to merchandise bought, and returns or request for service as a result of defects or operating failure.
- ■ Small local retailers — The third category represents small "mom and pop" retailers and local (nonchain) retail operations. These retailers are often in direct conflict with the retail chains identified above, and tend to focus on highly personal customer service and support as the primary mechanism for attracting customers. In general, these stores do not have the buying "clout," enabling them to return goods to the distributor or manufacturer simply because they have not been sold off their shelves. In order to support their business profitability, they need much closer control over their inventories and must focus on inventory turnovers. The small stores are generally required to charge more for their products than the equivalent larger chains and mass merchandisers, or their marketing and sales approach tends to be extremely highly focused (such as a single product line as in the case of women's wear, shoe dealers,

paint dealers, etc.) or focused on a narrow price segment, such as dollar stores.

In general, the retail organizations with the greatest incentive to fully manage their RL processes are the major retail chains, since the mass merchandisers can essentially pass on the return process to the manufacturer/distributor and the small local retailer lacks the financial and economic leverage to optimize their returns process. Thus, the most important type of retailer concerned with RL activity in the consumer products field are the retail chains. Their ability to manage and control both customer service and satisfaction on the one hand and returns on the other can directly influence the profitability, market share, and revenue growth of the organization. This is not to suggest that there are business opportunities for improvement through concentration on RL in all segments of the retail market, but rather that by focusing on the primary interest of the retail organizations most affected by a RL and customer service strategy, we can effectively highlight the management processes, principles and procedures employed.

The typical retail organizational structure of a chain highlighting the key roles and functions concerned with RL, as shown in Figure 5.2, helps to focus on the management issues facing their retail chain operations.

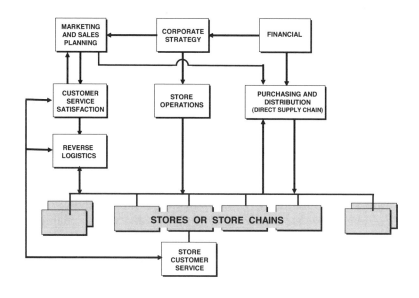

Figure 5.2   Operating relationships in retail chain organizations involved in reverse logistics.

Currently the retail organization, particular with a large number of stores or chains, must be able to manage the direct supply chain including purchasing, driven by its corporate strategy envision, marketing plans, and financial situation. The objective of the direct supply chain of the retailer is to make sure that the right products and goods are provided to the right stores as a function of the corporate strategy envision, specific marketing and product plans, customer demands — which may vary by season or geography — and other factors. The role of customer service and customer satisfaction and support on the one hand, and RL on the other, in a typical large retailer is undergoing some significant change. Originally, this role was managed at the local store level by the store customer service organization, which established store policy and dealt with returns, which are affected by both the actual store policies and corporate or chain or subchain policies. However, growing recognition of the importance of customer service and customer satisfaction support and RL in retail chains has now led to the creation of new corporate level organizations designed to cover all stores in a single chain or multiple stores in multiple chains depending upon the size and dimensions of the large retailer. There are several reasons for the need for a corporate level management of the customer service and returns process in any retail establishment, but particularly in larger retail chains. They come from several consumer goods lessons, learned over the years, which have a great impact on the efficiency and productivity of the returns process in a consumer goods environment. These include:

- Retail returns policy — In general, most retail establishments will take anything back in almost any condition due to store or chain policy to have a liberal returns process and the fact that increasingly, retail sales personnel are not trained to examine the reason for returns or to be technically helpful in fixing the issues that caused the return.
- Return rules and policies impacting on RL activity — Because of the general store level desire to have a very liberal returns policy and the inability of sales personnel to technically help and support the individual customers, it has been found to be important to establish return rules and policies to the lowest level possible and to enforce those rules, establishing specific guidelines for proper return by the customer, not only designed to reduce the volume of returns and improve the quality of returns, but also at the same time to improve customer satisfaction whenever possible.
- Use of built-in computer register and point-of-sale structure for empowering return rules — Computer driven cash registers and point of sale terminals may be used to build-in specific rules in

the retail return process, which could limit, or at least advise, the retail sales associate as to the proper handling of a customers return.

■ Impacts of seasonal returns — Since a very high percentage (50% or more) of sales occur in the Christmas and other major holiday seasons, the returns process tends to follow that pattern. Special return policies, particularly in specialized seasons, such as restocking fees, may be used to influence return experience and pattern.

Under any circumstance, management control and coordination of returns can be particularly important to the bottom-line profitability and individual store margins through a corporate wide analysis and evaluation of overall revenue logistics strategy with respect to customer service and satisfaction policies, and manufacturer agreements.

For example, establishing an agreement with manufacturers as to credit only or "destroy on-site" approaches, which reduce the need for product returns to the manufacturers, can be advantageous for both manufacturers and the retailers. The key issue is to manage and control how this is done. However, several studies have shown that the cost of returns may well outweigh the value of the product itself once it has been through the RL process. In essence, retail chains, in particular, can gain an economic advantage by managing its own return policies in the context of its existing and potential distribution channels and an availability of third party logistics providers rather than full dependence on its manufacturer suppliers. Experience in the use of CLSC processes in the high tech market suggest that retailers can gain a significant economic advantage by introducing their own management approach to RL through a combination of using its supply chain capabilities (transportation, distribution, warehousing, and refurbishment) and in-store customer service and support practices and policies, rather than dependence upon the manufacturer's return loop policies for reimbursement. Because of the fact that CLSC process in consumer goods (see Figure 5.3) allows for redistribution of returned goods through separate retail channels, the retailer may well find that greater value can be obtained through establishing secondary distribution channels rather than returning goods to the manufacturer for credit.

In summary, as indicated above, the RL and CLSC processes in the consumer goods area and market, must take into consideration the roles, responsibilities, and dynamics of both the manufacturer of consumer goods and the distributor/retailer of consumer goods. Studies of this market clearly demonstrate that this is not a zero sum game in which whatever the manufacturer loses the retailer gains, and vice versa. In essence, by establishing well-coordinated and substantiated return policies and practices based upon actual returns experience, a more effective strategy for

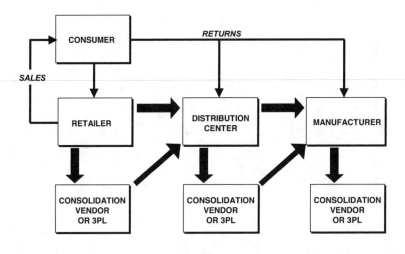

Figure 5.3   Flow of consumer goods products.

RL can be developed for both the manufacturer and the retailer in individual markets that can have a higher payoff for both. This is particularly true with respect to the difference in managing RL for durable goods items rather than groceries and other perishable items, as well as drugs and pharmaceuticals. Most grocery items are managed by jobbers or other local stocking agreements, such as independent stocking companies that deal explicitly with perishable goods returns. Thus, a consideration of use of established retail third party RL companies in specific markets can affect the organizational and operational structure of the RL management process in the retail establishment. In addition, specialized products, such as prescription pharmaceuticals need to be controlled in the U.S. under U.S. Food and Drug Administration (FDA) regulations, which establishes clear requirements and systems processes for coordination of returns/recalls. Thus, the RL process and management approach for consumer goods must take into account the kinds, types, and number of stores in their locations, the products and goods sold, existing systems in place, and general corporate strategy for market segment focus and customer service and satisfaction objectives, as well as government regulations, if any.

CONSUMER GOODS RETURN RATES

General return rates for consumer goods are a function of product life cycle, which varies as a function of product type (brown goods, home computer technology, white goods, pharmaceutical/cosmetics, food, clothing, etc.), as shown in Table 5.2. In addition, as shown in Figure 5.4, for

Table 5.2 Life Cycles of Consumer Products

Type	Examples	Life Cycle (Years)	Factors Affecting Life Cycles
Consumer electronics (brown goods)	• TV • DVD/VHS equipment • Audio equipment • Games	4–8	• Obsolescence • Flexibility • Connectivity • Ease of use
Personal computer technology	• PDAs • Laptops • Desktops • Printers and peripherals	5–7	• Technology • State-of-the-art • New applications
Major appliances (white goods)	• Washer/dryer • Refrigerator • Ranges • Air conditioner	10–15	• Reliability • Maintainability • Product quality
Consumable goods (food, drugs, cosmetics, clothing, etc.)	• Fruits and vegetables • Meats • Bread • Medicines • Cosmetics • Men's and women's apparel • Other furnishings	0.1–1	• Fashion and style • Obsolescence • Spoilage • Low or erratic sales demand

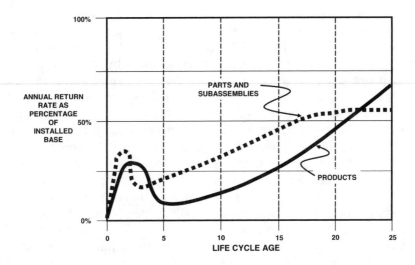

Figure 5.4 Product life cycle vs. product and parts/subassemblies, returns, and disposals. (From Blumberg Associates, Inc. (Appendix B and Appendix C.)

many consumer products,* both whole units and parts/subassemblies may return to either the higher level distribution channel (wholesalers) or to the manufacturers over time. As we will see below, these returns are caused by more than just defective or failed units (as in the case of high tech support). They also are caused by other factors, such as retail stock redistribution and clearing, recalls, obsolete or out of warranty products, "buyers remorse," and so forth.

Organization and Structure of Consumer Goods Reverse Logistics

In the consumer goods market, service issues, while under warranty, are usually handled by the retailer or dealer through either sales or customer service. Usually small units (brown goods) and consumables are returned to the stores while large white goods are supported by field service technicians who specialize in replacing parts and subassemblies. It is the exception when an in-use unit, and particularly white goods, are returned. This leads to the issue of parts and subassemblies returned by the customer or the field service or customer service organization. In general, major consumer appliances experience a return rate of approximately 4.5%, parts and subassemblies of these units can have a much higher rate of returns (between 20 and 25%) over the product life cycle.

---

* As well as high tech industrial and commercial products.

Typically, the parts failures rate spikes in the first 2 years to over 30%, dropping in years 3 through 5 to under 20% and gradually raising over the life of the product life, as shown in Figure 5.2. Due to the need to repair and refurbish these parts and subassemblies by the retailer, dealer, independent service provider, or even OEMs, a major secondary or after-market business in this market for these types of parts has developed.

In addition to the products themselves, the type of retailer also affects returns, as shown in Table 5.3. For the major mass retailer, consumer goods can be and are returned to the dealer or OEM, simply to "clean the shafts." The relationship between manufacturers/distributors and small- to medium-size retailers has changed over the past several years. These small and medium retailers are now "paid" not to return sold products to the manufacturer. If a product is returned to a dealer he will either repair it (through his own service force or a third party) or return to wholesaler or dispose of it directly. One of the reasons for these fundamental changes is the fact that manufacturers are not really manufacturing white, brown, and other consumable goods any longer. They are assembling the end product from modules and subassemblies manufactured at multiple locations throughout the world. Therefore, the cost and time to ship a unit back to the manufacturer is not justified. It is for this reason a very robust third party repair and sales market has developed for consumer electronics, appliance, and home IT.

Another important relationship is that between the consumer goods sales organization and the service organization. If the retail sales group has faith in the corporate (or a contracted third party) repair service organization, they will tend to accept fewer returns and have the item fixed in the field. Many factors affect this issue, such as speed of repair, parts availability, testing, and the issue of identifying the real reasons the product is not working properly or has been rejected by the buyer.

In general, the more liberal the return policy of a retail organization, the higher the return rate. The reason rarely involves the reliability of the product; in many cases, it is often masked by the general customer comment "It doesn't work," or "I can't use it." Recently, changes to retail return policy, such as a restocking fee, have reduced some of these returns.

One phenomenon seen in the high tech service industry, but not yet seen in the consumer white and brown goods market, is dependence on "modular repair of units" in the field, using a pull-and-replace repair philosophy based on product design. In the high-tech service industry there is a close relationship between rate of returns from service technicians and the research and development and product design groups. These product developers (particularly in high tech) closely examine the impact of modular design and reliability on field service requirements after product deployment. This generated the need for design of maintainable/reliable products with

Table 5.3 Summary Return Rate Impact of Retail Distribution Alternatives

Type of Retail	Examples	Estimated Market Share	Average Return Rate	
			Consumer Electronics	White Goods
Mass discount merchandisers	Target K-Mart Wal-Mart	58%	31%	5%
Major retail chains with service capabilities	Sears Circuit City Best Buy	37%	19%	4%
Small local retailers	Local retailers and appliance dealers	5%	17%	4%

Source: From Blumberg Associates, Inc. (Appendix B and Appendix C).

easily removable and replacable functional modules or circuit boards. The consumer electronic and home appliance field is only gradually moving into understanding this need/relationship.

The Relationship between Consumer Product Life Cycles and Product and Parts Returns

Product returns, as well as parts and subassembly returns, have a general relationship to the overall product life cycle. As shown in Figure 5.2, at the early introductory stage, returns can rise rapidly as a percentage of the installed base, due to early failures, poorly designed or unreliable components, and so on. In a short period of time, these problems are overcome through product redesign, engineering changes and revision, and product upgrades. This is particularly true if the returns are tracked in the early warranty stage.*

After this initial rapid increase in returns, the returns rates fall back to a more stable level. As the life cycle continues and product wear and lack of continuing service and support (such as preventative and predictive maintenance usually found in industrial products), failures, obsolescence, and other factors begin to take over, the return rates rise increasingly as the "end of life" approaches. This pattern does vary by type of product and its product life cycle design targets. This is due to the fact that certain products, such as "white goods" are designed for long life and high reliability, and others are designed for shorter life and/or built in obsoleteness (see Table 5.2).

Consumer Good Return Rates and Life Cycle

No known parametric relationship exists between product return rates and life cycle for brown, white, or consumable goods in general. Return rates are effected more by:

- Presence or lack of a reputable service organization to quickly repair inoperative (or partially operative) products
- Return policy of retailer from which the product was purchased
- Ease of use, connectivity, user friendly instructions and documentation, etc.
- Rate of obsolescence or new product development
- Shelf life and purchase value for consumables
- Other factors

---

* See Chapter 7 for additional discussion on warranty process and returns.

Life expectancy of both white and brown goods has changed in the past several years. At one time major appliances (white goods), washer, dryer, and refrigerator stores would last more than 20 years. The current and rapidly growing technology and color and style issues have significantly reduced this parameter.

In general we can classify nonconsumable consumer products into three groups:

- Consumer electronics (brown goods) — These include TVs, DVDs/VHS, audio equipment, and games. Consumer electronics have a life expectancy of 4 to 8 years. Factors affecting their life cycle include obsolescence, flexibility, connectivity, and ease of use.
- Personal computer technology — These include PDAs, laptops/desktops, printers, and so on. Personal computers have a life expectancy of 5 to 7 years. Factors affecting their life cycle include technology, state of the art, and new applications.
- Major appliances (white goods) — These include washers/dryers, refrigerators, stoves, air conditioners. Major appliances have a life expectancy of 10 to 15 years.

In the past 10 years, improvements in technology have changed the white and brown goods product returns. The gradual migration from analog to digital technology and related changes in the cost of manufacturing has reduced the life cycles of certain types of consumer products.

- White goods, in general, have retained the longer life cycle (more than 10 years). However, issues involving returns of white goods primarily occur in the first 30 days after delivery, thus, not really affecting long-term life cycle issues.
- Brown goods have a shorter life cycle due to more rapid technology advances, but again, most returns occur in the first 30 to 60 days unless a service contract was sold with the product.

The size, weight, and complexity of certain products (primarily major appliances), also affect returns at the product level. Traditionally, when a large white good (washer, dryer, refrigerator, home air conditioner, etc.) is delivered, it is returned only if:

- It has been obviously damaged via shipment
- It does not operate when initially installed (plugged in)
- It is not the correct size or color (too big, too small), or operating characteristics

In general, consumer goods reliability has increased significantly in the past decade. Products rarely are returned solely for reliability and failure issues. While this reason is often given, questioning the consumer directly often leads to uncovering issues regarding problems in complexity to operate, connectivity with other equipment, simple dissatisfaction (buyers remorse), and so on. Surveys undertaken in the past 5 years indicate 60 to 70% of the returned smaller products (typically brown goods) have nothing wrong with them.

Effect of Branding on Consumer Goods Returns

Brand is the proprietary visual, emotional, rational, and cultural image that associates with a company or a product. When we think Volvo, we might think safety. When we think Nike, we might think of Michael Jordan and "Just Do It." When we think IBM, we might think "Big Blue." The fact that we remember the brand name and have positive associations with that brand makes the product selection easier and enhances the value and satisfaction we get from the product.

Brand is not a newfound marketing gimmick. It has provided a guarantee of quality since the beginning of commerce. Brand is much more than a trademark or a logo; it is often a "Trustmark," a promise of quality and authenticity that customers can rely on. The purpose of a brand is to:

- Uniquely identify a company and its products, differentiating them from competitors
- Enhance the perceived value, quality, and satisfaction a customer will experience
- Provide a springboard for new products
- Contribute to stable, long-term demand
- Maximize profitability

Technology branding is different from consumer branding. While consumer products are often simple commodities, technology-based products are complex. Because of this, consumer brands, like soap, must magnify small differences (e.g., Ivory Soap: 99.44/100% So Pure, It Floats), while technology branding must focus on simplifying product messages in order to reduce buyer confusion (e.g., "Intel Inside").

The economics of product branding is changing. A survey by McKinsey & Company and Intelli-Quest, a high tech research firm, quantified the premium price that PC buyers will pay for alternative brands of PCs. At the time this research was conducted, IBM, Compaq, and Apple could command a premium price of $295, $232 and $195, respectively, over an average price of $1250 on a particular configuration of PC. This premium can be measured as the amount the average customer was willing to pay for an identical product over a "second tier" brand and name.

Although brand-related price premiums can be substantially reduced in some markets and products over time due to increased competition, it is important to note that even small differences can have a tremendous impact on the bottom line, as well as the level of support and logistics service that can be provided. For example, the ability to charge a $232 premium on a PC with an average selling price of $2500 adds 9.3% to the bottom line. In today's competitive markets, this can mean the difference between profit and loss at the corporate level, or the ability to improve after sales service.

The modeling of brand choice and switching behavior has a long history for frequently purchased consumable goods. Comparable efforts with consumer durable goods, however, have not received as much attention. Appliance and brown goods brand loyalty has been generally shown to be a function of, at least partially, the quality of the product line. In addition, retailer branding (such as Circuit City — where service is "state of the art"), may be used to create a service and return policy differentiation for products sold from that channel.

An example of the issue of quality and brand loyalty and its impact on RL is seen in the transformation of Frigidaire. Founded in 1916, Frigidaire is one of three major white good manufacturers in the U.S. It was for many years owned by General Electric, but in 1979 General Electric sold Frigidaire to a holding company, White Consolidated Industries. This, in turn, was purchased by Electrolux in 1987. When taken over by Electrolux, Frigidaire was a manufacturing-oriented company with only minimal investment in design. The company competed basically on price and had, according to one of their industrial designers, "a culture of churning out cheap products." Although once considered a Cadillac, the high product repair rate in the first 3 to 5 years made it more of an Edsel.

Given Electrolux's commitment to quality, design, and the importance of environmental factors in the company's European markets, big changes might well have been expected at Frigidaire. The new U.S. management sought to transform the company into a "customer-focused culture" with investment in industrial design being a crucial element in this process. Through the use of these processes, Electrolux was able to produce and sell a quality product. One of the indications of success in this endeavor was the reduction of warranty claims by 20% and an increase in annual sales by 25%.

The increase in product returns is slow to affect a product brand which has achieved its status over a number of years or in one industry. For example, Sony Electronics introduced its Trinition model of television in the early 1970s. This product line, although on the higher end of the price scale became known for quality/longevity and an almost "no repair need" reputation. In the early 1990s a number of changes in the design and manufacturing process at Sony significantly decreased the overall quality of their consumer electronic (TV) product lines. However, the reputation and brand loyalty developed over two decades masked these issues and did not result in an immediate downward level of customer satisfaction or increase in returns. This "halo effect" can be seen in white good products also. The reputation Maytag has developed in the white good industry for quality and service support is legendary. Consumers are much more accepting of a quality problem in Maytag products because of their overall history of producing well-engineered, quality appliances. General experience in the consumer goods field is that products with a high brand reputation for quality will be returned at a lower rate than the average product. In effect, buyers are willing to stay with a product if its reputation is high.

Access to the Internet and increased awareness of product quality and reliability by consumers has accelerated the exchange of performance information on consumer goods. Magazines, websites, surveys, and television reports by organizations such as Consumer Reports have provided relatively up-to-date performance data to interested consumers. These phenomenons have formalized "word of mouth" reputations on product quality, reliability, and service support, and have in turn affected brand loyalty.

In general, as indicated previously, brand loyalty is influenced by manufacturers or retailers:

- Return policy
- Service and support strategy and delivery
- Reliability
- User friendliness
- Product quality
- Price performance

Brand loyalty does not appear to directly impact or affect physical returns by itself. Rather, current conventional wisdom allows that high brand loyalty will not result in lower returns; instead the overall returns experience affects brand loyalty.

Consumer Goods Industry Return Rate Averages and Metrics

As discussed in the previous section and illustrated in Table 5.3, there are three major groups of retailers that supply brown and white goods to consumers:

- Major mass market retailers such as Wal-Mart and Target
- Midsize retailers such as Best Buy, Circuit City, Costco, Sears, and other department stores
- Small and local retailers operating on a stand-alone basis or in small strip malls

The differentiator affecting returns is not so much the size of the stores, location, or sales volume, but how the products are sold and supported after sale. There are three major ways products are sold by retailers:

- Mass marketers sell products without any after market support. Consumers must deal with a manufacturer or an independent third party supplier, separately contracted on any repair issue.
- Midsize retailers usually offer a service network to their customers (either in-house or third party).
- Small merchants/dealers typically operate in the same general way as the second category, but stress local service. They are very rapidly being moved out of the white/brown goods market by the national midsize and mass market retailers.

The most important reason used for product return varies with the size, complexity, and price of the unit, as shown in Table 5.4.

Product type variations include:

- White goods are returned primarily due to damage in transit, color/size issues, or because they do not work at all when initially activated.
- Brown goods are returned more due to issues such as complexity, operational, failure, inability to connect with other pieces of similar equipment, availability or similar goods at lower prices, and so on.

When estimating the impact of the various factors on returns, the greatest is the dealer/retailer's commitment to service and product warranty,* followed by buying factors (ease of use, connectivity, user friendliness of instructions, etc.) and product returns on warranty policy of manufacturer/retailer. Product reliability is seen as one of the least significant reasons for the return of a product from the perspective of the manufacturer. In general, end users expect all products to break.

In general, return rates for consumer goods fall into two categories:

---

* Issues of warranty and extended warranty are discussed in Chapter 7.

Table 5.4   Factors Affecting Consumer Brown and White Goods Product Returns

Factors	Estimated* Impact	Comment
Product return policy	7	Liberal policy creates highest return rate
Retailer/dealer commitment to service/service response	8	Level of retail service and support will directly influence product returns, but may increase part and subassembly action
Physical factors (size, weight, complexity)	5	Large and heavy white goods are returned less than consumer electronics
Product reliability	4	Increasing move to digital and modular design has increased reliability
Buying factors (ease of use, connectivity, user friendliness of instructions, etc.)	7	User unhappiness and "remorse" increasing in importance
Price	4	Higher priced units are returned more frequently

*Scale of 1–9 (9 = highest impact).

Source: From survey of retailer return experience, Blumberg Associates, Inc. (Appendix B and Appendix C).

- Products defective
- Products not defective

An overall analysis of return rates for white and brown goods, shown in Table 5.5, shows that return rates for brown goods (electronics) are much higher than for white goods. However, the cause is less due to defective factors (which is the primary factor for industrial and commercial products), than for nondefective factors.

Actual return rates for white goods and brown goods, based on surveys from the Department of Agriculture, as shown in Table 5.6, provide further detail by product line. Other return experience is shown in Table 5.7.

Other Consumer Product Return Issues

As discussed, consumer products are returned for many reasons:

- Product does not work (either partially or totally)
- Product damaged in shipment or when opened
- Product is too complex to operate/instructions not user friendly
- Product is not compatible with other items in providing a desired result or level of performance
- Product is wrong color or size
- Product was damaged during shipment
- Product price too high (ranges from cannot afford to find better/less expensive product)
- Other customer remorse reasons (changed my mind, really only wanted to "rent/try it out," etc.)
- Mass retailers need to clear shelves

Unrealistic charges involve discrepancies between the original price and requested credit. These include:

- Damaged in return freight
- Return of older, discounted models
- Not sent back on time (untimely delivery)
- Missing required paperwork

Contractual reasons include reasons such as:

- Returned merchandise is under a certain dollar amount
- Contract specifies that the returned merchandise should go to a third party (supplied with parts by manufacturer) for service

Table 5.5 Consumer Goods Returns Experience (By Cause)

Causes of Returns		Annual Percent Returns	
		Consumer Electronics (Brown)	Consumer Appliances (White)
Defective	Failure	9.4%	1.5%
	Shipment damage and other cause	2.3%	1.2%
Nondefective	Stock balancing and store returns	3.6%	0.5%
	Shipping errors	3.2%	0.3%
	Customer returns and non-satisfaction	7.5%	1.0%
Total		26.0%	4.5%

Source: From Blumberg Associates, Inc. surveys, consumer electronics retail survey, interviews with major retailers.

Table 5.6 Major Appliance and Consumer Electronics Product Return Rates*

Category	Defective		Nondefective			Total**
	Product Failure	Damaged in Shipping	Stock Balancing	Shipper Error	Customer Return (Nonsatisfactory)	
Major appliances (white goods):						
Washers/dryers (all)	19%	37%	5%	2%	37%	3.5%
Ranges (all)	20%	39%	7%	2%	35%	3.9%
Dishwashers (all)	24%	41%	3%	1%	31%	3.6%
Microwave ovens (all)	28%	46%	1%	1%	24%	6.8%
Air conditioners (room size)	39%	40%	2%	2%	16%	4.7%
Garbage disposals/trash compactors (all)	31%	30%	2%	1%	29%	4.5%
Water heaters (all)	36%	35%	3%	2%	27%	4.4%
Refrigerators (all)	21%	41%	2%	1%	35%	4.6%
Major appliances avg.	27%	39%	3%	2%	29%	4.5%
Consumer electronics (brown goods):						
Televisions (all)	32%	12%	18%	16%	38%	18.6%
Stereos (complete single units)	38%	4%	16%	14%	34%	28.9%
VHS players/recorders	40%	4%	16%	14%	26%	29.3%

Table 5.6 Major Appliance and Consumer Electronics Product Return Rates* (continued)

| Category | Defective | | | Nondefective | | Total** |
	Product Failure	Damaged in Shipping	Stock Balancing	Shipper Error	Customer Return (Nonsatisfactory)	
Desktop computers	35%	10%	14%	12%	28%	23.6%
Laptop computers	32%	8%	10%	8%	28%	25.8%
DVD players	37%	8%	10%	8%	24%	26.8%
Consumer electronics avg.	36%	8%	14%	12%	30%	26.0%

*Rates of manufacturers.

**As a % of products shipped.

Source: From U.S. Department of Agriculture, and Blumberg Associates, Inc. (BAI).

Table 5.7   General Returns Experience by Consumer Goods Product Lines (Mean Percentage)

Product	Annual Returns as Percent of Shipments by Manufacturer	Annual Returns as a Percent of Average Retailer Inventory Maintained
Car/truck batteries	97%	16%
Cans and bottles	55%	41%
Tires	26%	38%
Magazines	48%	29%
Books	22%	19%
Electronic components	11%	15%
Peripherals (printers, displays, etc.)	9%	10%
Automotive parts	4%	7%

Source: From Blumberg Associates, Inc. surveys, average of reports from various sources, etc., see Appendix D.

The *errors on shipment* category groups reasons such as:

■ Quantity discrepancies (less items sent back than disputed)
■ Wrong model shipped back (not the one specified in paperwork)
■ Merchandise sent back is missing items

In looking at the return rates of specific products in each of the major appliance categories (Table 5.6), we see the following:

■ Items in the major appliance category that experience the highest product failure rate are room-size air conditioners and water heaters (39 and 36%, respectively).
■ Washers and dryers, ranges, and refrigerators (at 19, 20 and 21%, respectively) had the lowest return rates.
■ Difference in the damages in shipment category were much less dispersed, averaging 39%, but ranging only between 30% (garbage disposal/trash compactors) to 41% (dishwashers and refrigerators).
■ Breakout of stock balancing and shipment errors by product showed no significant differences.
■ While the average customer return (nonsatisfactory) was 29%, the range of difference was very significant. The lowest at 16% was room air conditioners and the highest between 35 and 37% were washers and dryers, refrigerators, and ranges.

In summary, looking at specific products in the consumer electronics category, we see:

■ Relatively uniform product failure data — average 36% (ranges 32 to 40%)
■ Relatively large difference in the damaged in shipment category (average 8%) (TVs and desktops — 12 and 10%, respectively)
■ Stock balancing and shipping error results were fairly uniform throughout the six categories.
■ Consumer return category average of 30% had for its extreme 38% for televisions and 26% for VHS players/recorders.

Consumer Goods Reverse Logistics Practices

Experience in the consumer goods industry, involving the management, coordination, and control of RL tends to be very fragmented and has all been dictated by a specific set of events or participants coming together with a special set of requirements. For example, in the grocery industry prior to 1979 returns were handled on an ad hoc basis at the retail level, typically between the store manager and the individual salesperson. Up until this time, the individual salesperson was responsible for his or her own department and often was compensated on the basis of incentives. Thus, the individual salesperson had a strong interest in minimizing returns from their customers. In the 1980s and beyond, both the number of people and the quality of the vendor's sales force and the retail sales store personnel were significantly reduced resulting in the emergence of a concept of centralizing the return process. This centralization approach at the individual store or chain store level tended to result in passing the cost of return processing to the manufacturer or supplier.

This move to centralized management of the returns process in the 1980s and beyond also began to produce more accurate information as to the scope of returns. Return values were determined to be on the order of 0.3 to 0.5% of individual store or store chain retail sales. As these returns to a manufacturer began to impact sales budgets, the issue of the need for management control of this RL process began to take effect, and by the late 1980s, the grocery industry commissioned a series of studies on a most effective method to process returns.

This joint industry study, and other research by manufacturers and distributors, brought even more focus on the cost and effectiveness of returns with a view of identifying how to prevent the returns. It has been clear for the past few years that the average returns across the entire grocery industry is in the range of 1 to 1.5% of sales, and is growing. Therefore, new strategies are being employed, such as off invoice allowances where the retailer gets credit for damaged items before they are actually damaged. In reality, if invoice allowance credit is calculated as determined to be less than the actual rate of the damage, thus, producing a shortage for the retailer, and thereby reducing the returns of the product from the store leaving it at the retail level. The pressure on the manufacturer to reduce returns from their retail distribution channels has gained significant visibility in the manufacturer's organization. Management has begun a search for new solutions to reduce the returns or at least control the cost. It is quite clear that invoice allowance approach does not change the physical return process at the retail level and, therefore, the retailers have continued to attempt to recoup their cost via alternative tactics, such as markdowns and liquidation. This, in turn, creates a strong tendency to put branded products back onto the market and shelves in less than perfect condition, which, in turn, impacts first run sales and can also affect the image of the branded products.

Thus, it is very clear that the battle between the manufacturer attempting to reduce returns and still maintain brand quality and the retailer concerned with margin erosion due to returns, and lack of comprehensive return policy on a part of the manufacturer, places both parties at competitive odds. The actual participation by the players in this process is shown in Table 5.8.

Table 5.8 Retail Goods Product Flow by Distribution Channel

Distribution Channel	Product Field

Retail	• Back to shelf
	  – At full price
	  – Open box — reduced
	• Employee sale
	• Donate
	• Have vendor/supplier pick-up (RA#/ship)
	• Send to DC

Distribution	• Negotiate with vendor/supplier to consolidate and ship back • Destroy and charge back vendor or supplier • Return to stock • Liquidate in traditional markets or with online resellers
Manufacturer	• Return to stock • Rework/refurbish • Internally or outsource • Liquidate in traditional markets or with online reseller • Destroy

Consolidation center	• Return to stock
	• Return to vendor/supplier based on agreement
	• Reworked/repaired
	• Liquidated
	  – Resellers/secondary market
	  – Online auctions
	• Donate
	• Destroy

In essence, the grocery industry is beginning to recognize that the management of the return process requires participants from both the manufacturer and retailer side within the framework of accepting the principle that returns will always exist and that these returns impact all aspects of both businesses. The growing recognition of this problem has resulted in the industry beginning to establish an executive or team in charge of tracking returns within a company at both the retail and manufacturer level, as well as to educate and orient all levels of both organizations as to how to best manage and control the process. It is also clear that the customer is an extremely important participant in this process, and that any management strategy to be implemented must clearly communicate to the customer/buyer the return policies and practices available, and the store commitment to the appropriate management of the return process. In essence, as shown in Figure 5.4, in the consumer goods market, and particularly for grocery products and other perishables, the physical flow of the product is affected by the consumer, the retailer, the manufacturer, and the distribution consolidation centers. Because of the critical time dimensions, particularly in perishable goods, this process needs to be controlled in real time, making it an even more complex and sophisticated task.

The situation in general department stores is significantly different. In general, up through the 1990s, most large general department stores and department store chains handle their own returns at the store level, generally finding it to be an extremely complex and costly process because of the very large vendors and items to manage. As a result, there was almost no recovery for defective merchandise since the stores lack the tracking mechanisms and managing control processes to respond to the manufacturer's requirements in order to get credit for the defective returns. In general, as a result, most of the returns to the store went into land fill with the disposal costs handled by the store.

Starting in the 1990s, several store chains attempted to simplify the RL and return process by establishing standards for return and implementing options for the control returns at point of sale, or utilizing electronic cash registers or computerized cash systems. The starting point in this process was to establish tracking on clearly defined inventory to achieve accountability by stock-keeping unit and individual store sales department. The starting point with this control is to focus on direct customer returns as opposed to returns to clear shelves or reallocate merchandise. The most important step was to establish centralized management of the return process. This involved obtaining and describing the defined vendor return policies embedded in the general buying agreements along with the recognition that returning policies should be negotiated as part of the purchasing arrangements.

- Establish a data base description and describe physical flow and processes as a basis for tracking and control of the retail inventory from store receipt to shelf to customer sale to returns
- Establish store level management options for return and disposition, ultimately converting this into chain policy
- Set up the appropriate systems and infrastructure to track the entire process above

The initial focus of the centralized approach was to be concerned only with the processing of defective merchandise return by customer. Some store chains have established their own consolidation and recovery centers to help the returns while others are utilizing third party vendors, such as Genco, Usco, and UPS.

At the same time that retail general merchandise stores have gone after establishing management control over merchandise returns from customers, they have also moved toward management control and liquidation of liability inventory — essentially new merchandise that has not moved off the shelves. This process now involves:

- Retail to consumer item auctions using the Internet and e-Bay or retail and surplus deals
- Direct auctions through the retailers own Internet system
- Redeployment to other stores, distribution channels, and secondary markets
- Bulk liquidation both domestically and off-shore
- Auctions by power level via third party logistics Internet operators

General merchandise stores are now moving toward the next step in logistics control, which will include focusing on improving product quality and vendor quality as well as utilizing the RL process as an additional source of income and profitability. Specific plans include:

- Improving product quality through utilizing data from the system to calculate quality information about individual products and to provide this information to both the consumers and the vendors. In essence, the concept is to make use of the RL tracking analysis and evaluation processes of the store and store chain as a basis for product testing.
- Establishing customized processing relationships for individual vendors on the RL equation — another major initiative is to recognize the opportunity for a win-win situation between the retailer and the vendor by establishing a specialized relationship making use of the data and experience of the store with respect to returns and

failure to clear shelves in order to reduce costs and increase revenues of both parties. This could also serve to eliminate duplicate work done by both the store in consolidation of returns and the vendor in receipt and ultimate disposition of returns.

■ Using the Internet and managed process to generate new revenues and profits. A third initiative now under consideration is to establish an e-commerce/Internet capability to move groceries and perishable consumer merchandise directly from the vendor to the consumer on a managed basis utilizing the retailers position and market control. Under this concept, the retailer passes on to the vendor the responsibility for servicing and supporting the inventories on both the direct and reverse side through a consolidation of similar objectives by both the store/store chain and the vendor.

SUMMARY

It is very clear that in the consumer goods market for perishables and durables, the early 1990s was a turning point for viewing returns to the retailer as a store salesperson problem. The growing problem of returns and the decision to reduce both the number and quality of the sales personnel led to centralization of the returns process through the establishment of both vendor manufacturer and store driven return policies, and the creation of centralized customer service and returns operations. The directions that have been taken in the full implementation and roll out of the new RL strategy in the consumer goods market have varied as a function of the type of product, the store distribution channels and the types of retailers under consideration. As indicated, the mass merchandiser stores, focusing on price discounting as the major sales mechanism, tend to turn over the fullest responsibility for returns to the vendor. We, therefore, see that the general store chains, as opposed to the individual mom and pop stores or the mass merchandisers, will probably take the lead establishing new and advanced RL processes, technology, infrastructure, and strategy over the next decade.

6

DEPOT REPAIR AND ITS ROLE IN CLOSED LOOP SUPPLY CHAINS AND REVERSE LOGISTICS

INTRODUCTION

The business of depot repair* has experienced significant changes over the last 30 years, particularly as related to its role in the high tech market. As indicted in earlier chapters, depot repair is a key element in the reverse logistics (RL) and closed loop supply chain (CLSC) processes, taking returned material, parts, subassemblies, and whole units in, repairing or refurbishing them for reuse, or cannibalizing or disposing of them in secondary markets. This industry has experienced four phases of growth since the early 1980s. During the first phase (pre-1980s) of the market life cycle, traditionally the business of centralized depot repair was typically done by the original equipment manufacturer (OEM) as a service to its customers. These internal depots were operated as cost centers in support of product sales and were usually inefficiently run as "job shop" operations by the manufacturing organization, typically using excess labor capacity in slow production periods. Relatively low priority was given to this work, and, thus, depot repair cycle time from receipt to completion of repair was very slow (measured in minutes). As manufacturers moved to reduce the life cycle of their products in order to encourage more new product

---

* Repair depots operating independently are sometimes called "fourth party" maintainers.

and systems sales, depot repair was generally downsized or, in some cases, eliminated by the manufacturer. In addition, many manufacturers refused to provide depot repair services for competing independent service operations and third party maintainers.

In the 1980s, the second phase of the market life cycle began as manufacturers retreated from component level repair and third party maintainers were forced to develop their own depot repair operations. Individual bench technicians and depot repair managers left idle by OEM depot repair downsizing or outsourcing trends formed their own independent depot repair businesses. These new repair depots, independent of manufacturers, were given the name "fourth party" maintainers, as a play on a so-called third party maintenance market because these new repair depots neither manufactured nor used equipment and, in general, saw their primary markets as the third party maintainers. Thus began the fourth party maintenance market as we know it today; it emerged and evolved in both the U.S. and Europe (primarily the U.K.) over the last 20 years.

The second phase of the market life cycle was characterized by a large number of small depot repair organizations supporting a broad array of computer technology and components. Initially, this second phase was primarily oriented toward smaller "mom and pop" operations with relatively low margins. These smaller depot operations were also located close to the field service forces in order to minimize travel and transportation time and costs. As these smaller organizations began to demonstrate some success, some companies in the service market reasoned that economies of scale or specialization could potentially turn the low margin business into higher margins, resulting in a number of acquisitions and consolidations, such as by DecisionOne, Genicom (through a leveraged buy-out from General Electric), etc. However, a great majority of these organizations tended to continue to focus on depot bench repair, with primarily a data processing orientation (EDP equipment, peripherals, circuit boards, etc.), in which the primary competitive differentiator was *lower price*.

By the early 1990s, the market began to capture the attention of large companies. A new type of depot repair organization began to emerge, which signaled the beginning of the third phase. The third phase is characterized by firms who offer a broad portfolio of *logistics and value-added services*, as opposed to just bench repair, taking a more aggressive approach to the market. Examples of this class of organization include Aurora, which was eventually acquired by Cerplex, and Data Exchange. This new level of competition in the market drove large- and medium-size operations to broaden their portfolio of service offerings, creating an increasingly distinguishable segmentation of the market based on breadth and service portfolio beyond basic depot repair.

The broader market orientation has caught the attention of new classes of competition from the physical transportation, warehousing, distribution logistics, contract manufacturing, and e-commerce market spaces (such as UPS, FedEx, etc.). This has resulted in a maturing of the fourth party market. As the market enters its fourth stage of growth, we are beginning to observe a further consolidation of vendors through mergers and acquisitions.

Overall, the depot repair market is large and has continued to experience growth for some time. Clearly, the consolidation has resulted in intense competition from large and efficient providers. This could result in market shake-out or further consolidation among the smaller or more troubled providers.

STRUCTURE OF THE DEPOT REPAIR MARKET

In order to fully understand the structure and trends in the depot repair market, it is essential to examine the overall channels of distribution for products and service repair and support concerning both warranty and after-warranty service. These channels of distribution, as illustrated in Figure 6.1, include the flow of products directly from product technology OEM to large systems OEM, that repackage the individual product and technology subassemblies and components into overall systems. In many instances, contract manufacturing firms manufacture technology and perform the assembly process on behalf of larger OEMs. Products also flow directly to major distributors and to small manufacturers. Distributors and small OEMs also sell products and systems to value-added resellers (VARs), systems integrators, and other independent contractors. The OEMs (both small and large), with the exception of contract manufacturers, VARs, systems integrators, and contractors, sell their products, systems, and services directly to the end users.

The end user is obviously concerned about service and support after sale. Initial service under warranty is sometimes done directly by the service organizations of the OEMs, VARs or systems integrators, and, in some cases, distributors. Increasingly, both in and out of warranty services are provided by third or fourth party firms who may be either depot repair organizations, logistics providers, or the original contract manufacturer, either directly or through subcontracts or outsourcing agreements with OEMs.

Over the 1980s and 1990s, the class of multivendor equipment service (MVES) providers emerged. These providers operated out of OEMs, out of distributor organizations, or independently. All provided after-warranty service and some in-warranty services. This broad cluster of groups involved in the distribution and use of systems technology, including large and small OEMs, distributors, value-added resellers, systems integrators,

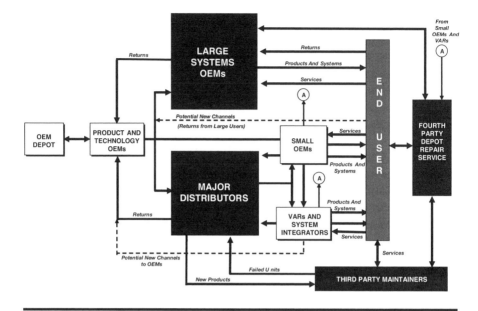

Figure 6.1   Distribution channels for products and service depot repair (warranty and after warranty).

end users, and third party maintainers, all have a need for depot repair refurbishment of parts, subassemblies, and whole units.

As mentioned above, this depot repair work was originally done almost exclusively by the internal repair depots of the product and technology OEMs or the large systems OEMs.* These internal operations were largely run as cost centers in support of product sales. Profit-driven independent fourth party depots have sprung out of existing third party maintenance organizations or OEMs and, in addition, new vendors have been created out of internal depot operations. In the 1990s, a variety of product and technology OEMs aggressively expanded their depot refurbishing or repair operations into general fourth party depot repair services as they witnessed the viability of profit-based depot repair operations. Some of these operations were sold or spun off into independent companies as OEMs in some markets returned to their "core business" or wished to take advantage of the market value of their depot operations as a way to raise new capital. However, as the profit margins on products continued to erode, many OEMs spun off or outsourced their entire manufacturing and depot repair operations to the emerging class of contract manufacturing electronic manufacturing service (EMS) providers, such as Selectron, Celestica, and Jabil.

---

* Some very large end users who had a sizeable base of equipment to support also operated their own repair depots as part of their internal plant maintenance and support operations, but by the mid-1960s this was the exception rather than the rule.

Taking into account this complex array of channels of distribution, it is also of interest to examine the general structure of the repair service depot market. The depot repair market consists of three major dimensions:

- Technology is the normal definition of depot maintenance and repair evolved around the type of technology repaired or refurbished, such as printed circuit boards and printed wire boards, displays, terminals, power supplies, disks and heads, tapes and drives, and keyboards.
- Market segments and applications also represent a dimension, including data processing, process control and plant automation, telecommunications, and medical electronics.
- Vendor type is a third segment defined in terms of market position, including third party maintainers, OEM and manufacturers, value-added resellers, dealers and distributors, and end users.

The depot repair service market is multidimensional in terms of the numbers and types of product technologies, market segments, and vendor types. Among the major segments of the depot repair market are the following:

- Computers and EDP components and peripherals, which is a large and growing segment, highly competitive, saturated with suppliers, (including many very large suppliers) but characterized by several attractive, narrowly defined growth segments, such as medical electronics, and government.
- Process control, plant and building automation, also representing a high growth opportunity, with specialized suppliers, relatively few depot firms, and good revenue and profit growth.
- Military and Department of Defense (DOD) technology, which is highly fragmented, and has historically been characterized with fairly stagnant growth, declining margins and highly specialized niche opportunities; however, the DOD segment is growing faster than other government sectors, largely because the military's new focus on outsourcing of life cycle system and component support.
- Telecommunications and CPE, which is dominated by very large and specialized suppliers focusing almost exclusively in the telecom area, with little crossover from data processing/office automation suppliers into this particular segment.
- Office products and office automation, which is highly competitive, with many suppliers and distributors, primarily involving electro-mechanical technology (as opposed to high tech) and reflecting relatively low returns on investment; it generally requires a strong product distribution market presence as well.

■ Medical electronics, a highly specialized and rapidly growing segment reflecting relatively high margins for specialized suppliers; however, a sharp delineation of focus exists between the medical instrumentation itself and data processing/office automation system add-ons, and there has been a resurgence of major OEMs and TPMs as depot service providers, making competition intense.
■ All other categories (including metrology/instrumentation, electromechanical equipment, other electronic equipment and instrumentation, and ATE software and fixturing), generally involving miscellaneous equipment and instrumentation, and generally characterized by numerous small local service providers in this market.

Depot Repair Operating Models

Repair depots operating in support of CLSCs and high tech products, which are typically embedded in RL and CLSC systems, can be run in one of two ways:

■ Job shop — In which individual bench techs are assigned to fully repair parts or subassemblies received from the field, test and check out, and then return for shipment.
■ Just in time — In which repairs are made using a productive line model in which material received in the field is first analyzed to determine if there is no trouble found (NTF), and thus, can be immediately returned to the field, or if failed is placed into a work in process (WIP) inventory. As orders to specific stock-keeping units (SKUs) are received, the appropriate material is taken from WIP to a "front end" diagnostic or triage process, resulting in a specific repair schedule and sequences. Based on this schedule, repair is done in a manufacturing line fashion. At the completion, the final SKU is then independently checked and tested, and if okay, is shipped out.

A comparison between these two markets is show in Figure 6.2.

Benchmarking of these two alternative models — job shop (Figure 6.2 top) vs. just in time (Figure 6.2 bottom) — is shown in Table 6.1 and Table 6.2. As indicated, the just in time product process is much more efficient then the typical job shop process from both a cost and operational standpoint to the extent that the repair depot is able to increase its volume by selling its services as an independent fourth party maintenance depot and achieve economies of scale. The performance differences are even greater.

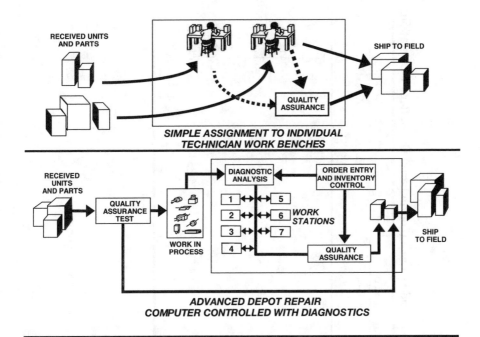

Figure 6.2   Depot repair alternatives.

Depot Repair Practices in Support of Closed Loop Systems

Depot Repair as part of the RL or CLSC can be used to either repair a part, subassembly, or whole unit, or disaggregate it into its component parts down to raw materials to either reuse or sell. A typical decomposition flow for a personal computer as shown in Figure 6.3 illustrates the individual values that can be produced through "tear down" or "cannibalization" of a whole unit which is no longer required or is not totally repairable. These components, parts, and subassemblies can be returned to the field for use, in closed loop systems, or sold in secondary markets* in pure RL systems.

Depot Repair and Reduction Process in Simple Reverse Logistics Operations

The role of depot repair in the closed loop system differs from a similar role in the simple RL process. As shown in Table 6.3, the role in the closed loop system is to refurbish, recondition, repair, and return the product, subassemblies, and parts back into the full logistics support

---

* Secondary markets are discussed in Chapter 8.

Table 6.1 Benchmark Parameters for Operations of Internal Repair Depot and External (Fourth Party) Depot Repair Operations

Parameters	Internal Depot		External Depot***	
	Average Experience	"Best Practices" Efficiently Run	Average Experience	"Best Practices" Efficiently Run
Profit or contribution of depot repair	0 (breakeven)	5%	14%	26%
Average unit repair cost	$79	$60	$53	$41
Repair time turnaround (in days)	10	5	4	3
Field dead on arrival (DOA)*	3%	2%	2%	1%
Receipt no trouble found (NTF) at recovery**	6%	18%	11%	22%
Bench tech labor and supplier costs as a % of total costs	47%	42%	35%	26%
Transportation costs as a percent of total cost	12%	8%	11%	8%

*Measure of repair quality.

**Measure of receiving processing quality.

***Run as a line of business.

Source: From Blumberg Associates, Inc. benchmark data — 1995–1998 based on 32 repair depots.

Table 6.2 Benchmark Parameters for Operations of Internal Repair Depot and External (Fourth Party) Depot Repair Operations (Logistics Support — Operation Experience)

Parameters	Internal Depot		External Depot	
	Average Experience	"Best Practices" Efficiently Run	Average Experience	"Best Practices" Efficiently Run
Average number of weekly parts/repair requests processed from customers per CSR	12.7	9.6	30.3	47.8
Average length of time per week required to process customer requests per CSR	3.3	2.4	3.6	3.8
Average number of weekly parts/repair requests processed from field engineers per CSR	40.0	26.0	17.6	12.1
Average length of time per week required to process field engineer requests per CSR	9.0	8.8	2.2	1.3
Average number of complaint calls per week per CSR	4.5	3.1	2.7	2.2
Average length and time per week to process complaint calls per CSR	1.1	0.7	0.8	0.6
Average number of weekly calls requiring technical assistance per CSR	5.2	4.6	3.9	3.3
Average length of time per week spent providing technical assistance per CSR	3.1	2.1	2.0	1.3
Average number of units processed by bench technician per week	10.0	13.8	15.9	19.4

Table 6.2 Benchmark Parameters for Operations of Internal Repair Depot and External (Fourth Party) Depot Repair Operations (Logistics Support — Operation Experience) (continued)

Parameters	Internal Depot		External Depot*	
	Average Experience	"Best Practices" Efficiently Run	Average Experience	"Best Practices" Efficiently Run
Average number of weekly repairs per bench technician	9.5	13.2	15.7	19.4
Average time to repair all units per week (in hours) by bench technician	33.3	30.0	34.5	34.9
Percent of requests requiring replacement parts	55.7%	53.4%	48.1%	43.3%
Percent of units that go through all initial quality test	48.9%	57.2%	94.5%	100.0%
Percent of times that trouble ticket description does not reflect actual problem	51.2%	44.1%	30.6%	24.1%

*Run as a line of business.

Source: From Blumberg Associates, Inc. benchmark data 1995–1998 based on 49 repair depots.

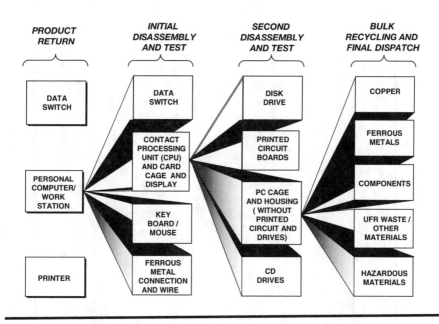

| PRODUCT RETURN | INITIAL DISASSEMBLY AND TEST | SECOND DISASSEMBLY AND TEST | BULK RECYCLING AND FINAL DISPATCH |

Figure 6.3   Disassembly stages for a personal computer/work product.

system as rapidly as possible, and at the lowest cost. In essence, the role is one of a pump designed to take the returned goods, treat them and return them to service. In this case, the role is very similar to a filtration system in a water treatment process.

The alternate role views the depot as the "end of the line." The depot in this case is focused on maximizing the value of the returns and final disposal of the residuals. In this type of depot, the job is to take the products, goods, trash, and waste through a process designed to break up the returned goods into component parts or even materials.

In the high tech repair depot, the decomposition and "demanufacturing," shown in Figure 6.3, provides a guide for "when to stop"; that is, what is to be done to achieve the most rapid and efficient return on the RL output back into the service logistics supply chain. However, for the stand-alone depot in the basic RL process, the same decomposition approach is used to determine how to maximize value of the return through resale of the components. In effect, the repair depot will move down the decomposition procedure to produce the material that has the largest resale value for the processing costs, rather than focusing on return of parts, subassemblies, and whole units into the full closed loop system.

In the basic RL role, the depot repair activity is a business of its own; this was the preview of the junk or reclamation businesses, buying up all used materials of a given type, for the purpose of processing for resale. Usually these organizations specialize in certain materials, such as:

Table 6.3 Comparison of Repair Depot Operations in Different Roles

Factor	Repair Depot in Closed Loop High Tech Operations	Repair Depot in Basic Reverse Logistics Operation as an End User
Primary objective	Return required whole units, parts and subassemblies rapidly at lowest cost of repair	Maximize value and revenue from processing and disposal
Type of operation	Use of bench techs operating as – Job shop – Just in time production	Production line process using maximum level of fragmentation and decision structure processes, including – Compacting – Heating – Grinding
Typical operational environment	Tech labor office type environment, including "clean rooms" — environmentally clean	Typical "junk yard" environment accompanied by – Dust and dirt – Noise Environmentally dirty
Value added service	• Analysis and evaluation of failure rates, repair times, causes of failure • Forecasting • Sourcing options	• Land or sea fill dumps • Knowledge of buyer sources • Refuse/trash collection

- Clothing and rags
- Paper
- Tires
- Batteries
- Raw materials, such as copper

Usually, these basic processes involve compacting, heating and melting, grinding, and so forth, all designed to reduce the acquired material into its most basic components for ease of resale into secondary markets, or as materials to act as raw material for basic production process (i.e., scrap steel, copper, aluminum, etc.).

7

WARRANTY MANAGEMENT, RETURN PROCESS, AND BENCHMARKS

INTRODUCTION: TYPES OF WARRANTIES

The role of warranty and extended warranty support service as part of the reverse logistics (RL) or closed loop supply chain (CLSC) process is neither well understood nor well managed in most industrial and commercial firms. The reasons for this are complex, but they primarily relate to the inability to fully understand the strategic value of warranties and the requirements for the appropriate infrastructure to manage and, in fact, optimize warranty and postwarranty support service. It is also important to understand the critical importance of perceptions (from both the purchaser's and the seller's points of view) in successfully managing the warranty and extended warranty process, as part of the overall RL system.

Starting with perceptions, we need to recognize that (in the minds of the buyer) the warranty is a guarantee of performance, in general, and specific form, fit, and function for products and services in particular. It is intended to be an "insurance policy" provided to the buyer by the seller that the purchased goods (and/or services) will be consistent with the marketing or sales offer made. This guarantee or insurance could be broadly implemented in terms of two mechanisms:

- Payment of compensation — Financial compensation represents one mechanism for warranty support. In essence, an amount is paid to the buyer in the event of the failure of the product or service to perform or meet the sales commitment. This is often tied in consumer products to the product return or RL process.

This approach is often used for small appliances and inexpensive consumer goods (such as clothing, cosmetics, household cleaners, food, etc.) with a warranty often stated as "return for full (or partial) refund in the event of dissatisfaction." It is also generally applied to small returnable goods in which excess wear or partial failure of these can be physically determined (such as the case of return warranty on tires based upon the date of purchase and observed tread wear). This warranty mechanism is also used between manufactures and wholesalers, and wholesalers and retailers on the return of unpurchased goods (books, clothing, pharmaceuticals, etc.) with the initial buyer "compensated" or credited for returns, and the return goods are sold in a secondary market.

■ Remedial or repair service — The second mechanism for satisfying the warranty commitment is to provide the appropriate services either in the field or at some defined depot repair location to fix or remediate the deficiency or problem in the products or services sold. As in the case of the payment mechanism, this process will also involve RL. However, it also requires a combination of proactive and reactive response to either, effect a fix or repair rapidly, replacement, or to prevent the failure in performance of occurring at all. This is obviously the more complex and sophisticated guarantee, because it is intended to leave the buyer with full satisfaction with the product, rather than a simple cash payment.

In essence, there is a significant difference between the warranty strategy involving repayment on a partial or full basis or exchange, in which the warranty acts very much as a simple insurance policy, vs. the more sophisticated service supported warranty process, in which the selling organization commits to making the repair or fix within a given timeframe. Both approaches need to be managed and involve a RL component. However, only one, the service warranty support, requires the seller or his dealer to set up and operate a complete RL or CLSC service organization and infrastructure (Table 7.1).

Managing the Strategic Value of the Warranty Process

Looking at this general model for warranty support, we need to also recognize that in both warranty and (in the case of service support) extended warranty performance, the process, if appropriately managed, can have strategic value. Actual experience in the retail field, such as consumer electronics, for example, shows that warranties can be extremely profitable. Circuit City and Sears have found that buyers tend not to make

Table 7.1 Warranty Strategies

Warranty Guarantee	Required Structure		Functional Services Received as Part of Warranty			Business Model(s)
	Policy Procedures	Infrastructure and Systems	Field	Reverse Logistics	Depot	
Payment in cash for failure	Payment for loss of use of replacement of equivalent produce/services	• Management structure • Reverse logistics	No	No	No	Insurance
Remedial or repair services	Service level commitment	• Full service management system – Call handling – Logistics – Etc.	Yes	Yes	Yes	Service line of business

as much use of service warranty guarantees as they might be entitled to for the following reasons:

- Unit purchased simply does not fall in the warranty or extended warranty timeframe
- Buyer fails to remember that a warranty exists
- Buyer moves to a new geographic region where warranty service is not available
- Purchased unit is sold to a third party or is no longer used

Experience also indicates, especially in well-planned warranty offers, based on accurate failure forecasting, that actual warranty service offer is often used less than was planned for in initial product cost allocations. This is due to the impact of product improvements and production changes, based on early warranty return experience. This could make the margin or profitability of warranties and extended warranties quite high. One can immediately see the result of this by simply going to any large consumer electronics or white goods (refrigerators, washing machines, air conditioning, etc.) retailer. In these organizations, once completing the product sale there is an immediate action by the sales person to add extended warranty coverage. This is due to the high incentive and margin associated with the warranty. On the other hand, poorly planned warranties can lead to both profit margin erosion and loss of market share. Thus, a warranty system that can track and identify failure rates of the whole unit, subassembly, and stock-keeping unit (SKU) levels, and can then proactively respond by either allocating parts properly, or making recommendations for engineering changes in the field or manufacturing changes to reduce future failure, will increase the profitability of the warranty or extended warranty function.

The key component in this evaluation and planning is that, in general, product failures are not constant over time. As shown in Figure 7.1, failures tend to be high in the early "burn in" stage in initial use of the product (typically, part or all of the warranty period), then stabilized with low level failures, particularly if engineering changes and retrofits and changes in parts reliability have been made in the field or production line based upon early mean time between failure experience. Finally, as the product begins to mature and age, or is not fully supported, failure rates again begin to rise. This idealized pattern depends upon the critical assumption that the initial warranty use period is monitored closely for failure. If this is carried out on a continuing real time and comprehensive basis, the ability to identify failure rate trends early in product introduction, take corrective action either at the manufacturing level or at the initial purchasing input, or installation, or in continuing preventative maintenance

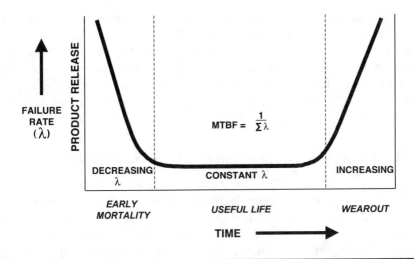

FAILURE RATE (λ)

PRODUCT RELEASE

MTBF = $\frac{1}{\sum \lambda}$

DECREASING λ

CONSTANT λ

INCREASING

EARLY MORTALITY

USEFUL LIFE

WEAROUT

TIME

Figure 7.1 Typical failure rate as a function of time. (From Blumberg Associates, Inc.)

in the field, the observed failure rates can be significantly limited or reduced and warranty profitability can increase.

This is perhaps the most important element of the warranty management process. The warranty systems and infrastructure should be designed and implemented such that it does provide continuous closed loop tracking of mean time between failures (MTBF), at the assembly, subassembly, and SKU levels, as well as to identify linkages between the part, assembly, and subassembly level failures. These failures should also be linked to problems and symptoms as reported by the user. This information is best collected starting in the warranty process. This data should be accurately collected and reported on a real-time basis, and then analyzed and evaluated to identify failure rate and trends, making use of advanced forecasting models and purchasing models.

Thus, the design of the warranty and post warranty offer needs to take into account:

■ Warranty's value to the buyer
■ Specific allocation of warranty-focused revenues — out of the total product price — to avoid either excess profits being attributed to the product or the underfunding of warranty support buy and offer; in essence, the warranty process should be tracked and evaluated as a separate profit center

The extended warranty support price to be offered also needs specific attention (too high implies poor reliability, too low could lead to losses);

extended warranty pricing should be based on market research on customer service perceptions, value, and willingness to pay. Extended warranty management also means engineering changes, part or subassembly replacement or upgrade, or some combination thereof in order to improve reliability in the field, paid for by the extended warranty charges and the need for predictive or preventive maintenance, paid out of warranty changes, to reduce high cost emergency repair.

The Importance of Perceptions in Managing Warranty and Postwarranty Service

Another real difference of critical importance in successfully managing the warranty and extended warranty process, is to recognize the very real differences in perception (and reality) on the part of the buyer vs. the seller. The seller wants to make the warranty guarantee as precise and specific as possible, and at the same time does not wish to suggest that the reliability or the quality of the performance of this product or service is at risk. The warranty specifications are thus usually written in extremely fine print and constructed utilizing legalistic phrases. The seller's policies and systems also tend to be focused on analysis and evaluation of submitted warranty claims and requests to limit exposure.

The buyer on the other hand perceives the warranty as a real guarantee of quality, reliability, and service support in the event of a problem. Warranty is generally viewed as a security blanket, and the buying customer assumes that the warranty provides an extremely high level of service and support commitment. The customer generally does not read the fine print, and in all probability does not understand, or is not aware, of the *caveat emptor* (let the buyer beware) framework in which the warranty is often stated. Specifically, however, if the general buyer group receives the service and support he or she needs or full payment as required during the warranty period, or if he or she never requires it, brand loyalty will increase, thus full service warranty support can lead to increased brand value and thus increased market share.

Once we can recognize this very real and critical difference between the buyer's and seller's perceptions, we can also begin to understand the strategic implications of those differences. The buyer's perception of a value of the warranty depends not upon individual events and experience in the future, but rather upon a series of past events based upon previous personal experience, experience of peers, and general market and industry experience, including common knowledge. The very high commitment of IBM to service under warranty and postwarranty support created a significant added value to the IBM brand name, leading strategically to higher market share, and the ability to maintain high prices in the presence of competition.

On the other hand, most sellers tend to view the warranty commitment as part of the sales process without seeing the added strategic value of the warranty service associated with the sale. They see customer complaints, particularly about product or service quality, performance, response, and so on, as a necessary evil or as a problem of a certain class of difficult to satisfy customers. This perception is made even more difficult as the manufacturer organizations report on their own output quality resulting in cases in which the product quality (MTBF), as measured by the manufacturing organization, can be seriously different from the observed mean time between failure as reported by the customer. This is made worse when the service organization fails to respond to a service call rapidly, or takes no preventive or predictive maintenance activity.

In addition, the difference between the customer's perceptions, which is holistic, in dealing with the *entire interface* between the customer (for the product/service purchase) and the manufacturer who deals with these problems in terms of explicit and specific events or factors can often be at odds in reporting the problems in dealing with each other. For example, an operator error of failure to follow an instruction may cause a copying machine to be viewed by the buyer as unreliable. The product seller tends to view this as a failure on the part of the customer to train his user personnel. Anyone with experience in product support also knows that most user organizations tend to focus on their perception of a product failure as the root cause of the problems being observed as opposed to their own personal performance and contribution to the problems at hand. It is, therefore, important to measure performance and reliability from the buyer's side.

Managing Warranty and Postwarranty Support in a Dealer Environment

The question of managing warranty and extended warranty service and support is made even more complex when indirect channels or dealers/distributors are involved. In the case of the direct distribution model, all of the above issues can be dealt with centrally and strategically by the manufacturer. However, in the presence of independent dealers and distributors, the problem is made much more complex in terms of the question of who takes responsibility for the strategy as opposed to the tactical issues of who pays for what.

Most indirect distribution strategies assume that the dealers/distributors have responsibility for both sales and service. In general, the manufacturer establishes the sales/product, form, fit, and function and the price. In many cases, the price to the dealer or retailer is "suggested" and can be modified by the individual dealer or distributor as a function of their specialized or additional cost of sales and service. Extrapolating from the general responsibility of the manufacturer for the product quality, it is generally the role of the manufacturer to also establish the warranty policy and processes. In most cases where the dealer is required to carry out warranty services on the part of the manufacturer, the manufacturer reimburses the dealer/distributor based on some type of claims processing system or procedures. Often the dealer/retailer takes direct responsibility for extended warranty, usually using their own or independent service providers.

A key question at this point is whether or not the manufacturer views the warranty and extended warranty and post warranty support as one integrated process and as part of a CLSC, or separates the overall service into two components; service under warranty, which is paid for by the manufacturer, and service out of warranty or under extended warranty, which is covered by the dealer. As indicated above, the warranty process, if properly managed, can give great insight into failure and repair characteristics and can be highly useful in determining optimum service parts logistics allocation, provisioning, and sparing in the CLSC. Separation by the manufacturer's management team of control under just the warranty period vs. coverage for full warranty and postwarranty service can lead to suboptimization.

Another important issue is whether the participants in warranty, extended warranty, and post warranty support (the manufacturer and the dealers) see the warranty process as a zero sum game in which the OEM vs. the dealers are at odds, or a full win-win/lose-lose situation in which both class of organizations can either win or lose depending upon their synergistic relationship.

Actual pragmatic experience suggests that the zero sum game view is still prevalent even though it can be clearly pointed out that both the warranty and extended or postwarranty pricing and service portfolios are interactively affected from the buyer's viewpoint. In addition, actions for engineering change and changes in manufacturing process or parts purchased, and so on, to improve field reliability can directly effect profit margins after the initial warranty period.

Resolution of this issue must also give specific weight to recent trends in the general market for outsourcing. In many markets the traditional internal plant and building maintenance service organizations have been eliminated through outsourcing. This reduces the ability of the buyer (for many types of technologies and products) to turn to the existing internal service force to effect minor repairs or to act rapidly. The trend is clearly to depend more and more on the manufacturer or the dealer/distributor (in the indirect channel model) for a full array of services. Thus, a very critical effect of the general outsourcing trend, particularly for companies utilizing an indirect distribution channel, is to significantly increase the amount of field service that the dealer/distributor must provide under the warranty and extended warranty, and postwarranty period.

If the manufacturer, in these circumstances, continues to see the process as a zero sum game, it is quite clear that a major conflict could arise between the manufacturer and the dealers relative to dealer profitability and level of service provided particularly for returns and field repairs. In essence, the impact of outsourcing requires the manufacturer to give much more serious attention to dealer service under either extended warranty or after warranty, including but not limited to insuring service parts resupply on an efficient basis. It also requires a much more elaborate and sophisticated analysis and evaluation of the entire warranty process including the policies, procedures, and systems infrastructure in order to ensure optimization of both the manufacturer and dealer/distributor support under both warranty and postwarranty periods, for the full CLSC or RL processes.

The bottom line is that management of the warranty, extended warranty, and postwarranty process requires:

- Clear understanding of the requirements for and degree of interest on the part of the customers in both the form and type of the warranty (repayment vs. corrective services).
- Importance of the full service guarantee as opposed to the reimbursement guarantee to the buyer group and individual segments.
- Understanding the long-term strategic value of the full service warranty commitment — The use of the full service approach in the warranty and extended warranty commitment process and guarantee needs to be related to overall long-term higher perceived reliability and quality and increased revenues and profits. Since the service organizations can directly identify, measure, and correct failures in the field if the appropriate infrastructure and systems are in place to control the problem/symptom/cause/corrective action relationships in the call opening, tracking, and close out process, and in the RL process, it can build a strong and accurate database to increase MTBF and reliability through optimizing purchase of stocking materials, recommend engineering changes and modifications that could result in extending the product MTBF and to identify other changes and modifications including on-board diagnostics to significantly improve mean time to repair (MTTR).
- Recognizing the strategic value of warranty and postwarranty service in terms of generating revenues and profits from service performance in the CLSC — In essence, the initial warranty coverage if properly managed, marketed, and priced, could provide a starting point for the sale of a longer term extended warranty or

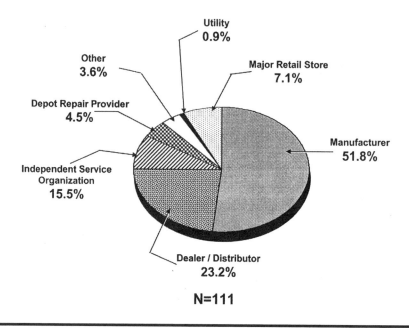

Figure 7.2   Distribution of benchmark study participants — by type of company.

after warranty service and support, at a substantial profit, through a more efficient CLSC covering warranty, extended warranty, and postwarranty support.

General Warranty Process Benchmark Analysis and Evaluation

Industry benchmark metrics were obtained using a combination of current benchmarking data and industry surveys. These surveys were designed to benchmark organizations involved in warranty processing activities, and were derived from a list of manufacturing and retail companies with $10 million or more of sales annually (Figure 7.2). Overall, the organizations benchmarked indicated that they were employing an average of eight warranty and claims personnel. The actual number of warranty claims processed each month from the survey ranged from 300 to well over 30,000, depending on the size and nature of each organization. General experiences in warranty management is summarized in Table 7.2

An interesting trend that emerged when conducting the benchmark analysis indicated that a small number of dealers and retailers do not submit or route any claims directly to manufacturer at all. Instead, these organizations are utilizing a combination of third-party services and internal processing departments to handle warranty claims.

The standard methods of routing warranty claims to manufacturers, whether from the customer or a dealer, as shown in Figure 7.3, are by:

Table 7.2 Warranty Management and Administration Benchmarking (Analysis and Comparison of Relevant Performance Metrics)

Performance Metrics	Industry	
	Average	Best of Class
Average claims processed per month	15,000	40,000
Rejection rate	12.6%	3%
Length of time to process each claim	8.7 days	2 days
Overall cost per claim	$125	$75
Processing cost per claim (fully automated)	$3.00	$0.34
Processing cost per claim (manual or semiautomated)	$10.42	$8.00
Number of claims processing personnel	18	2
Ratio of claims personnel to total employees	1:98	1:400
Time between claim filing and actual reimbursement	45 days	< 1 week
Claim severity (percent over budget)	3%	0%

Source: From Blumberg Associates, Inc.

Mail
Telephone
Fax
Electronic data interchange (EDI)
Internet

Of obvious popularity is the telephone claims submission method. In fact, the benchmark analysis found that approximately 35% of all claims are submitted using this method from the customer and dealer alike. The typical rejection rate of warranty claims submitted from both customers and dealers directly ranges from 2 to 40%, depending on the type and nature of the claim. An average rejection rate among industry participants is around 3%.

The number of days actually required to process a warranty claim, regardless of its origin, ranges from 1 to over 30 days, and is generally proportionate to the technologies and methods used to submit and process each claim. Costs to process individual warranty claims also range in value, from $0.05 up to $20 each. An average cost among most industry players is $11.80 per claim (mostly those using manual methods).

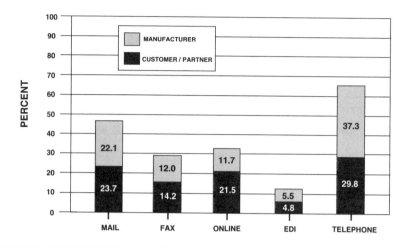

Figure 7.3   Methods for processing claims. (From Blumberg Associates, Inc.)

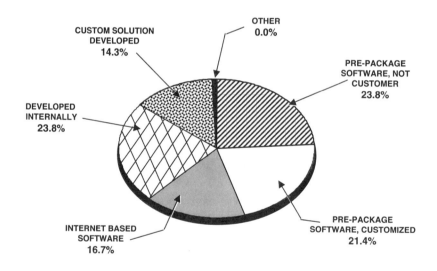

Figure 7.4   Use of software and Internet-based warranty management systems. (From Blumberg Associates, Inc.)

Table 7.3 Percentage of Improvement in Performance Received from Utilizing Integrated Warranty Management Software

Outcome	Percent of Improvement Received
Greater accuracy of claims	27.1%
Improved cash flow	22.6%
Improved productivity	21.0%
Reduced warranty processing costs	17.9%
Reduced rejection rate of claims	15.9%
Reduced cost of service parts processing and emergency delivery	23.1%

Source: From Blumberg Associates Inc.

From the standpoint of warranty management systems, it is interesting to note that slightly over 42% of all firms benchmarked said that their organizations were using manual, or at best spreadsheet, methods to track and manage warranty claims for those that have automated the process (Figure 7.4). Most said that they recovered their initial warranty management systems investments within 6 to 24 months after the purchase of the system. Those that recently purchased newer, more advanced systems reported several large improvements in their claims processing performance management and return on investment of less than 18 months. The primary improvements observed are shown in Table 7.3.

Benchmarking was also conducted of independent warranty claims management firms. These organizations take responsibility for outsourcing of the warranty claims process. They have generally evolved through a combination of individual vendors as shown in Figure 7.5 In general, claims management firm's price on a cost-plus basis, establishing flat fees for product warranties using the insurance cost as a basis for the markup. This process results in target margins for the claims business of between 8 and 15%, however realized margin per claim varies widely, from $0.08 per claim to $0.68 per claim, depending on vendor and industry. This implies a cost per claim of approximately $6 to $8.

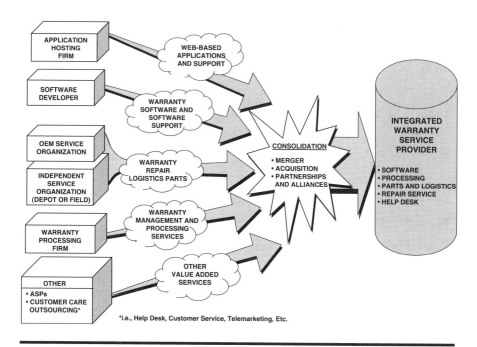

Figure 7.5   Evolution of warranty processing service organizations. (From Blumberg Associates, Inc.)

8

SECONDARY MARKETS AND FINAL DISPOSAL OF RETURNED PRODUCTS AND MATERIALS

INTRODUCTION

We discussed in previous chapters the return process through either a closed loop supply chain (CLSC) or simple reverse logistics (RL) operation (Chapter 4 and Chapter 5). We have also discussed the role of the depot in repair, refurbishment, remanufacture, and decomposition of the return goods (Chapter 6). Our analysis has also shown that products, goods, and materials can be returned for a variety of reasons, including:

- Parts or subassembly failures in the field
- Products or materials damaged in shipping or transit
- Products or materials returned to clear shelves
- Products or materials returned due to obsolescence, age, manufacturing issues/recalls
- Products or goods returned for other reasons, such as customer remorse

In the CLSC operation, a significant portion of these returns are repaired, refurbished, and sent back to the end user. Some materials and products are simply disposed of as waste or trash leading to:

- Material recycling
- Destruction by fire or chemical means
- Burial in land or sea deposits

In addition to these options, another return channel involves reselling to secondary markets. This chapter deals with the creation and use of secondary markets and mechanisms for disposal of returned products and materials, which continue to have value as is, or with refurbishment, repair, or remanufacture.

As a direct result of the significant increase in CLSC and RL processes, a number of secondary markets have been created. It originally started in certain specific industries and product areas, including automobiles, building and housing materials, industrial machinery, furniture and household goods, clothing, and personal computers. In general, these secondary market businesses operated nationally or regionally, and were primarily involved in the purchase of unwanted returned goods at significant discounts, for purpose of resale. The automotive after market resulting from the reconditioning of automotive parts, components, and subassemblies (engines, transmissions, etc.), as well as whole units is a perfect example of this process.

The increasing volume of RL and CLSC operations has also led to the development of new businesses* that provide the following services:

- Providing a buy/sell exchange increasingly supported through online Internet operations, such as e-Bay, and Wholesale Hub
- Organizations specializing in certain classes or types of products and materials, such as Processoverskott AB, Railway Logistics International Company, Inc., and Liquidity Services, Inc.
- Firms like Recover-ITT offering full services including, purchase of returned products and goods, refurbishing, transportation and delivery, and final sale and return products management (RPM)

A partial listing of these companies and firms representing secondary markets and disposal channels is outlined in Table 8.1.

OFFSHORE SECONDARY MARKETS

Primary disposal channels usually involve purchase and sale of products and goods in the same country or geographic region. Another alternative is to dispose of these products offshore through international transfers. Particularly in the case of consumer goods to be returned from mass merchandisers, often restrictions are placed on the disposition channels to avoid direct competition for the same products at discounted rates, which could compete with the mass merchandiser stores. This is usually resolved by remerchandising and marketing these goods in third world

---

* See Appendix D for a broader list of third party service providers.

Table 8.1 Organizations Providing Secondary Markets

Company	Services	Basic Process	Product or Technology Focus
Liquidity Services, Inc.	Management and sale of surplus assets	• Online auctions via Internet • Sealed bids	• Military equipment and supplies • Bulk product • Electronics
AAA Overstock 728 S.E. 9th St. Algona, IA 50511	Management and sale of overstock and department store returns	• Online ordering • Drop shipping	• Consumer goods • Department store returns • Overstocks • Overruns
Wholesale Hub	Acts as exchange broker using internet	• Buy-sell • Exchange	• Consumer goods
Processoverskott AB	Management and sale of excess and obsolete equipment	• Acquire at warehouse • Sell based on requests	• Industrial equipment for process industries
Railway Logistics International Co., Inc. North 9986 Newport Highway #282 Spokane, WA 99218	Repair/remanufacture management and sale of used industrial equipment	• Buy-sell • Exchange	• Railway and marine motive power • Power generating systems
Return Products Management (RPM)	Equipment returns and dismantling core returns, parts/assembly collections	• Repair and refurbishment • Scrap	• Industrial and commercial trucks and cars
Assetsmarket.com	Offers market for commercial and industrial equipment	• Online auction	• Second hand and excess business machinery

Table 8.1 Organizations Providing Secondary Markets (continued)

Company	Services	Basic Process	Product or Technology Focus
Pollution Prevention Information Resource for Industry Sectors (P2IRIS)	Information exchange for surplus materials Catalog listing	• Source and information clearing house	• Surplus materials and waste
Recover-ITT 767 kenrick – Suite 120 Houston, TX 77060	Full service For electronics technology including – Acquisition – Relocation/transportation – Packaging – Services	• Asset liquidation, removal, and sales	• Office equipment • Computers • Telecommunications equipment • Furniture
e-Bay	Provide market for buyers and sellers	• Buy-sell • Exchange	• No specialization

countries. A significantly increasing flow of goods and materials from one country to another to be resold at high discounts has been created. This may also require repackaging or minor modifications relative to electrical connections, power requirements, etc., in order to meet the regulations or requirements of these countries of sale.

Returned goods and products involving industrial/commercial, as well as consumer goods, can often be sold in secondary markets within the original country of origin or offshore, thus, turning valueless returns into economic value and, in effect, extending the life cycle of the original product. This ability to, in effect, recreate value from returns contributes to the increasing interest on the part of manufacturers, dealers, and distributors in the full CLSC and RL process. By more effectively and efficiently managing the entire logistics process, it is possible to recover significant value from what was once regarded as obsolete or unusable material to be trashed or destroyed.

USE OF THIRD PARTY SERVICE PROVIDERS

As indicated above, and in Table 8.1, a third party logistics organization already exists that is prepared to take responsibility for unwanted products and resell them, and also provide RL services. Because of the growing interest in RL as a business opportunity and as a result of the application of green law directives in Europe, it is clear that there will be a continuing growth in third party organizations focusing on the provision of RL services, including the ability to resell unwanted products into secondary markets. Organizations established for depot repair and RL support in free trade zones on the Mexican/U.S. border and in South America, the Middle East, South Africa, and Asia/Pacific (Hong Kong, Singapore, Malaysia, etc.) are now beginning to grow and expand as a result of recognition of the market opportunities available to it. In addition, the major global distribution organizations including UPS, FedEx, DHL, and others are also aggressively moving to expand their array of services and portfolio in order to make use of their worldwide distribution and support capabilities. Finally, third party maintenance organizations that currently operate their own depot repair and CLSC services to support their field operations are also in an excellent position to offer their closed loop services as an independent strategic line of business. It therefore seems very clear that all organizations interested in significantly improving the efficiency and effectiveness and ultimate distribution and delivery processes in RL will find available a broad array of third party contractors and service providers offering an expanded portfolio of service and support. Since so many organizations in this market already have large national, regional, or global transportation distribution warehousing and depot repair capabilities, it is clear that additional economies of scale will prevail in reducing the actual operating costs of RL processes.

E-commerce is a very hot topic with respect to the creation of efficient new secondary markets. Is it, however, simply a matter of building it and they will come? Apparently success in e-commerce is not a "slam dunk," says Tom Peck, president of Clinton, New Jersey–based Powersource Online, an electronic trading hub for the procurement of spare parts, "It takes time and money to build a trading hub, it has taken us 8 years."

Where do you find the right place to build an e-marketplace? In the old, old economy, a successful business depended on real estate. It is all about "location, location, location," a successful entrepreneur would tell you. The concept of location also applies to the new economy, but the real estate is not a physical presence. The best locations for building e-commerce is in industries where there are fragmented markets consisting of many buyers and sellers who must contend with inefficiencies in the market and in basic business processes. Given this formula for success, it seems that e-commerce has a good future in the service and support industry. Two areas with the most inefficiency and fragmentation are spare parts procurement and warranty claims processing. These have become new hot beds for e-commerce development. According to Alain Miquelon, CFO of Mediagrif, a leading developer and operator of business to business vertical marketplaces on the Internet, "Service industries have a lot of built-in inefficiency especially in the area of spare parts procurement. Open market systems also are a good place to look for market inefficiency. The ease of entry and encouragement of competition among participants characterize open markets. The multivendor IT services market is a good example of an open market system with much inefficiency, particularly in the area of warranty claims processing." Organizations that service and support products from multiple manufacturers must have a system in place to deal with each manufacturer's unique warranty claims processing procedures. According to Jack Smyth, director of planning and strategy for customer service at Compaq Corp., warranty claims processing is still a very manual process for most computer dealers/service providers. "Warranty claims processing is a very time consuming and costly process. Large dealers must have a different warranty team for each OEM because each warranty system is handled differently. There can be anywhere from 4 to 10 people on the team," notes Smyth who is also chairman of Comptia's electronic warranty claims initiative. Comptia, a consortium of over 5000 computer dealers and OEMs, is responding to these inefficiencies by creating a common electronic exchange standard for processing warranty claims. "We believe that Comptia can create one common standard for processing claims via the Internet. This standard will enable e-commerce vendors to create uniform electronic exchanges." The exchange that

Comptia is envisioning would function as a transfer station and work somewhat like airline booking systems such as Apollo and Sabre, which enable users to share and access data from multiple airlines. Now warranty claims processing has become a big opportunity for Internet firms. More importantly, warranty claims processing exchanges, such as those envisioned by Smyth, will help to improve the overall costs associated with field service dispatch and spare parts procurement, particularly during the warranty and extended warranty phases of the product life cycle.

Parts trading hubs and warranty exchanges are certainly a hot opportunity. The market for e-commerce based spare parts procurement and warranty claims processing is estimated to be a $12 billion and $2 billion market, respectively, by the year 2004. Over the last year, a number of firms have launched trading hubs and e-marketplaces to secure a large slice of the high tech service parts market. Traditional parts providers and depot repair vendors are using electronic trading hubs as a means of reinventing themselves as "clicks and mortar" firms.

An important key to success is the ability of trading hubs to differentiate themselves by adding value. All successful trading hubs agree on one thing, the best way to add value is by addressing critical business issues vis-à-vis the provision of content and information. For service parts this means the provision of accurate information on pricing and inventory availability. It could also be the provision of ancillary services such as quality testing and a 6-month warranty on all parts procured through its Internet-based reverse auction service. A reverse auction differs from traditional internet based auctions (such as e-Bay), by creating a forum whereby the sellers of parts bid on the lot specifications (e.g., part) and price requirements established by the buyer. For warranty claims processing exchange providers such as ServiceBench.com, this includes the provision of technical documentation and parts ordering capabilities into their exchange. For I-Service this means offering a broad array of system functionality in managing the warranty process from entitlement, to order entry, to reporting.

Despite the benefits of e-marketplaces and trading hubs, it has been an uphill battle in terms of persuading buyers and sellers to participate. The most obvious reason, when it comes to spare parts trading hubs, is uncertainty over the reliability and quality of participants. Most buying organizations have strict quality requirements for spare parts. They don't want to deal with thousands of nonqualified vendors. However, the most significant challenges facing e-marketplaces is the old NIH or "Not Invented Here" syndrome of the larger manufacturers and service providers. While managers and executives in these large companies may not necessarily be driving change, or championing the use of e-markets, this is not to say that they are not willing to contribute to their success. The reality is simply that e-marketplaces require organizations to reengineer or rethink the way they have traditionally done business. Managers and executives in the larger companies need to fully consider the implications of change on their day-to-day operations. Unfortunately, this does not occur overnight. However, this perceived reluctance does create a real catch-22; while the smaller firms are often the most anxious to utilize the e-marketplaces, it is the larger firms that have the most control and influence over the long term viability. It is not that the larger companies fear change. It is that they have so much invested in their existing systems and procedures for spare parts procurement and warranty processing that is often based on complex business rules and requirements. It is wishful thinking to presume that large companies are going to just toss out their current ways of doing business in favor of the newest new thing without giving it some careful consideration, particularly if this means relinquishing some control of their operations to a virtual third party.

Once the bigger firms get past this issue and make a decision to adopt the e-marketplace, the next challenge they run into is establishing interfaces with internal corporate information systems. Most firms want more then the ability to merely electronically bolt on the e-marketplace to their existing systems. What the larger firms are looking for is to actually have the trading hub embedded in their internal systems and processes. Their goal is to create a seamless interface, which permits online, real-time access to the trading hub, and eliminates human intervention. While most trading hub suppliers are delighted to provide this level of customization and integration, even on a pro bono basis, end user organizations often lack the internal IT resources to commit to these projects. The issue is a matter of prioritization and competition with other e-commerce initiatives that are going on within the organization. As a result, the use of trading hubs and warranty exchanges is becoming much more of a strategic outsourcing decision then many e-commerce entrepreneurs may have originally believed.

Many lessons must be learned from these early ventures into trading hubs and e-marketplaces. The first is that the creation of e-marketplaces takes time, effort, and commitment. It is a mistake to think that by simply flicking a switch the business will just flow. To work effectively, e-marketplaces must resolve inefficiencies shared by all market participants and demonstrate quantifiable benefits to users. Second, e-marketplaces must add value to end users and do more then simply bring buyers and sellers together in an electronic exchange. Third, e-marketplaces are an extension of the user's systemic infrastructure. As such, the e-marketplace vendor must be prepared to adapt its system to the needs of the user vis-à-vis consulting, integration, and customization services.

9

ADVANCED SYSTEMS AND TECHNOLOGY FOR MANAGING CLOSED LOOP SUPPLY CHAINS AND REVERSE LOGISTICS PROCESSES

INTRODUCTION

New software and systems vendors focusing on the development of new infrastructure technology and systems to support the full closed loop supply chain (CLSC) and reverse logistics (RL) process have emerged in the last few years. These organizations provide advanced tools and technology for optimizing service based RL operations. These systems include full capability for:

- Improving the accuracy of planning and forecasting
- Inventory and allocation control of whole units, parts, and subassemblies
- Tracking and coordination of the full service logistics pipeline down to and including service engineers "trunk" stocks, store or retail distribution stocks, and customer site stocks*
- Control, coordination, and scheduling of depot repair operations

---

* The material in the hands of field engineers in their car or van "trunks" or stored by them at a particular site.

These systems can either be acquired on a stand-alone basis or integrated into and delivered as part of customer relationship management (CRM) systems and field service management systems (FSMS). Integrating these advanced closed loop and RL optimizing and control systems and software into full CRM and FSMS technology can allow an organization to achieve improvements in efficiency and productivity.

Another new group of technologies being utilized to support the RL and repair process is made up of the Internet and e-commerce tools. Some vendors have developed shared systems based upon an application service provider (ASP) delivery model to allow any size organization to receive the full benefits of advanced systems functionality for CLSC operations. These e-commerce based approaches allow firms to acquire capabilities on a leased or activity-based basis at a fraction of the cost of acquiring a new stand-alone state-of-the-art system outright with the functional capabilities required. These web-enabled systems, utilizing Internet portals, trading hubs, and e-service solutions, have created a new management coordination environment where all the players and participants in the CLSC process can communicate and interact online and in real time. The result is significant improvement in the productivity of the RL parts provisioning and allocation process, as well as the creation of a "just in time" approach to repair and refurbishment.

SYSTEMS AND TECHNOLOGY FOR CONSUMER GOODS OPERATIONS

As indicated above, the more fragmented and larger consumer goods industry has moved in a number of different directions in terms of systems, technology, and infrastructure development as compared to the high tech market. Since groceries and other perishable items are typically managed by jobbers, or other stocking agreements for independent stocking and shelf management companies or agencies, these organizations have, themselves, developed their own systems for inventory, tracking, and control. This has generally taken the form of equipping jobber or stocking organization agents with wireless terminals or laptops enabling them to record the shelf status of the inventories under their management and direction. This process had been further improved through the use of bar code scanning. The information collected at the shelf sites is then relayed back over a wireless net or through wire downloading consensual computer facility, which tracks and compares changes in inventory status, as well as identifies those goods and items whose expiration date is rapidly approaching or has been approached. This analysis and evaluation is then utilized to provide directions to the agent in the field as to what actions are to be taken to approve the efficiency of the shelf space allocated.

For durable goods, such as white goods, brown goods, clothing, and so on, computerized cash registers or point-of-sale terminals have been used to build in rules for the return process, which is designed to limit the choice of the retail sales associate in handling the customers return. E-boomerang software for example is designed to deal with returns built around rules that control the return process, primarily focusing on original equipment manufacturer (OEM) type return policies. However, the same mechanisms could be utilized to support a retrial level return policy for the store or sales department per se.

A new technology area that appears to offer some very significant opportunities for improvement in the consumer goods area, relates to the use of the Internet and e-commerce capability to provide the network linkages and computational capabilities for supporting the RL process. Several web-based organizations are moving into the provision of a full Internet-supported service to control returns, including some of the larger distribution organizations, such as USF Processors, Ryder, Gatx, and UPS Logistics. A list of firms providing online RL through the Internet along with their Internet addresses is provided in Table 9.1. These firms are, in turn, utilizing specialized RL software designed for Internet operation from vendors such as ReturnCentral.com and Viewlocity.com, OrderTrust.com, and SubmitOrder.com. The primary advantage of utilizing the Internet and e-commerce in support of RL is that it allows the individual participants in the RL process, including organizations providing transportation, distribution, warehousing, depot repair, and second day market sales and disposition the ability to provide online status over the returns, as well as quotations on the ability to support individual processes. Some specific vendors are focusing even more narrowly on providing RL support for e-merchants who do not maintain their own physical store operations. These organizations, of course, require both a direct supply chain to provide delivery to the customer, as well as the capability for RL support. Return-View.com in Irvine, California has been focusing specifically on this area of the market.

HIGH TECH LOGISTICS SYSTEM FOR CLOSED LOOP SUPPLY CHAIN MANAGEMENT

The typical logistics or inventory management control system used in the CLSC process generally has architecture as shown in Figure 9.1. This system is designed to control the full logistics pipeline in a high tech environment:

- Down to the field engineer or customer site
- Back to depot repair and central inventory

Table 9.1   Firms Providing Online Reverse Logistics Services

Type Firm	Firm Name	Web Page ID
Web-based providers	Clickreturns	www.clickreturns.com
	E-RMA	www.e-ram.com
	First Attempt	www.firstattempt.com
	Ireturnit	www.ireturnit.com
	Return.com	www.return.com
	ReturnCentral.com	www.returncentral.com
	Returnview	www.returnview.com
	The Return Exchange	www.thereturnexchange.com
	The Return Store	www.thereturnstore.com
Traditional logistics providers	GATX Logistics	www.gatxlogistics.com
	Ryder Logistics	www.ryder.com
	UPS Logistics	www.upslogistics.com
	USF Processors	www.usfprocessors.com

Source: From Company reports; Bear, Stearns & Co., Inc.

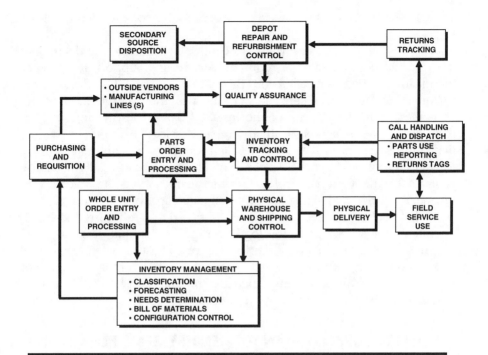

Figure 9.1   Logistics/inventory management and control system.

The key functions in the system include:

■ Forecasting
■ Planning
■ Inventory control, tracking, and delivery
■ Field resupply
■ Reverse and forward logistics
■ Depot repair

Historically, logistics system infrastructure has been implemented by service organizations to support product businesses within the context of a given budget. However, the increasing trend is toward operating service as an independent profit center within larger product based corporations, or as an independent service organization providing third party maintenance service or RL and depot repair services. The broad questions involved in designing and implementing logistics support management systems to run a profit making operation have become both critical and relevant.

In order to design the framework to analyze and evaluate the needs and requirements for CLSC and RL support service, it is essential to develop an analytical framework in which to examine the complex interrelationships.

The driving force is, ultimately, to control and manage the data about the installed equipment base requiring service and support, in terms of the mean time between failure (MTBF) of that equipment, the mean time to repair (MTTR), the technical characteristics and configuration of the equipment, and the density of the installed base. These factors will, in turn, dictate the demands for RL and repair services. To improve productivity and efficiency, it is necessary to introduce systems and mechanisms for full control of the total logistics pipeline from the central warehouse facilities to the regional or local district parts depots, to the service engineer's trunks and site stocks, as well as control of the return flow of parts, field subassemblies, and whole units to depot refurbish and repair operations for redelivery to the logistics pipeline, or final disposition.

Thus, the management system for the total logistics pipeline must be structured to significantly reduce the levels of inventory investment required, and at the same time, increase the ability to have the material at the desired level or site at the right time.

LOGISTICS SUPPORT MANAGEMENT SYSTEMS FUNCTIONS AND GENERAL SPECIFICATIONS

The required computerized field service logistics management systems (FSLMS) technology needs to be organized in terms of the following major functions or modules:

- Logistics management and control (LMC) — Includes parts order entry and order processing, inventory tracking and control, physical distribution, courier resupplies, and (as an option) depot repair or rehabilitation scheduling and control.
- Financial control and accounting (FCA) — Includes billing and invoicing to insure full revenues for logistic services rendered, including warranty, extended warranty, and service contract administration, and *financial control* of the revenue and cost components of service logistics operations.
- Logistics database management and reporting (DBMR) — Must include standard and *ad hoc* reporting, with 4GL capabilities, using a relational or networked database.
- Special logistics document and configuration control system — Supports need for drawings and configuration documents from the field. This may be satisfied by a corporatewide system or make use of a computer-aided logistics support (CALS) type technology.

- Contract life cycle management (CLCM) — Provides visibility of the complete span of customer relationships from the prospect and proposal stage though quotation to active service contract. The facility includes, in addition, configuration management and revision tracking.
- Logistics management and control (LMC) — Functionality required in the FSMS system should provide basic logistics management and support of the total inventory. The support should include techniques for managing and controlling the complete field inventory and spare parts pipeline, including central and regional depots, down to the field customer service engineer level, and trunk stock, and at field sites, and the return cycle to a central repair depot, to include the following:
  - Inventory tracking and control (ITC) — Full logistics pipeline (from central warehouse to the field customer service engineer level) and/or field site level to keep track of in-transit inventory, returned parts and equipment, borrowing control, repair and rehabilitation stock control. Data should be reported and tracked for effective and defective parts status, by stock-keeping unit (SKU).
  - Order entry and processing (OEP) — Includes online entry of orders, order pricing, order tracking and updating, allocation of inventory, automatic back ordering as required, generation of picking documents, shipping papers and transportation documents (shipment optimization, way bills, and freight manifests), and recording or capturing data for later billing and invoicing of the customer.
  - Parts management agreements (PMA) — Includes parts on customer site or in special stocking locations, monitor used parts and their replenishment, revision compatibility with customer equipment.
  - Equipment configuration maintenance (ECM) — Keeps track of the installed base of equipment and networks being serviced and supported, the manufacturer of the equipment in the case of third party maintenance, and any relocations of equipment and networks in the field. Wherever applies, the function will monitor the revision of the equipment installed and software used and be updated whenever they are revised.
  - Inventory forecasting and planning (IFP) — Includes all inventory stocking points, to better plan and forecast inventory and to optimize total inventory levels within the logistics pipeline.

  - Depot reworking/refurbishment operations control (DRROC) — Schedules, tracks, and processes material through the repair rework facility.
  - Inventory replenishment (IR) — Includes generation of material requisitions to the next higher inventory stocking level. Identification of primary and secondary sources of supply for spare parts and consumables, generation of purchase orders to vendors or replenishment order to manufacturing facilities, quality control processing, and receipt processing to update inventory.
  - Physical distribution (PD) — Includes management control, dispatch, tracking of physical delivery of parts to sites via courier, or dedicated mobile van. This function must link at a general level to the manufacturing systems and technology in order to automatically order proprietary product spares as required to maintain the service inventory at optimum levels, and report on product quality as delivered (i.e., "dead on arrival" in field, and product MTBF and MTTR).
■ Financial support, including billing and invoicing — Includes financial accounting and control, and profit and loss analysis to include the following:
  - Cost allocation — Includes direct and indirect logistics service expenses to accurately reflect the profitability of the logistics service organization by service portfolio as a whole, and by major element, by customer segments and for major customer accounts, service area, service technician/mechanic, or other criteria.
  - Customer credit checking — Validates the customer's credit status for time and material and contract service calls.
  - Profit contribution analysis — Determines profitability for the service organization and by portfolio segment, specific types of service call, service area, service technician/mechanic, customer, type of equipment being maintained, maintenance contract or any combination of the above. This function must be able to link to the corporate financial system, and administration systems, if required.
■ Logistics database management and reporting — Should include an integrated database management system, including a comprehensive structured database to provide timely, accurate, and flexible information for reporting to all levels of the field service management and service organization structure basic reports to be generated by the system.
■ Logistics and technical document storage and retrieval — Should include the capability to store and retrieve documents, and images, and other graphics and should be compatible and/or linked to the Corporate Engineering support document retrieval system.

- Logistics planning and forecasting functions — Should include the full capability for planning and forecasting at both the strategic and tactical level.
- Depot repair systems — Requires that computerized depot repair service management systems technology, should be organized into the following key functions, as shown in Figure 9.2. They include:
  - Repair entry processing (RFP) — Includes front-end screening for no trouble found units; repair entry, routing, tracking and control, identification of repair item, assignment of work order/control number, and routing by type of repair/type of unit.
  - Depot service planning and scheduling (SPS) — Includes the management requirements for doing simple and complex depot repair and refurbishment tasks such as contract repair management, system integration, and reverse engineering.

OTHER TECHNOLOGY SUPPORTING REVERSE LOGISTICS AND CLOSED LOOP SYSTEMS

Bar Coding

Bar coding is important to good CLSC operations.

- Bar codes allow tracking of parts at all levels of the distribution process and at any level of aggregation from pallet to individual part
- Bar coding has been measured to produce up to 300% improvements in volume of check in and inventory verification over manual methods
- Aside from setting the pace for just in time inventory practices, it has also provided for a significant improvement in data entry accuracy and data collection

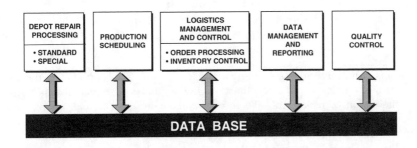

Figure 9.2 Depot management system functional structure.

Essentially, bar coding allows parts and components to be tracked in real-time or near real-time fashion throughout the logistics pipeline from the central warehouse to the field service and to end users. Bar coding is one of the technologies that has helped create a closed loop logistics pipeline essential to successful service logistics that is substantially different from production logistics. Bar coding is especially important in managing inventory in service operations due to the high value of parts in the return cycle.

Radio Frequency Identification System (RFID)

While bar coding has been extensively used for tracking status of whole units, subassemblies, and parts on both the direct and RL legs, there are some problems in its application and use. For example, in dirty or crowded environments, it may be difficult, if not impossible, to use optical scanning to obtain an accurate reading of identification. Dirt on the bar code label or on the scanning device itself can cause a misreading. The packages or pallets may be crowded together making it difficult to optically scan. In addition, the scanning process itself must be done in enough time to allow the scanning device to fully read the imprint.

A new development in this area involves a very inexpensive radio frequency base and coding, using fixed or embedded stickers or labels.* This technology, using very thin integrated circuitry, makes use of electronic rather than visual scanning technique in order to generate an identifiable tracking number as well as additional information concerning the product identification. Since RFID utilizes the electronic spectrum, dirt and congestion has less negative impact, and the scanning units need not be physically passed by the coding tag.

Scanning is also done much more rapidly. The downside of this technology is that at present the RFID labels are somewhat more expensive than bar code labels, and are subject to errors due to sparse** or even false electromatic signals. This technology is now being evaluated by organizations such as Wal-Mart and the U.S. Department of Defense, and may soon be available in less expensive and more secure formats. In either case, bar coding or RFID identifiers achieve the same goal, providing

---

* Stickers, anywhere from 2 to 4 square inches in size. A silicon chip in the center of the tag contains a unique identifier, a string of numbers that identifies the contents of the carton or pallet. An RFID reader sends a signal to the tag, asking for that information, and the tag's antenna, which is woven into the tag itself and attached to the chip, beams it back. Signals need not be read directly by a scanner, as bar codes are. Instead, masses of RFID tags can be read in seconds, greatly cutting the time needed to inventory packages.

** Due to electromagnetic interference.

a more efficient and effective tracking system to control the flow of goods and the material in both the direct supply chain and in the RL.

Repair Depot Applications of Bar Coding or RFID Scanning

In the manufacturing environment, parts usually flow in one direction — to the customer. In CLSCs, the return cycle, for most parts, (particularly those with the highest value) are usually returned to a central depot for repair or refurbishment. Parts that are sent back to the depot repair and refurbishment center can be tracked throughout the repair process via a bar coding or RFID system internally within the depot and during return to the field. In addition, the bar coding or RFID tagging of parts actually makes it possible to track not only the distribution cycle of parts and components, but in some instances, to track the entire life cycle of the product.

CONFIGURATION CONTROL

Configuration control systems are used in logistics-oriented service operations to effectively administer and control large installed equipment bases. They have the following advantages:

- Provide data as a basis for effective logistics support management
- Enable hardware and software upgrade programs to be planned effectively
- Carry out replacement and equipment moves, adds, and changes faster and with greater efficiency
- Easily identify engineering and software change modification candidates
- Facilitate fault identification by accurate knowledge of a systems hardware and software components

Typically, the following protocols must be observed with regards to configuration control:

- Configuration data should be held in two locations: the logistics management system itself and the help desk system.
- Data describing the hardware and installed software should be placed in the control file that is already being placed on each systems hard disk at initial productivity and during any refurbishment and reconfiguration program.
- Data on configuration should also be stored centrally.

- File should also contain the data on the bar code on the various system units.
- Data is then made accessible remotely by the logistics control center whenever needed.
- Same data is also held on the database of the call handling and help desk system to support the initial digital process.

Relatively new developments in configuration control, and advances in online real-time tracking of status and location of whole units, systems, and network configurations involving emerging device relationship management (DRM) technology like ZigBee are now being installed.

DRM is a specific technology for inexpensively linking devices and/or products into a full network system configuration, using very low cost, low power consumption, and low frequency communications between the individual device and the central configuration control net. More recently, an alliance of OEMs, systems, integrators, and users have come together as the ZigBee Alliance to create an open system architecture standard (IEEE 802.15.4 phy) and a framework for the broad interface or wireless devices. This standardized communication base for sensor, control systems and information technology products/boxes creates the frequency, power and functional standards to allow full interoperability. A major area of ZigBee focus is now on improving CLSC to support large and complex field configurations.

LOGISTICS MANAGEMENT SYSTEMS TECHNOLOGY STATE-OF-THE-ART

In general, the CLSC and RL management systems, as described above, are available in one of three forms:

- Logistics systems available as part of an overall FSMS or CRM systems
- General service logistics systems
- Stand-alone optimization systems for CLSC and/or depot repair

Generally, software packages including several or all functions for CLSC, RL, and depot repair are outlined above, but in varying degrees of sophistication. Some packages are more highly functional for specific areas. Examples of field service management systems that incorporate logistics capability are Service Alliance (Astea International); Metrix 4 (Metrix, Inc.); Flagship/Super Service (Pacific Decisions Sciences Corp.). Packages are developed on a number of databases (e.g., Oracle, Progress,

Sybase) and run on various platforms; several feature open systems architecture and others are migrating to open systems. Most packages run in a desktop environment, with base hardware requirements generally requiring Pentium II processor or greater and at least 32 megabytes of RAM, as well as on mainframe and LAN environments. A list of major software packages, current vendors, product offerings, and a brief description of products is provided in Table 9.2. Newer offerings include web-based architecture that allows software to reside on remote platforms and be accessed via a web browser over time. The following packages can potentially meet the needs of a high volume depot repair environment:

- "Depot Management" (Module Of Super Alliance), Astea
- "Super Depot," The Pacific Decision Sciences Corp.
- "Repair Center" (Module Of OpenUPTIME), Metrix

IMPACT AND VALUE OF ADVANCED LOGISTICS MANAGEMENT SYSTEMS

We have described above the role, functions, and software availability in order to articulate the current state of the art. A critical question is the effectiveness of these systems on the total CLSC and RL chain in terms of specific productivity improvements.

A survey of over 100 users of this type of technology provided a general assessment of the benefits and improvements of this technology over manual methods. The results of the survey are summarized in Figure 9.3.

Table 9.2 Selected List of Service Logistics Vendors (Background Information)

Company	Revenue and Size	Historic Data	Logistics Product Suite	General Description
Amdocs San Jose, CA 96134 www.amdocs.com	• $230.7M (public) • Comprised of: – 65% software license – 35% services	• Founded in 1991 developed a full suite of software • Purchased by Nortel in 2000 • Now offers a full solution hardware and software integration	• Amdocs logistics™	• Fully integrated service management system • Full functionality offered in all modules
Astea International Horsham, PA www.astea.com	• $33.M (public) • Comprised of: – 55% software – 45% service	• Founded in 1996 • Most recent product released in 1997 • Recent financial difficulties have slowed sales	• Servicealliance™	• Offers robust fully integrated service management solutions • Specialized in logistics functionality
Baxter Planning Systems Austin, TX www.bybaxter.com	• $50.0M (estimated) • Comprised of: – 45% software – 20% maintenance – 35% implementation services	• Founded in 1993 to file gap of planning and logistical solutions • Specially targeted to service parts industry	• Prophet™	• Core product is a comprehensive software point solution that offers companies with service parts inventories optimization functionality

Company	Financials	Notes	Products	Description
i2 Technologies Dallas, TX www.i2.com	• $1.12B • Comprised of: – 62% software licenses – 24% services – 13% maintenance	• i2 has experienced a steady growth in revenue over the past 5 years • Their net income has also increased steadily by over 100% each year	• Supplier Relationship Management (SRM)™ • Supply Chain Management (SCM)™	• e-Market solutions centered around manufacturing and supply chain management operations
Mapics Alpharetta, GA www.mapics.com	• $128.3M • Comprised of: – 60% software – 40% other	• Recently purchased Frontstep (SYMIC)	• Mapics (SCM)™	• Supply chain management solutions for manufacturing
Manugistics, Inc. Rockville, MD www.manugistics.com	• $268M • Comprised of: – 52% software – 27% services – 21% support	• 2001 revenue grew 76% from 2000 • Software revenue grew 131% through the same time period	• Supply Chain Management Optimization Suite™	• Markets themselves as the leading provider of enterprise profit optimization (EPO)
MCA Solutions Philadelphia, PA www.mcasolutions.com	• $2.0M (estimated) • Comprised of: – 80% consulting – 20% software sales	• Founded in 1999 • First software product introduced in 2000	• Service Optimization Suite (SOS)™	• Provides state-of-the-art planning engine for service supply chain management
Metrix, Inc. Waukesha, WI www.metrix.com	• $20.0M (estimated) • Comprised of: – 70% software – 30% service	• Founded in 1991 • Latest product Metrix 4™ introduced in 1999 • Privately owned company	• eProductservice™	• Integrated service management system

Table 9.2   Selected List of Service Logistics Vendors (Background Information) (continued)

Company	Revenue and Size	Historic Data	Logistics Product Suite	General Description

Mapics
Alpharetta, GA
www.mapics.com
	• $128.3M
	• Comprised of:
	  – 60% software
	  – 40% other
		• Recently purchased Frontstep (SYMIC)	• Mapics (SCM)™	• Supply chain management solutions for manufacturing

Pacific Decision Sciences Corp. (PDSC)
Santa Ana, CA
www.pdsc.com
	• Revenue $30.0M
	• Comprised of:
	  – 65% software
	  – 18% service
	  – 17% maintenance
		• Founded in 1973
		• Acquired by Applied Digital Solutions in 2000
			• Flagship Depot™	• Fully integrated service management system, specializes in logistics support and repair logistics

Peoplesoft
Pleasanton, CA
www.peoplesoft.com
	• Revenue of $1.4B
	• Comprised of:
	  – 50% software license
	  – 40% maintenance
	  – 10% solutions consulting
		• Founded in 1991 as Vantive
		• Purchased in 1999 by Peoplesoft SFA/HR vendor
			• Peoplesoft 8.0™	• Integrated service management system

Servigistics
Marietta, GA
www.servigistics.com
	• Revenue (4.0M (estimated)
	• Comprised of:
	  – 60% service sales
	  – 40% service maintenance
		• Founded in 1998
		• Privately held
		• Specialized in service parts requirements (niche market)
			• PARTSPLUS™
			• PARTSPLAN™
				• Provides the first service resource planning (SRP) that enables users to maximize parts availability

Company			

Siebel Systems, Inc.
San Mateo, CA
www.siebel.com
	• Revenue of $790.9M
	• Comprised of:
	  – 50% software license
	  – 40% maintenance
	  – 10% software
	    consulting
		• Founded in 1993
		• Service Management
		  Piece (SCOPUS)
		  purchased in 1999
			• Siebel Field
			  Service 7.5™
				• Integrated service
				  management system

Viryanet
Southborough, MA
www.viryanet.com
	• $19.0M (estimated)
	• Comprised of:
	  – 50% software license
	  – 45% service
		• Founded in 1993
		• Private firm
		• In forefront of web
		  enablement
			• Service Hub™	• Integrated service
				  management system

Xelus, Inc.
Fairport, NY
www.xelus.com
	• $50.0M
	• Comprised of:
	  – 55% software
	  – 30% implementation
	  – 15% support
		• Founded in 1970s as
		  LPA
		• Worldwide presence
		• Recent infusion of
		  investor capital
			• Xelus Plan™	• Leading provider of
				  service optimization
				  and e-commerce
				  solutions

FUNCTION	ESTIMATED IMPACT AREA	EXPERIENCE RANGE	COMMENT
RETURN LOGISTICS PIPELINE TIME	• REDUCTION IN TOTAL INVENTORY REQUIRED TO ADDRESS A GIVEN FILL RATE	• REDUCTION OF 10 to 50% IN TIME	• REQUIRES FULL CONTROL OVER RETURN PIPELINE • REPORTING OF SERVICE ENGINEER AT CALL CLOSE OUT
ACCURATE FORECASTING OF RETURNS	• IMPROVED ASSIGNMENT AND PROVISIONING OF PARTS • INCREASED SCHEDULING AND EFFICIENCY IN DEPOT	• IMPROVEMENT OF 15 to 35% IN FORECASTING ACCOUNTING	• NEEDS GOOD ESSENTIAL DATA AND ADVANCED FORECASTING MODELS
QUALITY CONTROL AND REPORTING AT RECEIVING DEPOT	• RECORD PIPELINE TIME - SENDING NTF BACK TO FIELD • IMPROVE RELIABILITY IN FIELD	• TYPICALLY 30 to 35% OF RETURNS ARE NTF* • QA AT RECEIVING CAN CUT WORKLOAD BY 30% OR MORE	• NEED TO TIE SERVICE ENGINEER RMA REPORT TO QUALITY ASSURANCE
IMPROVEMENT IN DEPOT REPAIR DIAGNOSTICS	• REDUCTION IN REPAIR TIME	• IMPROVEMENT IN DEPOT REPAIR TIME AND COST BY 30 to 40%	• CAN USE SAME DIAGNOSTICS AS EMPLOYED IN CALL HANDLING
OPTIMIZED SCHEDULING OF REPAIR FACILITY	• REDUCTION IN REPAIR TIME AND COSTS	• REDUCE COSTS BY 20 to 25% • REDUCE TIME BY 35 to 40%	• SEVERAL SCHEDULING PACKAGES AVAILABLE
IMPROVED CONTROL OVER WARRANTY VS. NON-WARRANTY COVERAGE	• DECREASE IN COSTS OF WARRANTY REPAIR	• REDUCE WARRANTY COSTS BY 28%	• NEED FOR GOOD WARRANTY DATA
IMPROVED COORDINATION OF SUBCONTRACTORS AND THEIR KEY SUPPLIERS	• REDUCE REPAIR TIME • IMPROVED INVENTORY UTILIZATION	• REDUCTION IN NUMBER OF SUBCONTRACTORS • REDUCTION IN SUBCONTRACT COSTS BY 23%	• NEEDS BOTH E -COMMERCE LINKAGES
OVERALL CONTROL OF REVERSE LOGISTICS PROCESS	• REDUCTION IN INVENTORY ACQUISITIONS AND CARRYING COSTS	• REDUCTION OF 30 to 35% IN INVENTORY WITHOUT AFFECTING FIELD FILL RATE	• CAN DIRECTLY IMPACT BOTTOM LINE PROFITS BY 10 to 18%

Figure 9.3 Key parameters to the reverse logistics and repair process in high tech service which can improve using advanced systems.

10

BRINGING IT ALL TOGETHER: MANAGING REVERSE LOGISTICS AND CLOSED LOOP SUPPLY CHAIN PROCESSES

INTRODUCTION

Our introduction to, and examination of, the reverse logistics (RL) and closed loop supply chain (CLSC) markets, processes, technology, and practices presented above have been designed to demonstrate both the existence of the market and the unusual or novel requirements and needs of the processes separating and distinguishing it from the normal direct supply chain operation.

In addition to outlining the alternative business models for RL and CLSC and market size and dimensions, we have also focused on:

- Specific requirements for high tech CLSC operations
- Managing of consumer goods RL processes
- Management and coordination of depot repair operations
- Warranty and extended warranty management
- Secondary markets
- Advanced systems and technology for RL and CLSC management

These all serve as the building blocks or modules by which a manager interested in the business opportunities for RL and CLSC can search in order to develop, implement, and produce an efficient business model and operating strategy. However, it is not enough to simply understand the component elements of the process or the existence of the market structure and business model. The manager must bring this together in orderly and logical process in order to ensure that the strategic direction is consistent with the trends and focus of the marketplace, the current and emerging state of the art, and competitive activities. The process of establishing both the strategy and tactics and management of a RL or CLSC business requires a step-by-step process, as outlined in Figure 10.1. As indicated, the process involves several steps or stages.

STAGE 1 — ESTABLISHMENT OF MARKET FOCUS

We have also already identified that a series of markets including high tech, consumer, green goods, packaging, and so forth, and products or technologies need to be examined in order to determine the optimum market focus. This should be based upon a consideration of both the existing organization and operating structure and business and other opportunities, as identified in Chapter 1 and Chapter 2.

STAGE 2 — COLLECTION OF DATA ON EXISTING PROCESSES AND STRUCTURES

Once the general focus has been established, the next step is to identify, analyze, and evaluate the existing internal capabilities, activities, and dynamics, as well as the market requirements and needs for RL and CLSC services. An example of the types of data required describing the typical consumer retail establishment are shown in Table 10.1. The collection of this information and analysis and evaluation of internal capabilities vs. market requirements and needs can then lead to the third stage or steps.

STAGE 3 — ESTABLISH STRATEGIC DIRECTION AND BUSINESS PLAN

Based upon the data collected in Stage 2 and the identification of third party service providers for RL and CLSC support and creation of secondary markets, as discussed above, as well as a review of the state of the art, found in Chapter 11, it is then possible to construct one or more strategic directions to create penetration in the specifically selected RL and CLSC market, identified in Stage 1.

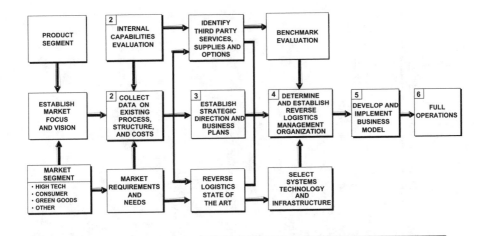

Figure 10.1   Steps in developing management and business strategy and plan for reverse logistics and closed loop supply chain operations.

STAGE 4 — DETERMINE AND ESTABLISH A MANAGEMENT ORGANIZATION AND OPERATING STRUCTURE

Leading directly from the selection of the optimum business strategy and model, the next step is to establish a management organization and operating structure based upon consideration of benchmarking targets established and a selection of the appropriate systems technology and infrastructure based upon a review of the state of the art.

STAGE 5 — DEVELOPMENT AND IMPLEMENTATION OF A BUSINESS MODEL

The full coordination and implementation of the management organization and operating structure, benchmarking targets, systems technology, and infrastructure will then lead to the development and implementation of the business model that meets the optimized strategic direction established in Stage 3.

STAGE 6 — FULL OPERATIONS

The final stage of this process is to convert the business model into day-to-day operations utilizing the systems infrastructure and benchmarking targets established in Stage 4.

Table 10.1 Data on Reverse Logistics Operations and Structure Required to Develop Consumer Goods Strategies

Number and size of stores by type (grocery, drug, etc.)	• Average sales volume by store type • Average cost of goods by store type • Average logistics (direct and reverse) expenditures by store type • Physical mapping of store locations (by region) • Average turnover of inventory by store type

Current logistics and distribution network and structure supporting stores	• Network map
	• Number and size of facilities
	• Operating costs
	  – Transportation
	  – Distribution
	  – Portion of logistics & distribution focused on returns (estimate of returns costs)

Primary suppliers to stores by type	• Major suppliers • Average annual sales by goods type • Estimated annual returns by goods type or average
Current external (third party service) providers of the logistics support, by store type for logistics and distribution returns, etc.	• Vendors • Budgets
Any statistics, internal studies, or evaluations of reverse logistics/closed loop supply chain processes	• Size and dimensions of problem • Returns/unsaleable experience • Issues or "pain problems"

General (or specific) return policies and/or commitments

- Overall cooperation
- Individual store type

Experiences with returns to vendors for credit

- Anecdotal
- Statistical

Existing systems in place that trace inventory to store, and/or returns

- Type of systems
- Extent of coverage (types of data tracked)
- Degree of centralization (one common corporate system) or fragmented
- New logistics and distribution systems being contemplated

Management directives, concepts, or justification for reverse logistics function (i.e., Why are the "drivers" creating the need for a reverse logistics strategy and management organization? What does top management want to accomplish, and desired time schedule for improvement?)

Corporate organizational structure, identifying key logistics, distribution, and reverse logistics and control functions, organizations, skill sets, and data bases

USE OF THIRD PARTY SERVICE PROVIDERS

Having developed your business model and strategy, do you make, buy, or outsource your service logistics solution? New advances have opened up a whole new world of options. Utter the words "service logistics" and, yes, you may notice some eyes glazing over. But in this new economy, service logistics can actually make or break your business, and what you don't know just may harm you — and help your competition. Here's what you may not know: That over the last 2 to 3 years, there have been many advances in the "state of the art" and best practices for improving the quality, efficiency, and productivity of service logistics. We are now seeing more providers, solutions, and services available than ever before. But what's driving this expansion — an expansion that can lead to improved operational and financial performance?

Believe it or not, it's the age-old business challenge that has consistently faced service logistics managers: "Should we make or buy a new solution?" In the service logistics arena, a make vs. buy decision boils down to whether a manager should create the knowledge and know-how (e.g., tools) internally, buy the tools and knowledge from someone else, or outsource the entire process to a more efficient and/or qualified vendor. What's new is that these types of decisions are now cropping up more frequently than ever in the field service area, and that's the result of three major market trends.

Trend 1: New Software Focus

The first major trend toward improving the quality, efficiency, and productivity of service logistics operations is a direct result of the growing number of software vendors that have focused on service logistics as a critical functional area for their systems. An in-depth analysis my firm recently conducted illustrates how major improvements in the "depot" and "logistics" management modules of customer relationship management (CRM) systems are providing unprecedented systems support to depot and service logistics operations. All the major vendors of customer relationship management software (e.g., Siebel, Clarify, Metrix, PDSC, and Astea) now include fully functional depot and service logistics management subsystems, including such functions as depot financial management, repair processing/depot workflow automation, data capture and analysis, and decision-support planning tools. Although the functionality in these systems was developed as an offshoot of call management applications, the systems do have capabilities to support the transaction and movement of parts, from receipt of call to delivery of part to the customer.

Trend 2: New Vendors, Advanced Tools

A new class of software vendors has also emerged that provides advanced tools and technology for optimizing service logistics and reverse supply chain operations. These stand-alone systems developed by next-generation software developers such as I2, Servigistics, I-Dream, and Xelus provide adjunct functionality in the areas of optimized allocation, planning, forecasting, and inventorying of service spare parts. By integrating these advanced systems into basic customer relationship management systems, an end user organization or independent logistics support provider (that is, an outsourcing vendor) can achieve significant improvements in the efficiency and productivity of its service supply chain. For example, end-to-end systems (that incorporate with CRM the types of logistics supply chain management systems that I've just described) allow a field service organization to manage, control, plan, and forecast the parts requirements for its entire logistics pipeline, from a strategic national level down to a local operational level, and from a national warehouse to its repair depots, stocking facilities, customer population — even down to the field engineers' trunk stock. More importantly, these systems utilize forecasting algorithms that reflect the true nature of the service logistics pipeline: a closed-loop system with spike demand periods and a high percentage of returns and recycled material.

Trend 3: Move to Real-Time Control

The advent of real-time control systems coupled with new and advanced online tracking and control (ZigBee) has opened up another new trend that is currently being explored in certain limited market segments. This involves the use of online real-time demand fulfillment as opposed to more standard forecasting mechanisms. Clearly as the ability of the RL system to manage, coordinate, and control the flow of material in real time increases, coupled with a reduction in delivery and resupply times through coordinated next flight out (NFO) or online controlled courier/van delivery service, the need for sophisticated and accurate forecasting becomes less important. This broad concept of utilizing ruggedized devices in the field to report on material returns and on request for resupply tied together with online real-time distribution center operations, can offer significant improvements in improving the entire return cycle. As indicated earlier, the U.S. Department of Defense — primarily the Army and Marines — have been experimenting with this type of real-time control in order to more effectively balance and allocate assets on the battlefield; thus, reducing the need for dependency on accurate forecasts in rapidly changing situations and environments.

Additional Factors

The Internet and E-Commerce

Also playing a major role in bringing increased improvement to the efficiency and productivity of the service logistics supply chain is the Internet and e-commerce. Web-enabled systems make it significantly easier for all players in the service-logistics supply chain to share and exchange information. Internet trading hubs and warranty aggregator hubs (such as those provided by Bid Vantage, ServiceBench.com, Powersource Online, and I-Service) bring buyers and sellers of parts together on an online basis, and thus minimize the need for a firm to hold large inventories of spare parts. Vendors of e-service solutions (e.g., Viryanet, iMedeon, and Antenna Software) have developed service management systems that incorporate wireless communications with Internet applications to create a service portal. These portals provide a virtual service environment where all the players and touchpoints in field service, depot repair, and the logistical support process can communicate and interact on an online and real-time basis regarding the status of a single, specific transaction — or a multitude of them — regardless of who owns the request, who is providing the solution, or where in time and space the transaction is occurring.

The by-product of all these technological innovations is the ability of a service organization to build end-to-end online solutions. For service logistics, this means that a manager can deal with spare-parts issues or emergencies, and provide contingencies on an online, live, just in time basis. Imagine having the ability to view the entire logistics pipeline and service delivery process from the comfort of your laptop computer — and being sure that everything is under control! The net result of these advances is an almost speed-of-light improvement in the productivity and efficiency of the spare-parts provisioning process, as well as the creation of reliable and dependable just in time logistical support systems.

Application Service Providers

The web-enabled systems — as described above, and when combined with the application service provider (ASP) model — further increase the number of options available to end users within the service logistics support services market. The ASP model essentially allows any organization to receive the full benefits of advanced system functionality on a "leased" basis, and at a fraction of the cost of acquiring a new system outright. By partnering with logistics and depot repair vendors, an ASP (or ASP end user organization) can obtain a best-of-breed logistics solution, on demand, without bearing the tremendous capital investment and learning curve challenges associated with more traditional approaches to building a logistics solution. And this leads to another interesting point concerning market trends, that is the role of the supplier in increasing efficiency through partnering.

The Role of the Supplier in Obtaining Increased Efficiency through Partnering

The tools and technology described above are available to depot repair and logistics support suppliers, as well as to end users. These tools make suppliers more productive and more efficient, thus more competitive and attractive to customers who wish to outsource their logistics operations. Outsourcing of logistics and depot repair activities has, for some time, been a strategy for improving the overall levels of service productivity and efficiency that are available to field service organizations. But now, the capabilities of depot repair and logistics support providers will increasingly improve in response to pressures from the market to offer better, more effective, and more competitive solutions. The new tools that are coming online will certainly make this a reality. A continuing increase in the numbers of strategic alliance and partnerships between vendors and major customers will be seen, primarily between the original equipment manufacturer (OEM) and major multivendor service-provider segments. New alliances will also be formed between outsourcing vendors and the suppliers of service tools and technology that I have described above. As a result, the overall complexion of the outsourcing environment is likely to continue to change quickly. Those organizations most effective in making improvements in service logistics efficiency and productivity via technology will be most successful in keeping pace with the constantly changing needs and requirements of end users.

Depot repair and logistical support providers (including trading hubs and software developers) will continue to occupy their place as an integral and profitable part of the service logistics pipeline. Although market pressures may force these vendors to partner and become increasingly indistinguishable from each other in terms of their service portfolios, it is clear that each supplier will bring to the picture a unique area of service expertise. That expertise may lie in efficient repair operations, reliable courier services, state-of-the-art systems, advanced communication networks, or comprehensive information and reporting capabilities. But is it also clear that some suppliers will focus on the entire service logistics pipeline, while others will target only selected activities or aspects. This is only one reason why, when considering the possibility of deploying a new service logistics infrastructure or outsourcing portions of an organization's service logistics pipeline, it is absolutely critical that logistical processes are carefully mapped out. From this vantage point, an evaluation of gaps of service logistics productivity and efficiency can be made, enabling an organization to define where gains are most needed, as well as identify which suppliers or vendors are best suited to meet those requirements.

To Outsource, or Not to Outsource?

In the end, the service logistics manager or the service VP is going to be faced with the decision to make — buy, or outsource? — or a combination of any or all of these choices. Decisions to outsource any portion of the service logistics pipeline are always made when an organization is convinced that productivity and efficiency gains are needed, but is certain that the solution is not available from in-house development or from a prepackaged system. Unfortunately, the new wave of service logistics software and advanced technology doesn't simplify this dilemma; it only adds greater implications and complexities to a more basic evaluation of make vs. buy. Ultimately, the selection of one outsourcing vendor to tool over another is dependent on the ability of the end user to clearly and effectively identify the components of the logistics pipeline/service supply chain where improvements in productivity and efficiency are most needed, and can be best supported by an external supplier. Regardless of whether end users choose to make, buy, or outsource any aspects of the logistics pipeline, the good news is that there are now a multitude of productivity and efficiency gains available in today's market. Your search starts here.

11

SUMMARY AND CONCLUSION: MANAGEMENT OF CLOSED LOOP SUPPLY CHAINS AND REVERSE LOGISTICS PROCESS DIRECTIONS AND TRENDS

INTRODUCTION

The full review of the closed loop supply chain (CLSC) and reverse logistics (RL) market, business models, processes, systems and technology, and functional areas have provided the framework and structure for examining management issues. This relatively new and emerging business opportunity is of growing importance with respect to two areas:

- Environmental concerns focusing on reducing waste, trash, hazardous, and other residue of consumer and industrial and commercial enterprise
- Economic value in terms of extending the product life, as well as the usability and uptime of goods and products manufactured

While considerable focus has been placed on the environmental issues and impacts, the economic side of the equation has received less attention. However, as discussed and described in the above chapters, both objectives (environmental and economic) can be achieved with the same business models, practices, and infrastructure. We have identified that the market for RL and repair on either a stand-alone basis or as part of a CLSC represents a significant and growing business opportunity and market. It has also been shown that by managing this process efficiently and with modern technology, both objectives can be met.

This concept, which marries both environmental and economic concerns through RL as one integrated approach, is being to some extent driven by recent developments in the European Union (EU). The EU has been aggressive in its concern over environmental impact resulting in the design, development, and implementation of green laws designed to protect the environment. These green laws were originally focused on purely environmental concerns, but as a result of extensive research, investigation, and study,* it became increasingly clear that effective control over environmental pollution, particularly from industrial, commercial, and consumer goods, would have to specifically take into account the RL and CLSC practices of manufacturers, dealers, distributors, retailers, and consumers. As a result new green laws began to emerge that focused on the role of the manufacturer ensuring that the ultimate disposition of its products and goods would not produce negative environmental impact or create hazardous situations for the population as a whole.

The EU has recently developed new directives and regulations that merges environmental and economic issues. For example, the recently developed Waste, Electrical, and Electronic Equipment Directive (outlined in Appendix E) places the responsibility for the ultimate disposition of all electrical and electronic products and technology in the hands of the manufacturer. The solution to these new regulations, which are about to be approved and issued throughout the EU in 2004 will have to be dealt with on a cost effective basis if they are to be workable. It appears clear that this will, in turn, increase the need for focus on developing efficient business models, technology and infrastructure for our CLSC and RL operations.

RL and CLSC processes in consumer electronics and white goods is both similar and different than for industrial and commercial product markets. The similarities are:

- Complex issues over disposal over the last decade (green laws) effect all product markets.
- Secondary markets have developed for products and material which have failed and need to be repaired and resold (third party rebuild and refurbish experience).

---

* See Appendix A and Appendix B.

- Many parts and subassemblies can be and are reused, thereby creating a *depot* repair market.
- Returns need to be defined more precisely in all markets. Traditionally, the perception is that an item is returned because it doesn't work properly or at all. In reality, this is probably one of the least frequent reasons for product returns.

The principal difference between these market segments is that consumer goods (especially white and brown goods) are returned for many different reasons than industrial and commercial items. Other differences between these two groups

- White goods are normally large expensive items for which delivery is a significant cost. Shipment damage, size, and color considerations are often the reasons for return.
- White goods are also repaired on site in the majority of uses when they fail. The rate of parts and subassembly returns must be considered.
- Brown goods are much more impulse purchases. They are returned for many different reasons.
- Many people *test* a product and return it if it is too difficult to operate or it doesn't meet the features/functionality advertised.
- People also *rent* items for short periods of time, returning same when the immediate need has passed. Liberal product return policies help create this behavior.

We can conclude from this that a firm interested in entering the white/brown goods appliance market needs to carefully consider the following issues in developing the administrative cost of product return issues:

- Need for the product to interface/integrate with other products to work as efficiently as promised
- Size and ease of setting up/using the product
- Susceptibility of the product to damage in shipment
- Potential shelf life span of product/model (will technology make older model difficult to sell without deep discounts)
- Overall reliability of product (especially with regards to power fluctuation)

LONG-TERM IMPACT OF GREEN LAWS

The EU has been heavily focused on the development and adoption of green laws to reduce or eliminate environmental impact. The initial focus was in Germany, and in Northern Europe (Norway, Denmark, and Finland) where environmental impact is an extremely important issue. Much of this focus was on waste materials and recycling, but in recent years the Germans in particular have adopted new green laws that focus on the ultimate disposal of products and technology. The essence of these new laws was that the original equipment manufacturer (OEM) of a product or technology would become ultimately responsible for the final disposition of that technology; the OEM could be held directly responsible if a failure to correctly dispose the technology resulted in economic or physical damage. In pragmatic terms, this could mean that a manufacturer of refrigerators could be held directly responsible if the ultimate buyer of that refrigerator simply put the refrigerator on a trash pile without taking off the doors, resulting in a child becoming trapped inside the refrigerator and dying.

While the enforcement of this type of green law has been fought and challenged, the basic idea of extending the green laws into products and technology, in addition to solid and fluid waste and hazardous materials, has certainly been on the agenda, particularly in certain of the EU states.

In the past 2 to 3 years this movement has grown substantially and in fact, particularly with the 2003 publication of the WEEE directive.* The WEEE directive puts some bite and clout into the concept of holding the manufacturer ultimately responsible for electrical and electronic product disposition. The directive requires OEM and vendors to take back obsolete or unwanted equipment on a one-for-one or like-for-like basis. In addition, if the vendor will not take it back, the end user must dispose of it, but it must be done in accordance with regulations and not just dumped on a trash pile. Of greater importance is that this directive has now been approved by not just a limited set of European countries, but by the broader EU including specifically the U.K. In fact, the WEEE directive is to become law in August 2005.

The WEEE directive, and other similar regulations now in development in the EU will have a very significant impact on the RL and CLSC industry. Obviously both EU-based companies and firms in the electrical and electronic product business, as well as multinational companies, including U.S. and Canadian firms selling into the European markets, will be faced with adapting to these new specifications and directives. In point of fact, a great deal of research and study on the issues of the impact, as well as technology, systems, and infrastructure for reverse logistics has been underway in Europe through Revlog, a EU consortium focused on these specific issues.**

---

* See Appendix E.
** Specific Revlog papers are identified in Appendix A.

We can draw from this analysis that the technology utilized in high tech CLSCs may also be applicable in consumer goods supply chains if the manufacturer or retailer is willing and able to establish a closed loop process and system. They have pointed out that this might be best accomplished at the present time by large retail chains that appear to be in the best position to take economic advantage of the business opportunities involved in the process. The key point is that systems and technology developed for the high tech closed supply chain business model and market may have very real applicability in specific areas of the consumer goods market. Unfortunately, at the present moment, these two communities generally do not share information about experience, practices, technology, state of the art, or statistics. This problem is now being overcome in the EU as a result of the new drivers created by the WEEE directive. We anticipate that this coalition of interest will also occur in North America in the near future. It is, however, clear that there is a great and growing need for exchange of information about RL trends, practices, metrics, and parameters. Analysis contained in this book is an attempt to bring together from a variety of different sources, outlined in Appendices A, B, and C, the basic data on the RL and CLSC processes in both high tech and consumer goods area. There is, however, a long way to go in terms of providing a full array of data and both theoretical and structural solutions for management, coordination, and control of these processes on a global basis. Of even greater importance is the need for both systems developers and third party logistics participants to recognize the broader opportunities that exist in RL and CLSCs across all market segments. At the present time, the very narrow focus on specific markets and specific products has to some extent inhibited the ability of all organizations to take advantage of the emerging state of the art practices, rules of thumb, and anecdotal experience in order to apply it to the broader market opportunity.

RECOMMENDATIONS

Based upon our evaluation of the market, business models, state of the art, and practices for RL and CLSCs, we strongly recommend that both current participants in both the high tech and the consumer products markets, as well as third party logistics vendors and systems technology suppliers, take a broader view of the opportunities available and gain a better appreciation for the market potential and economic value of managing RL and CLSC processes efficiently and effectively. Over the past 10 to 15 years, significant breakthroughs have been made in both the concepts, technology, systems, and control mechanisms in RL and CLSCs driven by different market issues and concerns, but ultimately coalescing in the emerging ability to efficiently and effectively manage, coordinate, and control the RL and CLSC processes in all markets.

In essence, the increased focus on RL as an extension of the basic direction supply chain concept is becoming increasingly important, driven by the recognition of both the environmental impact of incorrectly handling, managing, and processing returns, as well as the economic value of returns, which is increasingly lost. As senior executives and financial officers of major industrial, commercial, and consumer goods manufacturers become more aware of this opportunity, as well as to begin to look closely at new legislation and directives, they will recognize the need to establish the role of a logistics executive concerned with both the direct supply chain and reverse supply chain operations. This role has already been created in a number of high tech corporations such as Boeing, General Electric, General Motors, IBM, and so on. We now see a growing recognition of the need to take similar steps in the consumer goods area. This new focus is also being reenforced by the creation of new and/or expanded third party logistics providers offering new options for RL, coordination control, repair, and disposition. The continuing consolidation of physical distribution, depot repair and RL management and support organizations is seen through mergers and acquisitions, through both the activities of the very large global logistics and distribution organizations, such as UPS and FedEx, and through the growth of younger organizations now exceeding $100 to $200 million or more in annual revenues, including firms such as Genco, USCO, and so forth. This will also produce more strategic alliances between logistics organizations with strong skills in management, coordination, forecasting and planning, linked to organizations with core competence in specific physical activities such as depot repair, transportation, and distribution. The general market trends clearly suggest that RL outsourcing vendors will have to continuously improve the efficiencies and productivity of their operations in order to remain competitive. This will be achieved through emergence and consolidation of systems, technology, and software networks, and advanced logistics forecasting and planning tools that are specifically designed to deal with RL and CLSC operations, as opposed to straightforward inventory management and control requirements found in the typical manufacturing facility and support of manufacturing and production operations.

From the vendor perspective, one strategic solution is to specifically target key market segments (i.e., industrial, commercial, consumer, and manufacturer vs. retailer) in which the specific skill sets are most closely adapted to requirements of those specific segments. This approach to segmentation and targeting will allow the third party vendor to be most successful in meeting the constantly changing customer needs and requirements of those segments, as well as possess the understanding, knowledge, and skills associated with the RL dynamics of those particular segments. In this regard, our surveys and research clearly show that the high tech RL and CLSC not only exists, but has generally stabilized and continues to offer significant growth potential. Most importantly, it is fairly generic across the major product technology subsegments. On the other hand, the other major subsegments involving commercial and consumer goods are much less well defined and in the very early stages of development and, therefore, much less generic. In some subsegments, such as automotive, pharmaceutical, and perishable foods, the significant support and infrastructure has now emerged, offering both manufacturers and retailers interested in achieving greater control over the RL process immediate solutions. On the other hand, in other markets, decision makers may vary from company to company, service requirements may vary, and perhaps, most importantly, the technical knowledge and capabilities for management and control for the full RL process may differ significantly.

As pointed out above, these trends are not necessarily the case in the EU, where RL responsibilities are matter of law and new directives and regulations clearly establish the need for a managed approach. A number of vendors exist and in addition a great deal of attention is being placed on the subject by academic and research organizations, management organizations, and software vendors.

In essence, from the vendor perspective, the development of an optimized business strategy in RL and CLSCs must be built from three major dimensions:

- Market segment focus (i.e., portfolio of services to be provided)
- Geographic focus (countries and regions in which RL and CLSC services can be provided)
- Timing — the rate at which the strategies to be deployed and the timeframe by which the processes are to be carried out (i.e., over hours and days vs. weeks and months)

From the standpoint of the owner of the process (i.e., the manufacturer or the dealer, distributor, or retailer) the most immediate problem is to recognize the economic and financial importance of RL and the strategic need to manage the processes in terms of its effect on the bottom line of the organization. This, in turn, will not only push the responsibilities up the management train, but also identify the important, and, in fact, the critical need for collecting accurate data on RL processes, dynamics, costs, and opportunities for improvement.

In summary, the market potential and opportunity for managing RL and CLSC processes is large and growing, and has the potential for affecting profitability either from the standpoint of the manufacturer or the distributor/retailer. These actors must recognize the need for managing processes strategically as part of overall corporate operations, as well as for the management of third party logistics providers who recognize the emerging opportunity. Overall the future for RL and CLSCs appears to be bright. We have tried in this book to provide the building blocks and understanding of these new processes and conceptual approaches. It is, however, for the reader to understand that this a market undergoing significant and rapid change and, therefore, one in which it will be necessary to continuously update one's view of strategic opportunity. We have attempted in Appendices A, B, and C to identify reference and data sources that will help in this process.

APPENDIX A

CLOSED LOOP SUPPLY CHAINS AND REVERSE LOGISTICS BIBLIOGRAPHY

Andel, T. (1993). New ways to take out the trash, *Transportation & Distribution* 34(5): pp. 24–30.

Anonymous. (2000). Return to sender, *Modern Materials Handling* 55(6): 64–65.

Bagnall, R. (1992). Environmental management systems: Developing an IT strategy, *Logistics Information Management* 5(4):19–20.

Barros A.I., R. Dekker, and V. Scholten. (1998). A two-level network for recycling sand: A case study, *European Journal of Operational Research* 110(2):199–215.

Biddle, D. (1993). Recycling for profit: The new green business frontier, *Harvard Business Review* 71(6):145–156.

Blumberg, D. (1991). *Managing service as a strategic profit center.* New York: McGraw Hill.

Blumberg, D. (1999). Strategic examination of reverse logistics & repair service needs, market size & opportunities, *Journal of Business Logistics* 20 (2).

Blumberg, D. (2002). *Managing high-tech services using a CRM strategy.* New York: St. Lucie Press.

Brennan, J.R. (1994). *Warranties; Planning, analysis & implementation.* New York: McGraw Hill.

Byrne, P.M. and A. Deeb. (1993). Logistics must meet the "green" challenge, *Transportation & Distribution* 34(2):33–37.

Carter C.R. and L.M. Ellram. (1998). Reverse logistics: A review of the literature and framework for future investigation, *Journal of Business Logistics* 19(1):85–102.

Caruso, C., A. Colorni, and M. Paruccini. (1993). The regional urban solid waste management system: A modeling approach, *European Journal of Operational Research* 70:16–30.

Daugherty, P.J., C.W. Autry, and A.E. Ellinger. (2001). Reverse logistics: The relationship between resource commitment and program performance, *Journal of Business Logistics* 22(1):107–123.

de Brito M.P., S.D.P. Flapper, and R. Dekker. (2002). Reverse Logistics: A review of case studies, Econometric Institute Report EI2002-21, Erasmus University Rotterdam, The Netherlands.

de Brito, M.P. and E.A. van der Laan. (2002). Inventory management with product returns: The impact of (mis)information, Econometric Institute Report Series EI 2002-29, Erasmus University Rotterdam, The Netherlands.

de Koster, M.B.M., S.D.P Flapper, and H.K.W.S.V. (2002). Networks for the collection and processing of end-of-life large white goods (Submitted to Production and Operations Management).

de Koster, R.B.M , M.P. de Brito, and M. van de Vendel. (2002). How to organize return handling: An exploratory study with nine retailer warehouses, the Erim Report Series Report in Management (nr. ERS-2001-49-LIS), Erasmus University Rotterdam, The Netherlands. (Forthcoming in *International Journal of Retail and Distribution Management.*)

Del Castillo, E. and J.K. Cochran. (1996). Optimal short horizon distribution operations in reusable container systems, *Journal of the Operational Research Society* 47(1):48–60.

Dowlatshahi S. (2000). Developing a theory of reverse logistics, *Interfaces* 30:143–155.

Flapper, S.D.P. and T. Jensen. (2002). Logistic planning and control of rework. (Forthcoming in *International Journal of Production Research.*)

Fleischmann, M. (2001). *Quantitative models for reverse logistics.* Berlin: Springer-Verlag. ISB 0075-8450.

Fleischmann M., J.M. Bloemhof-Ruwaard, R. Dekker, E. van der Laan, J.A.E.E. van Nunen and L.N. van wassenhove. (1997). Quantitative models for reverse logistics: A review, *European Journal of Operational Research* 103:1–17.

Fleischmann, M., R. Kuik, and R. Dekker. (2002). Controlling inventories with stochastic item returns: A basic model, *European Journal of Operational Research* 138:63–75.

Fleischmann M., H.R. Krikke, R. Dekker and S.D.P. Flapper. (200), A characterization of logistics networks for product recovery, Omega, 28: (6) 653–666.

Fuller D.A. and J. Allen. (1997). A typology of reverse channel systems for post-consumer recyclables, in J. Polonsky and A.T. Mintu-Winsatt (Eds.), *Environmental marketing: Strategies, practice, theory and research.* Binghamton, NY: Haworth Press.

Ganeshan R., E. Jack, M.J. Magazine, and P. Stephens. (1999), A taxonomic review of supply chain management research, in S. Tayur, R. Ganeshan and M. Magazine (Eds.), *Quantitative models for supply chain management*, New York: Kluwer Academic Publishers.

Gen, M. and Cheng, R. (2000). *Genetic algorithms and engineering optimizations.* New York: Wiley.

Georgiadis, P., D. Vlachos, and I. Karatsis. (2002). Reverse logistics modeling: A new approach, using system dynamics. In *6th Balkan conference on Operational Research proceedings.*

Ginter P.M. and J.M. Starling. (1978). Reverse distribution channels for recycling, *California Management Review* 20(3):72–81.

Groggin K. and J. Browne. (2000). Towards a taxonomy of resource recovery from end-of-life products, *Computers & Industry* 42:177–191.

Guide, V.D., Jr. and L.N. Van Wassenhove. (2001). Managing product returns for remanufacturing, *Production and Operations Management* 10(2):142–154.

Guide V.D., Jr. and L.N. Van Wassenhove (Eds.). (2001). Business aspects of closed loop supply chains. Pittsburgh: Carnegie Mellon University Press.

Guide, V.D., Jr. and L.N. Van Wassenhove. (2002). Managing Product Returns at HP. INSEAD Case.

Guiltinan J. and N. Nwokoye. (1974). Reverse channels for recycling: An analysis for alternatives and public policy implications in R. G. Curhan (Ed.), *New marketing for social and economic progress*, Combined Proceedings, American Marketing Assoc.

Guintini, R. and T. Andel. (1995). Advance with reverse logistics, *Transportation & Distribution* 36(2): 73ff.

Guintini, R. and T. Andel. (1995). Reverse logistics role models, *Transportation & Distribution* 36(4): 97ff.

Gunger A. and S.M. Gupta. (1998). Issues in environmentally conscious manufacturing and product recovery: A survey, *Computers & Industrial Engineering* 36:811–853.

Harrington, L.H. (1994). Hazardous materials compliance: What you don't know can hurt you, *Inbound Logistics* 14(8):20–29.

Heisig, G. (2002). Planning stability in material requirements planning systems, Lecture Notes in Economics and Mathematical Systems 515, Berlin: Springer-Verlag.

Hoffman S., W. Kahler, and W. Wellman. (1995). The complete shipping paper rules, 2nd Ed. HazMat Shipping, c/o Tom Foster, Publisher, One Chilton Way, Radnor, PA 19089.

Inderfurth, K. (2002). Optimal policies in hybrid manufacturing/remanufacturing systems with product substitution, FEMM working paper 1/2002 University of Magdeburg, Germany.

Inderfurth, K. (2002). The performance of simple MRP driven policies for stochastic manufacturing/remanufacturing problems, FEMM working paper 6/2002 University of Magdeburg, Germany.

Inderfurth, K., S.D.P. Lambert, A.J.D. Rappig, and C.P. Voutsinas. (2002). Production planning for Product Recovery Management, FEMM working paper, University of Magdeburg, Germany.

Inderfurth, K., G. Lindner, and N.P. Rahaniotis. (2002). Lot sizing in a production system with rework and product deterioration, in *Operations Research Proceedings 2002*, Berlin: Heidelberg/New York: Springer.

Inderfurth, K. and Ruud H. Teunter. (2002). Production planning and control of closed-loop supply chains, in V.D.R. Guide et al. (Eds.) *Business prospectives on closed loop supply chains*.

Jahre, M. (1995). Household waste collection as a reverse channel: A theoretical perspective, *International Journal of Physical Distribution and Logistics Management* 25(2):39–55.

Jayaraman, V., V.D.R. Guide, Jr., and R. Srivastava. (1999). A closed-loop logistics model for remanufacturing, *Journal of the Operational Research Society* 50:497–508.

Jayaraman, V., R.A. Patterson, and E. Rolland. (2003). The design of reverse distribution networks: Models and solution procedures, *European Journal of Operational Research*, in press.

Kiesmueller, G.P. (2002). A new approach for controlling a hybrid stochastic manufacturing remanufacturing system with inventories and different leadtimes (forthcoming in European Journal of Operational Research).

Kiesmueller, G.P. (2002). Optimal control of a one product recovery system with leadtimes. (Forthcoming in International Journal of Production Economics.)

Kiesmueller, G.P. and C.W. Scherer (2002). Computational Issues in a Stochastic Finite Horizon One Product Recovery Inventory Model. (Forthcoming in European Journal of Operational Research.)

Kiesmueller, G.P. and S. Minner. (2002). Simple expressions for finding recovery system inventory control parameters (forthcoming in Journal of the Operational Research Society).

Kleber, R., S. Minner, and G.P. Kiesmueller. (2002). A continuous time inventory model for a product recovery system with multiple options, *International Journal of Production Economics* 79:121–141.

Kokkinaki, A.I., N. Karakapilides, R. Dekker, and C. Pappis. (2002). A web-based recommender system for end-of-use ICT products. Proceedings of the Second IFIP Conference on E-commerce, E-business, E-government, October.

Kokkinaki, A.I., R. Dekker, M.B.M. de Koster, and C. Pappis. (2002). Web applications for reverse logistics networks. (Forthcoming in Supply Chain Management, An International Journal.)

Kokkinaki, A.I., R. Dekker, M.B.M. de Koster, C. Pappis, and W. Verbeke (2002). E-business models for reverse logistics: Contributions and challenges. Proceedings of IEEE Computer Society (ITCC) 2002 International Conference on Information Technology, Las Vegas, Nevada, USA, pp. 470–476, April 2002.

Kopicky R.J., M.J. Berg, L. Legg, V. Dasappa, and C. Maggioni. (1993). *Reuse and recycling: Reverse logistics opportunities.* Oak Brook, IL: Council of Logistics Management.

Krarup, J. and Pruzan, P.M. (1983). The simple plant location problem: Survey and synthesis, *European Journal of Operational Research* 12, 36–81.

Krikke, H.R. (1998). Recovery strategies and reverse logistics network design, Ph.D. Dissertation, Enschede, The Netherlands: University of Twente.

Krikke, H.R., E.J. Kooi, and P.C. Schurr. (1999). Network design in reverse logistics: A quantitative model, in P. Stahly (Ed.) *New trends in distribution logistics.* Berlin: Springer Verlag, 45–62.

Lambert A.J.D. (2002). Determining optimum disassembly sequences in electronic equipment, *Computers and Industrial Engineering* 43(3):553–575.

Lambert A.J.D. (2002). Disassembly sequencing: A review. (Forthcoming in International Journal of Production Research.)

Lambert A.J.D. (2002). Generation of assembly graphs by systematic analysis of assembly* structures, Proceedings of 15th IFAC World Congress, Barcelona. Session: Assembly Line Design and Balancing. 6 pp. Proceedings on CD-ROM. Paper edition to appear (Elsevier Scientific).

Lambert, A.J.D. and F.A. Boons. (2002). Eco-industrial parks, *Technovation* 22(8):471–484.

Lambert, A.J.D. and S.M. Gupta. (2002). Demand-driven disassembly optimization for electronic products, *Journal of Electronics Manufacturing* 11(2):121–135.

Lambert, A.J.D., H.M. Boelaarts, and M.A.M. Splinter. (2002). Optimal recycling system design with an application to sophisticated packaging tools. (Forthcoming in Environmental and Resource Economics.)

Lindner, G. (2002). Optimizing single stage production in the presence of rework, working paper, Otto-von-Guericke-University Magdeburg, Germany.

Lindner, G. and U. Buscher. (2002). An optimal lot and batch size policy for a single item produced and remanufactured on one machine in the presence of limitations on the manufacturing and handling capacity, working paper, Otto-von-Guericke-University Magdeburg, Germany.

Melachronoudis, E., H. Min, and X. Wu. (1995). A multiobjective model for the dynamic location of landfills, *Location Science* 3(3):143–166.

Melissen F.W. & A.J. de Ron. (1999). Defining recovery practices — Definitions and terminology, *International Journal on Environmentally Conscious Manufacturing and Design* 8(2):1–18.

Min, H. (1989). A bi-criterion reverse distribution model for product recall. *Omega* 17(5):483–490.

Minner, S. and G.P. Kiesmüller. (2002). Dynamic product acquisition in closed loop supply chains, working paper, Otto-von-Guericke University of Magdeburg, Germany.

Mostard, J. and R. Teunter. (2002). The newsboy problem with resalable returns, working paper, Erasmus University Rotterdam, The Netherlands.

Muller, E. J. (1993). Environmental packaging: Reduce, reuse, recycle, *Distribution* 92(11):42–49.

Nash, Kim S. (2003). Getting it back, *Baseline*, Case 054.

Nemhauser, G.L. and L.A. Wolsey. (1988). *Integer and combinatorial optimization.* Chichester, England: Wiley.

Ottman, J.A. (1993). Green marketing: Challenges and opportunities for the new marketing age. Chicago: NTC Business Books.

ReturnBuy. (2000). The new dynamics of returns: The profit, customer and business intelligence opportunities in returns, White Paper, Ashburn, Virginia: ReturnBuy.com, December.

Reuse and Recycling-Reverse Logistics Opportunities. (1993). Transmode Consultants and Icf. Inc. by the Council of Logistics Management, 2803 Butterfield Road, Oak Brook, IL 60521.

Schmidt G. and W.E. Wilhelm. (2000). Strategic, tactical and operational decisions in multi-national logistics networks: A review and discussion of modeling issues, *International Journal of Production Research* 38(7):1501–1523

Schrijver, A. (2003). *Combinatorial optimization: Polyhedra and efficiency.* Berlin: Springer.

Shear, H., T.W. Speh, and J.R. Stock. (2003). The warehousing link of reverse logistics. Presented at the 26th Annual Warehousing Education and Research Council Conference, San Francisco, CA.

Smith, J.M.S. and G. Watts. (1993). A Framework for the environmental management, *The Journal of the Institute of Logistics and Distribution Management* 12(2):2–5.

Stock J.R. (1992). *Reverse logistics.* Oak Brook, IL: Council of Logistics Management.

Stock, J.R. (2001). The seven deadly sins of reverse logistics, *Material Handling Management* 56(3):5–10.

Teunter, R.H. (2002). Economic ordering quantities for stochastic discounted cost inventory systems with remanufacturing, *International Journal of Logistics* 5(2):161–175

Teunter, R.H. and S.D.P. Flapper. (2002). Lot-sizing for a single-stage, single-product production system with rework of perishable production defectives. (Forthcoming in OR Spektrum.)

Teunter, R.H. and E.A. van der Laan. (2002). On the non-optimality of the average cost approach for inventory models with remanufacturing, *International Journal of Production Economics* 79(1):67–73.

Teunter, R.H. and D. Vlachos. (2002). On the necessity of a disposal option for returned products that can be remanufactured, *International Journal of Production Economics* 75(3):257–266.

The Challenge of Going Green. (1994). *Harvard Business Review* 72(4, July/August):37–50.

The Franklin Report. Published by Franklin Associates, Ltd., 4121 West 83rd Street, Suite 108, Prairie Village, KS 66208.

Thierry M., M. Salomon, J. van Nunen, and L. van Wassenhove. (1995). Strategic sigues in product recovery management, *California Management* 37 (2):114–135.

Thierry, M. (1997). An analysis of the impact of product recovery management on manufacturing companies, Ph.D. Dissertation, Rotterdam, The Netherlands: Erasmus University.

Toktay, L.B. (2002). Forecasting product returns, forthcoming in Daniel Guide, Jr., Charles Corbett, Rommert Dekker, and Luk N. Van Wassenhove (Eds.) *Business Perspectives in Closed-Loop Supply Chains.*

Tsoulfas, G., C. Pappis, and S. Minner. (2002). An environmental analysis of the reverse supply chain of SLI batteries, *Resources, Conservation and Recycling* 36:135–154.

van der Laan, E. (2003). An NPV and AC analysis of a stochastic inventory system with joint manufacturing and remanufacturing, *International journal of Production Economics* 81-82:317–331.

van der Laan, E. and R. Teunter. (2002). Average costs versus net present value: A comparison for multi-source inventory models, in A. Klose, M. G. Speranza, L. N. Van Wassenhove, Eds., *Quantitative Approaches to Distribution Logistics and Supply Chain Management*. Lecture Notes in Economics and Mathematical Systems. Berlin: Springer-Verlag.

White, J.A. (1994). Reverse logistics moves forward, *Modern Material Handling* 49(1):29.

APPENDIX B

FORECASTING METHODOLOGY AND SPECIAL DATA SOURCES USED TO DEVELOP BENCHMARK AND MARKET FORECASTS

INTRODUCTION TO THE METHODOLOGY FOR ESTIMATING SERVICE MARKET POTENTIAL

The general estimation and forecasting methodology used in this research by Blumberg Associates, Inc. (BAI) revolves around the key assumption that, ultimately, all potential service spending is driven by levels and dynamics of four critical factors:

- Value of shipments of equipment or systems to be serviced
- Installed base value for equipment, systems, or products to be serviced
- Service requirements associated with this installed base
- Willingness to pay (both realized and unrealized in the market) for these services

It was generally assumed that service market potential in a given time period is a function of the installed base. In some more complex modeling efforts, we separately treated front end logistics service markets as a function of product/system shipments and all other services as dependent on installed base values.

Overall estimates of potential spending for services associated with a given product, product group, or major product class in a given geographic area were derived from a 5-step process:

1. Determine the (observed) value of equipment shipments and the installed equipment base for past time periods.
2. Forecast shipment and installed base values for time periods in progress and in the future.
3. Determine service requirements and estimate coefficient of spending for services, as a function of shipments and installed base values, in past periods.
4. Forecast willingness to pay for time periods in progress based on market services.
5. Calculate service market potential as a product of spending coefficient and shipments/installed base value, historically and in the future.

This general methodology provides reasonably accurate estimates and forecasts of the "top line" total *market* in the market segments identified.

Since line-item service spending data is rarely available in any useful (time series, longitudinal, or panel) form, segmentation of a given market segment below this "top line" level is then most often developed as a derivative of the top line estimates and forecasts. This is generally achieved by sampling cross sectional data from end users via market research surveys that provide some look at the relative size of spending by various service categories, line item services as a percent of total spending, or some similar measure, then extrapolating the relative content of service spending (usually with line items measured as a percent of total spending) year-by-year across the estimation and forecast period based on this sample data. Applying these structural extrapolations to the top line estimates then yields detailed segmentation of the market in a cost effective manner using the best available data.

A variation on this same procedure is often employed in cases where robust data on the revenue structure of service providers is available. Revenue structures of representative service providers give a reasonable view of segmentation of the external service market in any given market segment, and this segmentation basis is also often used in combination with end user spending data to contrast the total and available opportunities in a given market segment.

In cases where reliable line item time series are available, they can be employed to build a "bottom-up" estimate of the top line service potential, either as a primary method of estimation or as a check on the results of the more conventional top-down method discussed above. These cases are very rare and are generally limited to industry-specific data sets or service activities given their own 4-digit classification within the Standard Industrial Classification (SIC) system (or, for data published in 2000 or later from government sources, 6-digit classification within the North American Industry Classification System [NAICS]). Furthermore, this data will usually only reflect external market activities, rather than total market potential, since internal service spending is rarely captured in such data. In cases where only firm-by-firm service spending data is available, line-item or total service market estimates and forecasts were made by applying this data to projections of the size distribution of firms in a given market segment.

DATA SOURCES FOR ESTIMATES AND FORECASTS

As is evident from the discussion above, the general form, type, and availability of data is a major determinant of the ultimate choice of estimation and forecasting techniques, it is informative to begin with a discussion of the data used in various forecasts. BAI uses three primary sources of industry data in its study of U.S. markets:

- U.S. government data sets — Includes Economic Census reports, Current Industrial Reports, County Business Patterns, and a variety of others
- BAI primary market research — Includes data collected from the variety of market research and related surveys conducted each year by BAI on behalf of clients
- Trade association data and data from similar sources — Often provides narrow but deep information useful for studying specific market segments or niches in some detail

BAI also uses purchased installed base and shipment product data from various outside sources, such as market research and consulting organizations with focus in specific regions or industries.

Specific Data Sources

Specific data sources used are discussed in this section.

Formal Primary Market Research Surveys

Three different types of market surveys were conducted over the period from 1996 to 2003:

- Surveys of *end users of closed loop supply chain and reverse logistics* covering consumer goods and other low tech products
- Surveys of *high tech service organizations* involved in closed loop supply chain process and the field service process
- Vendors and providers of closed loop supply chain and reverse logistics services and support processes (i.e., third and fourth party logistics firms)

The surveys were designed to provide:

- Demographic data by market segment
- Internal and external expenditures (or revenues) on closed loop supply chain and reverse logistics
- Future plans
- Benchmark measurement of closed loop supply chain and reverse logistics processes and procedures

In-Depth One-on-One In-Person and Telephonic Interviews

- 32 reverse logistics and closed loop supply chain industry specialists, conducted in 2001 and 2002 in the U.S. and Europe
- 16 reverse logistics and closed loop supply chain vendors and suppliers in U.S. and Europe
- 18 reverse logistics specialists focusing on global supply chain and reverse logistics operations

Literature and State-of-the-Art Research

Primary data sources in this category are found in Appendix A and Appendix B.

General Forecasting Methodology Employed

In general, three methods were used to generate future forecasts from data series gathered or estimated as part of the market modeling process:

- Simple linear or exponential growth trend projections
- Exponential smoothing forecasts
- Moving average forecasts

In principle, some analysts would prefer the application of more complex and technically robust forecasting methods to situations encountered in service market analysis (such as forecasting based upon ARIMA or Distributed Lag models). In practice, however, it is not clear that a correct underlying model specification is known in most cases for service market segments. More importantly, it is very likely that, should such a more robust structural model be known and properly specified, sufficient data (in both quantity and quality) for proper estimation and application of the model is not at all likely to be available. Furthermore, trend projections and exponential smoothing forecasts provide cost-effective methods of forecasting with sufficient accuracy for many common applications in business, social sciences, engineering, and other fields.

Exponential smoothing is BAIs preferred method for forecasting market size from known or estimated data series. This model allows for inclusion of trend and cyclical (by adapting methods used to allow for seasonality) characteristics of the series, within a computationally simple iterative framework (using minimum MSE criteria to identify the smoothing, trend and seasonal parameters, as needed). Generally, the forecasts were designed for an overall goodness of fit standard of mean absolute percentage error (MAPE) of 10% or less for its exponential smoothing forecasts.

In summary, the market size and forecasting provided in this report are based on the following methodology:

- Bottom-up extrapolation of current and future internal and external expenditures based on survey sources from end users
- Top-down determination of external expenditures based on extrapolation of results of surveys of vendors

The overall forecasting methodology is outlined in Figure B.1.

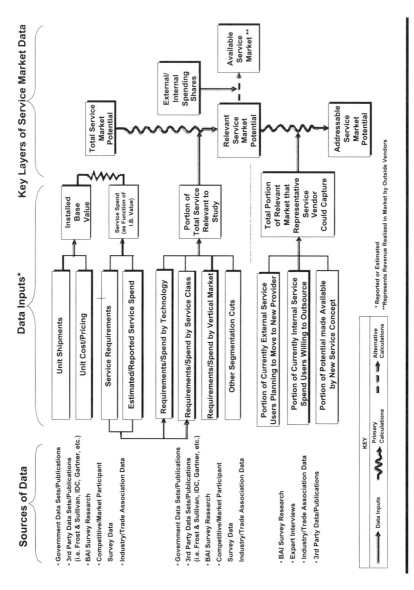

Figure B.1 General service market estimation and forecasting methodology.

APPENDIX C

ADDITIONAL DATA SOURCES ON REVERSE LOGISTICS AND CLOSED LOOP SUPPLY CHAIN OPERATIONS AND PERFORMANCE

- *The Joint Industry Unsaleables, Committee,* "Unsaleables Benchmarking Study," sponsored by Food Distributed International, Food Marketing Institute, and Grocery Manufacturers of America.
- *RevLog (Reverse Logistics),* research effort sponsored by the European Commission, including the European working group on Reverse Logistics (REVLOG):
  - Erasmus University, Rotterdam (coordinating the Netherlands Group)
  - Aristoteles University of Thessaloniki, Greece
  - Eindhoven University of Technology, The Netherlands
  - Insead Business School, France
  - Otto-Von-Guericke University, Germany
  - University of Piraeus, Greece
- Industry Council for Electronic Equipment Recycling (ICER).
- International Association of Electronics Recyclers (IAER).
- The Reverse Logistics Executive Council Center for Logistics Management, University of Nevada, Reno, NV.
- UPS Center for Worldwide Supply Chain Management, University of Louisville, KY.
- Fishman Davidson Center for Service & Operations Management, Wharton School, University of PA, Philadelphia, PA.
- Reverse Logistics Trends, Inc. (RLTI), 39510 Paseo Padre Parkway, Suite 390, Freemont, CA.
- Consumer Electronics Association (CEA).
- American Home Appliance Maintenance Association (AHAMA).
- Association of Home Appliance Manufacturers (AHAM).
- U.S. Department of Agriculture Life Cycle Evaluation Report.
- *Twice Magazine.*
- *Home Furnishing Daily.*

APPENDIX D

FIRMS PROVIDING REVERSE LOGISTICS SERVICES

Firm	General description	Product Focus/Technology	Service Focus
Click Returns, Inc. 8001 Irvine Center Drive, 4th Floor Irvine, CA 92618 949-679-8599 www.clickreturns.com	• End-to-end outsourced reverse logistics and asset recovery solution for industry • Offers "sell and forget" solution to resellers, distributors, and manufacturers	• Core business model based on patent pending virtual returns interface (vri) technology • Web and EDI • Enabled product allows seamless data flow	• Support both retail and commercial clients • Supports e-customers • Available in ASP version • Specializes in integration to legacy systems
Genco Distribution Systems 100 Papercraft Park Pittsburgh, PA 15238 800-224-3141 www.Genco.com	• Offers worldwide total solutions in reverse logistics, supply chain management, and asset recovery services • Special emphasis on asset recovery services	• Asset recovery services offer: – Bulk liquidation program – B-to-B automation – Consumer-directed auctions	• In addition to asset recovery services • Provides a full range of value added services: – Supply chain analysis – Post cause analysis – Policy development – Hidden damage assessment
Recover-ITT 767 Kenrick Road Suite 120 Houston, TX 77060 281-448-0022 www.recover-itt.com	• Offers Full Range Of Services For IT industry clients • Services include: – Pre-delivery – Installation – Maintenance – Deinstalled – Disposition	• Services broad array of IT technology: – Desktop computer – Laptops – Servers – Printers – POS units – Routers and switches	• Adds features to typical installation/maintenance portfolio to include: – Predelivery – Deinstallation – Disposition

Firm	General description	Product Focus/Technology	Service Focus
Reverse Logistics Trends 39510 Paseo Padre Parkway Suite 309 Fremont, CA 94538 www.reverselogistictrends.com	• Provides a clearing house for information on reverse logistics and closed loop supply chain issues • Offers cost effective source of current information on all above issues	• Specializes in latest trends on: – Repair – Customer service – Parts management – End-of-life manufacturing – Return processing – Order fulfillment	• Services all manufacturing verticals with special emphasis on third party service providers (3psp)
Surplus Village.com 1610 Colonial Parkway Inverness, IL 60067 800-424-5030 www.surplusvillage.com	• Assists corporations, product manufacturers, and resellers with recovering maximum value of new, used, overstocked and/or underutilized products • Specializes in high tech office and consumer items	• Acts as clearing house for all services involved in redistribution of excess high tech office and consumer items • Offers refurbishing services to enable user to get full value for excess assets	• Service offerings include: – Audit and refurbishing – Purchase/trade-in – Returns management – Remarketing – Quick quote
Wipro Technologies (USA Headquarters) 1300 Anttenden Lane 2nd FLOOR Mountain View, CA 94043 650-316-3555	• Global technology services division of Wipro Ltd. (India based) • Worldwide foot print – 30 offices – Over 21,000 IT practitioners • Specialized in quality programs – Six sigma – PCMM – CMMi – CMM (level 5)	• Offers full service IT portfolio: – IT consulting – Application development and maintenance – Package implementation – Total outsourcing – System integration	• Specializes in providing high end (Fortune 500) companies IT support from planning to execution includes: – Both forward the reverse logistics – Product deign service – Business process outsourcing

Company	Description	Capabilities/Services
E-RMA 2355 Oakland Road Suite #9 San Jose, CA 95131 (408) 955-0272 FAX (408) 955-0299 www.e-rma.com PARTNERS: EXODUS, GIZMO.COM, MATRANET	• RMA is an application service provider (ASP) that provides an efficient business process with a focus on B2B. E-RMA delivers a global e-commerce infrastructure to manage product returns between enterprise businesses, their customers, and their strategic business partners.	Capabilities: • Complete functionality without system integration • Value-added features with erp integration • Usability by all partners in the supply chain • Ability to configure or personalize • Ability to accommodate new products, additional customers, change of operational and approval flows, or other changes without utilizing it staff. • Ability to dynamically add business rules to improve the return process at any time without extensive programming • Scalable and secure architecture

Company	Description	Capabilities/Services

Keystone Internet Services
1500 Harbor Blvd.
Weehawken, NJ 07087
800-669-3535
FAX 717-633-3199
www.keystonefulfillment.com
	• Keystone seamlessly ties all areas of your operation together from purchasing to:
	  – Customer services
	  – Credit card processing
	  – Warehousing
	  – Distribution
	  – Data management
	  – Accounting
	• Keystone is the direct link to customers.
	• Their specialized customer service system is real time and large order processing.
	• It's a 24-hour-a-day, seven-days-a-week online service.
	• Integrated with a call response system to provide detailed, up-to-the-minute reporting on all aspects of account activity.
	• Over 750 stations in our national call centers can handle over 10,000 calls an hour.
	• Ability to access all long distance carriers and toll-free numbers - as well as ability to takes orders via mail, fax and the internet.
	• Keystone builds partnerships that offer a multitude of innovative solutions to e-commerce logistics, such as warehouse-within-warehouse delivery that lets your product ship closer to your customers' ultimate destination. Keystone also takes the time to get to know your brand, offering a menu of brand-building services from web site design to integrated supply chain solutions
		Information technology:
		• Customized software
		• Real-time inventory
		• Professional technical staff
		• Reliable backup
		Customer service:
		• State of the art facilities
		• Detailed reporting
		• Comprehensive training
		Fulfillment:
		• Capacity
		• Integrated systems
		• Cost effective shipping
		• Pick pack and ship
		Logistics solutions:
		• Warehouse-within-warehouse
		• Warehouse-within-container
		• Warehouse-within-mall
		• Warehouse-within-network
		Returns/liquidations:
		• Liquidations
		• Website distribution network
		• Warehouse and jobber sales
		Web development:
		• Design and creative
		• Production and technology
		• Project management
		• Redesign

Liquidation World
3880 - 29th Street, N.E.
Calgary, Alberta
Canada, T1Y 6B6
1-877-728-3289
1 (403) 250-1222
www.liquidtaionworld.com

- Provides a broad range of asset recovery services including the liquidation of merchandise from distress situations (insolvencies, insurance claims, closeouts), throughout a chain of retail locations across North America.

- Auctions
- Closeouts/surplus
- Insolvency
- Insurance claims
- Inventory appraisals:
  – Fair market value
  – Forced sale value
- Reverse logistics:
  – Product liability management
- Strategic downsizing/going out of business

Liquidation.com
Division of Liquidity Services, Inc.
22131 K Street NW, 4th Floor
Washington D.C. 20037
800-310-4604
Richard Rieman
Sales Director
X283
www.liquidation.com

- Provides large, complex organizations with comprehensive, innovative, customer-focused solutions to convert surplus property into cash. Headquartered in Washington, D.C., the company serves Fortune 500 companies, large federal agencies, and state agencies. Liquidation.com employees are experts in surplus asset liquidation, with extensive background in asset management, logistics services, wholesale merchandising, asset remarketing, sales, and customer support.

- Services as the exclusive surplus partner of the U.S. Department of Defense through its subsidiary, government liquidation LLC and as the primary surplus sales partner for the sale of surplus aircraft, ship and armored vehicle parts for the U.K.'s Ministry of Defense (U.K. mod) through its subsidiary, U.K. surplus.
- Liquidity Services, Inc., employs more than 225 people and is headquartered in Washington, D.C. with corporate offices in Scottsdale, AZ and Taunton, England.

Company	Description	Capabilities/Services
Product Management Canada Inc. 170 HWY #7 West UNIT 6 Brampton, Ontario, L7A 1A1 (905) 456-8344 or (888) 259-4712 FAX (905) 456-2687 www.pmcinc.org	• Product Management Canada Inc. (PMC) specializes in reverse logistics and product liability management services for the following industries: – Pharmaceutical – Health and beauty – Food and consumer products • Since 1997, PMC has managed the reverse supply chain needs of many of Canada's largest manufacturers, wholesalers, and distributors of these types of products.	Reverse logistics: • Depackaging and sorting of seasonal and promotional product prepacks for destruction, recycling, or redistribution • Reworking nonperishable food or health and beauty overruns for redistribution • Assistance with duty drawbacks and canadian food inspection agency recalls • Depackaging waste products, recycling of the packaging components, and bulking of the solid and liquid products for secure destruction • Emptying and bulking of packaged waste fragrances for alcohol recovery • Sorting of mixed wastes streams (e.g., returns, unsaleables, production material, obsolete inventories) to ensure waste products are sent to the correct licensed disposal facility • Refurbishing seasonal over-the-counter products (e.g., sunscreens, insect repellents; allergy medications, etc.) Product liability management: • A regularly scheduled PMC audit program of all facilities where clients' products are handled transferred or destroyed. PMC clients are welcome to schedule facility audits at any time. • A compliance program that ensures all PMC activities conform with applicable regulations, guidelines, laws and conventions at all levels of government, in all jurisdictions where PMC operates. • Compliance with documented standard operating procedures for all activities. • An emphasis on high-level security systems at all PMC facilities.

- Appropriate levels of insurance (comprehensive general, pollution and environmental impairment, W.S.I.B.)
- A waste characterization process for all waste products to determine regulatory compliance and the correct end disposition

PMC product destruction options include:

- Consolidation and transfer of waste to secure, licensed disposal facilities in Canada and the U.S.
- Incineration of nonhazardous and hazardous consumer products, cosmetics and pharmaceutical waste including: production waste, bulks, samples, clinical trial material, returns, damages, short-dated and unsaleable products
- Secure shredding of food and consumer products, cosmetics and pharmaceuticals (liquids and solids)
- Incineration in Canada of narcotics and controlled drugs and other sensitive materials
- Denaturing of narcotics and controlled drugs
- Complete product destruction and conversion of waste products to energy through incineration at any of american Ref-fuel's six waste-to-energy plants

PMC and American Ref fuel:

- PMC can now offer manufacturers, distributors, and wholesalers of these products a cost-effective option for transportation and complete destruction of waste products through american Ref-fuel's special waste services program.

Company	Description	Capabilities/Services
The Return Exchange 8001 Irvine Center Drive, 4th Floor Irvine, CA 92618 949.585.9495 FAX: 949.585.9499 www.thereturnexchange.com	• The leading technology provider of fraud and abuse detection for retailers" signature product, Verify-1°, utilizes an ASP model to provide return authorization services that are initiated by either a Verifone° or similar type platform on a retailer's POS system. • A driver"s license or state I.D. card is swiped through these devices to initiate a product return, and similar to credit card or check verification, the data is transmitted to the return exchange"s host server for an approval for return authorization. • they detect fraud through utilization of deterministic rules, statistical models and a shared return information database.	• Verify-1°, merchants are able to enforce a consistent return policy while monitoring consumer return transaction patterns to identify fraudulent and/or abusive customers. Bringing ease-of-use rules and predictive statistical modeling together, the return exchange offers this leading tool to both improve customer service and lower return rate with consistent deployment of your return policy. • Through the use of Verify-1°, merchants are given the ability to access a basic rule set to enforce their return policy. Return information collected at the terminal is processed real time, against a database of customers across multiple retailers. The authenticity of returns is automatically verified while ensuring compliance with all your return policies. If the return is authorized, a return authorization code is immediately sent back to the terminal for continued processing. If a pattern of unusual return activity is detected, a decline code is sent back to the terminal, and the consumer is offered a courtesy notice directing them to contact customer service at the return exchange. • Verify-1®, by the Return Exchange, is compliant with the Fair Credit Reporting Act (FCRA) and Verifone° certified to run on all Verifone° models using the Verix operating system.

Returnbuy
Purchased by Jabil Global Services
Jabil Circuit
10560 Dr. Martin Luther King Jr. St.,
North St. Petersburg, FL 33716
727-577-9749
www.jabil.com

- Jabil designs, manufactures and services electronics products by managing a global supply chain and delivering world-class quality.
- Their full range of services allows them to deliver business value to their customers, but ultimately, they believe their enterprise-wide commitment to understanding customers' needs is what sets them apart in other industries.
- They are responsive, flexible and accountable and that is reflected in their culture and execution.
- Jabil Global Services (JGS) is Jabil's postmanufacturing services subsidiary offering returns management and warranty repair services to Jabil customers.
- JGS provides closed-loop analysis feedback on manufacturing and design processes, resulting in a truly integrated product life cycle solution.

Returncentral
2300 Windy Ridge Parkway,
Suite 700
Atlanta, GA 30339

(770) 955-7070
FAX(770) 955-0302

www.manhattanassociates.com

- Manhattan Associates provides powerful application suites which are integrated to address execution from the point of source to the point of consumption.
- Companies use the joint strength of their trading partner management (TPM), Transportation Management Systems (TMS) and Warehouse Management Systems (WMS) application suites not only to manage operations within the four walls, but also to blend and synchronize processes with suppliers, consolidators, customers and transportation providers.
- Trading Partner Management synchronizes business processes across your trading partner network by extending execution capabilities to your suppliers, hubs, carriers and customers.
  - Allows for secure, accurate and electronic exchange of critical business documents, such as purchase orders and advance ship notices (ASNS), and the remote printing of compliant bar code labels, RFID tags and shipping documentation for your vendors and factories.
  - Provides end-to-end returns management capabilities, which automate each step of the returns process regardless of disparate technology systems.

Company	Description	Capabilities/Services

		• Transportation Management Systems application suite integrates transportation processes, maximizing profitability and strengthening communication between shippers and carriers with optimized procurement, integrated planning and execution and carrier management capabilities.
		  – Gives both shippers and carriers complete control over the resources in their transportation network.
		• Warehouse Management Systems provides advanced warehouse management functionality — supporting the full spectrum of execution processes that are part of everyday business realities, including:
		  – Warehouse management
		  – Workload planning and balancing
		  – Labor monitoring and measurement tools
		  – Optimal slotting and space utilization
		  – The ability to track and bill key cost drivers within the warehouse with comprehensive billing management capabilities.

Shipxact
Acquired by DDS Distribution
  Services, Ltd.

DDS Ltd.
20770 Westwood Drive
Strongsville, OH 44149

(440) 572-0725
FAX (440) 572-0815

www.ddsltd.com

- North America's premier fulfillment, distribution and direct mail company with over 2 million square feet of warehouse space.
- With facilities located in Albuquerque, Atlanta, Chicago, Cleveland, Dallas, Los Angeles, Oklahoma City, Philadelphia, St. Louis, and Toronto, they are the only full service fulfillment company with a national footprint.
- At DDS Distribution Services, it's their combination of people, technology and process that sets them apart. For more than 30 years they have provided innovative fulfillment and distribution solutions to Fortune 500 companies in a variety of industries

- Business to business fulfillment
  - Warehouse management
  - Order management
  - Transportation management
  - Technology tools
  - Ancillary services
- Consumer fulfillment
  - Rebates and refunds
  - Premium and merchandise
  - Continuity and loyalty
  - Sweepstakes, games and contests
  - Database marketing
  - Sampling
  - Call center solutions
  - Technology tools
- Pharmaceutical services
  - Web-based ordering
  - Direct-to programs
  - Personalized correspondence
  - Ancillary services
- Direct mail
  - Automation compatible postal software
  - List hygiene
  - Merge/purge
  - Programming capabilities
  - Printing
  - Bindery/inserting
  - Mail processing
  - Operations
- Textbook depository operations

Company	Description	Capabilities/Services

UPS Supply Chain Solutions Transportation and Freight, Logistics, and Distribution Services UPS Supply Chain Solutions 12380 Morris Road Alpharetta, GA 30005
 	
1.866.822.5336
 	
www.ups-scs.com
	• A single source can synchronize the flow of goods, funds, and information for your company. UPS Supply Chain Solutions has resources for every aspect of supply chain networks, from transportation and distribution to customs brokerage and design consulting.
	• Their experience and coverage provides global 500 and growing companies alike with flexibility of modes and scheduling, scalability of design and resources and global reach.
		• Transportation and freight
		• Logistics
		  – Distribution
		  – Design and planning
		• International trade
		  – Customs brokerage
		  – Compliance consulting
		  – Trade consulting
		  – Tariff consulting
		• Mail services
		• UPS Consulting

USF Processors 4055 Valley View Lane Dallas, TX 75244 (972) 980-7825 FAX (972) 239-1062 www.usfreightways.com/logistics/home/about_usf_processors.jsp	• A USF Logistics Services Operating Group, USF Processors is a solutions driven reverse logistics organization. With over 20 years of experience in implementing and servicing returns programs for manufacturer, wholesale/distributor, and retail clients, USF Processors offers a comprehensive range of solutions that will deliver value to your business. • USF Processors designed the first robust reverse/returns software technology and processing capabilities that centered on a vision to attach accountability to unsaleable products. This vision not only pioneered reverse logistics but the concept quickly spread to a multitude of industries that ranged from controlled prescription drugs to general merchandise to web-based consumer direct purchases.	• Asset recovery • Rx manufacturer services • General manufacturing services

APPENDIX E

THE WASTE ELECTRICAL AND ELECTRONIC EQUIPMENT (WEEE) DIRECTIVE OF THE EUROPEAN UNION

DIRECTIVE 2002/96/EC OF THE EUROPEAN PARLIAMENT AND OF THE COUNCIL
of 27 January 2003
on waste electrical and electronic equipment (WEEE)

THE EUROPEAN PARLIAMENT AND THE COUNCIL OF THE EUROPEAN UNION,

Having regard to the Treaty establishing the European Community, and in particular Article 175(1) thereof,

Having regard to the proposal from the Commission (¹),

Having regard to the Opinion of the Economic and Social Committee (²),

Having regard to the Opinion of the Committee of Regions (³),

Acting in accordance with the procedure laid down in Article 251 of the Treaty in the light of the joint text approved by the Conciliation Committee on 8 November 2002 (⁴),

Whereas:

(1) The objectives of the Community's environment policy are, in particular, to preserve, protect and improve the quality of the environment, protect human health and utilise natural resources prudently and rationally. That policy is based on the precautionary principle and principles that preventive action should be taken, that environmental damage should as a priority be rectified at source and that the polluter should pay.

(2) The Community programme of policy and action in relation to the environment and sustainable development (Fifth Environmental Action Programme) (⁵) states that the achievement of sustainable development calls for significant changes in current patterns of development, production, consumption and behaviour and advocates, *inter alia*, the reduction of wasteful consumption of natural resources and the prevention of pollution. It mentions waste electrical and electronic equipment (WEEE) as one of the target areas to be regulated, in view of the application of the principles of prevention, recovery and safe disposal of waste.

(3) The Commission Communication of 30 July 1996 on review of the Community strategy for waste management states that, where the generation of waste cannot be avoided, it should be reused or recovered for its material or energy.

(4) The Council in its Resolution of 24 February 1997 on a Community strategy for waste management (⁶) insisted on the need for promoting waste recovery with a view to reducing the quantity of waste for disposal and saving natural resources, in particular by reuse, recycling, composting and recovering energy from waste and recognised that the choice of options in any particular case must have regard to environmental and economic effects but that until scientific and technological progress is made and life-cycle analyses are further developed, reuse and material recovery should be considered preferable where and in so far as they are the best environmental options. The Council also invited the Commission to develop, as soon as possible, an appropriate follow-up to the projects of the priority waste streams programme, including WEEE.

(5) The European Parliament, in its Resolution of 14 November 1996 (⁷), asked the Commission to present proposals for Directives on a number of priority waste streams, including electrical and electronic waste, and to base such proposals on the principle of producer responsibility. The European Parliament, in the same Resolution, requests the Council and the Commission to put forward proposals for cutting the volume of waste.

(6) Council Directive 75/442/EEC of 15 July 1975 on waste (⁸) provides that specific rules for particular instances or supplementing those of Directive 75/442/EEC on the management of particular categories of waste may be laid down by means of individual Directives.

(7) The amount of WEEE generated in the Community is growing rapidly. The content of hazardous components in electrical and electronic equipment (EEE) is a major concern during the waste management phase and recycling of WEEE is not undertaken to a sufficient extent.

(8) The objective of improving the management of WEEE cannot be achieved effectively by Member States acting individually. In particular, different national applications of the producer responsibility principle may lead to substantial disparities in the financial burden on economic operators. Having different national policies on the management of WEEE hampers the effectiveness of recycling policies. For that reason the essential criteria should be laid down at Community level.

(¹) OJ C 365 E, 19.12.2000, p. 184 and OJ C 240 E, 28.8.2001, p. 298.
(²) OJ C 116, 20.4.2001, p. 38.
(³) OJ C 148, 18.5.2001, p. 1.
(⁴) Opinion of the European Parliament of 15 May 2001 (OJ C 34 E, 7.2.2002, p. 115), Council Common Position of 4 December 2001 (OJ C 110 E, 7.5.2002, p. 1) and Decision of the European Parliament of 10 April 2002 (not yet published in the Official Journal). Decision of the European Parliament of 18 December 2002 and Decision of the Council of 16 December 2002.
(⁵) OJ C 138, 17.5.1993, p. 5.

(⁶) OJ C 76, 11.3.1997, p. 1.
(⁷) OJ C 362, 2.12.1996, p. 241.
(⁸) OJ L 194, 25.7.1975, p. 47. Directive as last amended by Commission Decision 96/350/EC (OJ L 135, 6.6.1996, p. 32).

(9) The provisions of this Directive should apply to products and producers irrespective of the selling technique, including distance and electronic selling. In this connection the obligations of producers and distributors using distance and electronic selling channels should, as far as is practicable, take the same form and should be enforced in the same way in order to avoid other distribution channels having to bear the costs of the provisions of this Directive concerning WEEE for which the equipment was sold by distant or electronic selling.

(10) This Directive should cover all electrical and electronic equipment used by consumers and electrical and electronic equipment intended for professional use. This Directive should apply without prejudice to Community legislation on safety and health requirements protecting all actors in contact with WEEE as well as specific Community waste management legislation, in particular Council Directive 91/157/EEC of 18 March 1991 on batteries and accumulators containing certain dangerous substances (¹).

(11) Directive 91/157/EEC needs to be revised as soon as possible, particularly in the light of this Directive.

(12) The establishment, by this Directive, of producer responsibility is one of the means of encouraging the design and production of electrical and electronic equipment which take into full account and facilitate their repair, possible upgrading, reuse, disassembly and recycling.

(13) In order to guarantee the safety and health of distributors' personnel involved in the take-back and handling of WEEE, Member States should, in accordance with national and Community legislation on safety and health requirements, determine the conditions under which take-back may be refused by distributors.

(14) Member States should encourage the design and production of electrical and electronic equipment which take into account and facilitate dismantling and recovery, in particular the re-use and recycling of WEEE, their components and materials. Producers should not prevent, through specific design features or manufacturing processes, WEEE from being reused, unless such specific design features or manufacturing processes present overriding advantages, for example with regard to the protection of the environment and/or safety requirements.

(15) Separate collection is the precondition to ensure specific treatment and recycling of WEEE and is necessary to achieve the chosen level of protection of human health and the environment in the Community. Consumers have to actively contribute to the success of such collection and should be encouraged to return WEEE. For this purpose, convenient facilities should be set up for the return of WEEE, including public collection points, where private households should be able to return their waste at least free of charge.

(¹) OJ L 78, 26.3.1991, p. 38. Directive as amended by Commission Directive 98/101/EC (OJ L 1, 5.1.1999, p. 1).

(16) In order to attain the chosen level of protection and harmonised environmental objectives of the Community, Member States should adopt appropriate measures to minimise the disposal of WEEE as unsorted municipal waste and to achieve a high level of separate collection of WEEE. In order to ensure that Member States strive to set up efficient collection schemes, they should be required to achieve a high level of collection of WEEE from private households.

(17) Specific treatment for WEEE is indispensable in order to avoid the dispersion of pollutants into the recycled material or the waste stream. Such treatment is the most effective means of ensuring compliance with the chosen level of protection of the environment of the Community. Any establishment or undertakings carrying out recycling and treatment operations should comply with minimum standards to prevent negative environmental impacts associated with the treatment of WEEE. Best available treatment, recovery and recycling techniques should be used provided that they ensure human health and high environmental protection. Best available treatment, recovery and recycling techniques may be further defined in accordance with the procedures of Directive 96/61/EC.

(18) Where appropriate, priority should be given to the reuse of WEEE and its components, subassemblies and consumables. Where reuse is not preferable, all WEEE collected separately should be sent for recovery, in the course of which a high level of recycling and recovery should be achieved. In addition, producers should be encouraged to integrate recycled material in new equipment.

(19) Basic principles with regard to the financing of WEEE management have to be set at Community level and financing schemes have to contribute to high collection rates as well as to the implementation of the principle of producer responsibility.

(20) Users of electrical and electronic equipment from private households should have the possibility of returning WEEE at least free of charge. Producers should therefore finance collection from collection facilities, and the treatment, recovery and disposal of WEEE. In order to give maximum effect to the concept of producer responsibility, each producer should be responsible for financing the management of the waste from his own products. The producer should be able to choose to fulfil this obligation either individually or by joining a collective scheme. Each producer should, when placing a product on the market, provide a financial guarantee to prevent costs for the management of WEEE from orphan products from falling on society or the remaining producers. The responsibility for the financing of the management of historical waste should be shared by all existing producers in collective financing schemes to which all producers, existing on the market when the costs occur,

contribute proportionately. Collective financing schemes should not have the effect of excluding niche and low-volume producers, importers and new entrants. For a transitional period, producers should be allowed to show purchasers, on a voluntary basis at the time of sale of new products, the costs of collecting, treating and disposing in an environmentally sound way of historical waste. Producers making use of this provision should ensure that the costs mentioned do not exceed the actual costs incurred.

(21) Information to users about the requirement not to dispose of WEEE as unsorted municipal waste and to collect WEEE separately, and about the collection systems and their role in the management of WEEE, is indispensable for the success of WEEE collection. Such information implies the proper marking of electrical and electronic equipment which could end up in rubbish bins or similar means of municipal waste collection.

(22) Information on component and material identification to be provided by producers is important to facilitate the management, and in particular the treatment and recovery/recycling, of WEEE.

(23) Member States should ensure that inspection and monitoring infrastructure enable the proper implementation of this Directive to be verified, having regard, *inter alia*, to Recommendation 2001/331/EC of the European Parliament and the Council of 4 April 2001 providing for minimum criteria for environmental inspections in the Member States (¹).

(24) Information about the weight or, if this is not possible, the numbers of items of electrical and electronic equipment put on the market in the Community and the rates of collection, reuse (including as far as possible reuse of whole appliances), recovery/recycling and export of WEEE collected in accordance with this Directive is necessary to monitor the achievement of the objectives of this Directive.

(25) Member States may choose to implement certain provisions of this Directive by means of agreements between the competent authorities and the economic sectors concerned provided that particular requirements are met.

(26) The adaptation to scientific and technical progress of certain provisions of the Directive, the list of products falling under the categories set out in Annex IA, the selective treatment for materials and components of WEEE, the technical requirements for storage and treatment of WEEE and the symbol for the marking of EEE should be effected by the Commission under a committee procedure.

(27) The measures necessary for the implementation of this Directive should be adopted in accordance with Council Decision 1999/468/EC of 28 June 1999 laying down the procedures for the exercise of implementing powers conferred on the Commission (²),

HAVE ADOPTED THIS DIRECTIVE:

Article 1

Objectives

The purpose of this Directive is, as a first priority, the prevention of waste electrical and electronic equipment (WEEE), and in addition, the reuse, recycling and other forms of recovery of such wastes so as to reduce the disposal of waste. It also seeks to improve the environmental performance of all operators involved in the life cycle of electrical and electronic equipment, e.g. producers, distributors and consumers and in particular those operators directly involved in the treatment of waste electrical and electronic equipment.

Article 2

Scope

1. This Directive shall apply to electrical and electronic equipment falling under the categories set out in Annex IA provided that the equipment concerned is not part of another type of equipment that does not fall within the scope of this Directive. Annex IB contains a list of products which fall under the categories set out in Annex IA.

2. This Directive shall apply without prejudice to Community legislation on safety and health requirements and specific Community waste management legislation.

3. Equipment which is connected with the protection of the essential interests of the security of Member States, arms, munitions and war material shall be excluded from this Directive. This does not, however, apply to products which are not intended for specifically military purposes.

(¹) OJ L 118, 27.4.2001, p. 41.

(²) OJ L 184, 17.7.1999, p. 23.

Article 3

Definitions

For the purposes of this Directive, the following definitions shall apply:

(a) 'electrical and electronic equipment' or 'EEE' means equipment which is dependent on electric currents or electromagnetic fields in order to work properly and equipment for the generation, transfer and measurement of such currents and fields falling under the categories set out in Annex IA and designed for use with a voltage rating not exceeding 1 000 Volt for alternating current and 1 500 Volt for direct current;

(b) 'waste electrical and electronic equipment' or 'WEEE' means electrical or electronic equipment which is waste within the meaning of Article 1(a) of Directive 75/442/EEC, including all components, subassemblies and consumables which are part of the product at the time of discarding;

(c) 'prevention' means measures aimed at reducing the quantity and the harmfulness to the environment of WEEE and materials and substances contained therein;

(d) 'reuse' means any operation by which WEEE or components thereof are used for the same purpose for which they were conceived, including the continued use of the equipment or components thereof which are returned to collection points, distributors, recyclers or manufacturers;

(e) 'recycling' means the reprocessing in a production process of the waste materials for the original purpose or for other purposes, but excluding energy recovery which means the use of combustible waste as a means of generating energy through direct incineration with or without other waste but with recovery of the heat;

(f) 'recovery' means any of the applicable operations provided for in Annex IIB to Directive 75/442/EEC;

(g) 'disposal' means any of the applicable operations provided for in Annex IIA to Directive 75/442/EEC;

(h) 'treatment' means any activity after the WEEE has been handed over to a facility for depollution, disassembly, shredding, recovery or preparation for disposal and any other operation carried out for the recovery and/or the disposal of the WEEE;

(i) 'producer' means any person who, irrespective of the selling technique used, including by means of distance communication in accordance with Directive 97/7/EC of the European Parliament and of the Council of 20 May 1997 on the protection of consumers in respect of distance contracts (¹):

    (i) manufactures and sells electrical and electronic equipment under his own brand,

---
(¹) OJ L 144, 4.6.1997, p. 19.

    (ii) resells under his own brand equipment produced by other suppliers, a reseller not being regarded as the 'producer' if the brand of the producer appears on the equipment, as provided for in subpoint (i), or

    (iii) imports or exports electrical and electronic equipment on a professional basis into a Member State.

Whoever exclusively provides financing under or pursuant to any finance agreement shall not be deemed a 'producer' unless he also acts as a producer within the meaning of subpoints (i) to (iii);

(j) 'distributor' means any person who provides electrical or electronic equipment on a commercial basis to the party who is going to use it;

(k) 'WEEE from private households' means WEEE which comes from private households and from commercial, industrial, institutional and other sources which, because of its nature and quantity, is similar to that from private households;

(l) 'dangerous substance or preparation' means any substance or preparation which has to be considered dangerous under Council Directive 67/548/EEC (²) or Directive 1999/45/EC of the European Parliament and of the Council (³).

(m) 'finance agreement' means any loan, lease, hiring or deferred sale agreement or arrangement relating to any equipment whether or not the terms of that agreement or arrangement or any collateral agreement or arrangement provide that a transfer of ownership of that equipment will or may take place.

Article 4

Product design

Member States shall encourage the design and production of electrical and electronic equipment which take into account and facilitate dismantling and recovery, in particular the reuse and recycling of WEEE, their components and materials. In this context, Member States shall take appropriate measures so that producers do not prevent, through specific design features or manufacturing processes, WEEE from being reused, unless such specific design features or manufacturing processes present overriding advantages, for example, with regard to the protection of the environment and/or safety requirements.

Article 5

Separate collection

1.   Member States shall adopt appropriate measures in order to minimise the disposal of WEEE as unsorted municipal waste and to achieve a high level of separate collection of WEEE.

(²) OJ 196, 16.8.1967, p. 1. Directive as last amended by Commission Directive 2001/59/EC (OJ L 225, 21.8.2001, p. 1).
(³) OJ L 200, 30.7.1999, p. 1. Directive as amended by Commission Directive 2001/60/EC (OJ L 226, 22.8.2001, p. 5).

2. For WEEE from private households, Member States shall ensure that by the 13 August 2005:

(a) systems are set up allowing final holders and distributors to return such waste at least free of charge. Member States shall ensure the availability and accessibility of the necessary collection facilities, taking into account in particular the population density;

(b) when supplying a new product, distributors shall be responsible for ensuring that such waste can be returned to the distributor at least free of charge on a one-to-one basis as long as the equipment is of equivalent type and has fulfilled the same functions as the supplied equipment. Member States may depart from this provision provided they ensure that returning the WEEE is not thereby made more difficult for the final holder and provided that these systems remain free of charge for the final holder. Member States making use of this provision shall inform the Commission thereof;

(c) without prejudice to the provisions of (a) and (b), producers are allowed to set up and operate individual and/or collective take-back systems for WEEE from private households provided that these are in line with the objectives of this Directive;

(d) having regard to national and Community health and safety standards, WEEE that presents a health and safety risk to personnel because of contamination may be refused for return under (a) and (b). Member States shall make specific arrangements for such WEEE.

Member States may provide for specific arrangements for the return of WEEE as under (a) and (b) if the equipment does not contain the essential components or if the equipment contains waste other than WEEE.

3. In the case of WEEE other than WEEE from private households, and without prejudice to Article 9, Member States shall ensure that producers or third parties acting on their behalf provide for the collection of such waste.

4. Member States shall ensure that all WEEE collected under paragraphs 1, 2 and 3 above is transported to treatment facilities authorised under Article 6 unless the appliances are reused as a whole. Member States shall ensure that the envisaged reuse does not lead to a circumvention of this Directive, in particular as regards Articles 6 and 7. The collection and transport of separately collected WEEE shall be carried out in a way which optimises reuse and recycling of those components or whole appliances capable of being reused or recycled.

5. Without prejudice to paragraph 1, Member States shall ensure that by 31 December 2006 at the latest a rate of separate collection of at least four kilograms on average per inhabitant per year of WEEE from private households is achieved.

The European Parliament and the Council, acting on a proposal from the Commission and taking account of technical and economic experience in the Member States, shall establish a new mandatory target by 31 December 2008. This may take the form of a percentage of the quantities of electrical and electronic equipment sold to private households in the preceding years.

Article 6

Treatment

1. Member States shall ensure that producers or third parties acting on their behalf, in accordance with Community legislation, set up systems to provide for the treatment of WEEE using best available treatment, recovery and recycling techniques. The systems may be set up by producers individually and/or collectively. To ensure compliance with Article 4 of Directive 75/442/EEC, the treatment shall, as a minimum, include the removal of all fluids and a selective treatment in accordance with Annex II to this Directive.

Other treatment technologies ensuring at least the same level of protection for human health and the environment may be introduced in Annex II under the procedure referred to in Article 14(2).

For the purposes of environmental protection, Member States may set up minimum quality standards for the treatment of collected WEEE. Member States which opt for such quality standards shall inform the Commission thereof, which shall publish these standards.

2. Member States shall ensure that any establishment or undertaking carrying out treatment operations obtains a permit from the competent authorities, in compliance with Articles 9 and 10 of Directive 75/442/EEC.

The derogation from the permit requirement referred to in Article 11(1)(b) of Directive 75/442/EEC may apply to recovery operations concerning WEEE if an inspection is carried out by the competent authorities before the registration in order to ensure compliance with Article 4 of Directive 75/442/EEC.

The inspection shall verify:

(a) the type and quantities of waste to be treated;

(b) the general technical requirements to be complied with;

(c) the safety precautions to be taken.

The inspection shall be carried out at least once a year and the results shall be communicated by the Member States to the Commission.

3. Member States shall ensure that any establishment or undertaking carrying out treatment operations stores and treats WEEE in compliance with the technical requirements set out in Annex III.

4. Member States shall ensure that the permit or the registration referred to in paragraph 2 includes all conditions necessary for compliance with the requirements of paragraphs 1 and 3 and for the achievement of the recovery targets set out in Article 7.

5. The treatment operation may also be undertaken outside the respective Member State or the Community provided that the shipment of WEEE is in compliance with Council Regulation (EEC) No 259/93 of 1 February 1993 on the supervision and control of shipments of waste within, into and out of the European Community (¹).

WEEE exported out of the Community in line with Council Regulation (EEC) No 259/93, Council Regulation (EC) No 1420/1999 (²) of 29 April 1999 establishing common rules and procedures to apply to shipments to certain non-OECD countries of certain types of waste and Commission Regulation (EC) No 1547/1999 (³) of 12 July 1999 determining the control procedures under Council Regulation (EEC) No 259/93 to apply to shipments of certain types of waste to certain countries to which OECD Decision C(92)39 final does not apply, shall only count for the fulfilment of obligations and targets of Article 7(1) and (2) of this Directive if the exporter can prove that the recovery, reuse and/or recycling operation took place under conditions that are equivalent to the requirements of this Directive.

6. Member States shall encourage establishments or undertakings which carry out treatment operations to introduce certified environmental management systems in accordance with Regulation (EC) No 761/2001 of the European Parliament and of the Council of 19 March 2001 allowing voluntary participation by organisations in a Community eco-management and audit scheme (EMAS) (⁴).

Article 7

Recovery

1. Member States shall ensure that producers or third parties acting on their behalf set up systems either on an individual or on a collective basis, in accordance with Community legislation, to provide for the recovery of WEEE collected separately in accordance with Article 5. Member States shall give priority to the reuse of whole appliances. Until the date referred to in paragraph 4, such appliances shall not be taken into account for the calculation of the targets set out in paragraph 2.

2. Regarding WEEE sent for treatment in accordance with Article 6, Member States shall ensure that, by 31 December 2006, producers meet the following targets:

(a) for WEEE falling under categories 1 and 10 of Annex IA,

— the rate of recovery shall be increased to a minimum of 80 % by an average weight per appliance, and

---

(¹) OJ L 30, 6.2.1993, p. 1. Regulation as last amended by Commission Regulation (EC) No 2557/2001 (OJ L 349, 31.12.2001, p. 1).
(²) OJ L 166, 1.7.1999, p. 6. Regulation as last amended by Commission Regulation (EC) No 2243/2001 (OJ L 303, 20.11.2001, p. 11).
(³) OJ L 185, 17.7.1999, p 1. Regulation as last amended by Commission Regulation (EC) No 2243/2001.
(⁴) OJ L 114, 24.4.2001, p. 1.

— component, material and substance reuse and recycling shall be increased to a minimum of 75 % by an average weight per appliance;

(b) for WEEE falling under categories 3 and 4 of Annex IA,

— the rate of recovery shall be increased to a minimum of 75 % by an average weight per appliance, and

— component, material and substance reuse and recycling shall be increased to a minimum of 65 % by an average weight per appliance;

(c) for WEEE falling under categories 2, 5, 6, 7 and 9 of Annex IA,

— the rate of recovery shall be increased to a minimum of 70 % by an average weight per appliance, and

— component, material and substance reuse and recycling shall be increased to a minimum of 50 % by an average weight per appliance;

(d) for gas discharge lamps, the rate of component, material and substance reuse and recycling shall reach a minimum of 80 % by weight of the lamps.

3. Member States shall ensure that, for the purpose of calculating these targets, producers or third parties acting on their behalf keep records on the mass of WEEE, their components, materials or substances when entering (input) and leaving (output) the treatment facility and/or when entering (input) the recovery or recycling facility.

The Commission shall, in accordance with the procedure laid down in Article 14(2), establish the detailed rules for monitoring compliance, including specifications for materials, of Member States with the targets set out in paragraph 2. The Commission shall submit this measure by 13 August 2004.

4. The European Parliament and the Council, acting on a proposal from the Commission, shall establish new targets for recovery and reuse/recycling, including for the reuse of whole appliances as appropriate, and for the products falling under category 8 of Annex IA, by 31 December 2008. This shall be done with account being taken of the environmental benefits of electrical and electronic equipment in use, such as improved resource efficiency resulting from developments in the areas of materials and technology. Technical progress in reuse, recovery and recycling, products and materials, and the experience gained by the Member States and the industry, shall also be taken into account.

5. Member States shall encourage the development of new recovery, recycling and treatment technologies.

Article 8

Financing in respect of WEEE from private households

1.   Member States shall ensure that, by 13 August 2005, producers provide at least for the financing of the collection, treatment, recovery and environmentally sound disposal of WEEE from private households deposited at collection facilities, set up under Article 5(2).

2.   For products put on the market later than 13 August 2005, each producer shall be responsible for financing the operations referred to in paragraph 1 relating to the waste from his own products. The producer can choose to fulfil this obligation either individually or by joining a collective scheme.

Member States shall ensure that each producer provides a guarantee when placing a product on the market showing that the management of all WEEE will be financed and that producers clearly mark their products in accordance with Article 11(2). This guarantee shall ensure that the operations referred to in paragraph 1 relating to this product will be financed. The guarantee may take the form of participation by the producer in appropriate schemes for the financing of the management of WEEE, a recycling insurance or a blocked bank account.

The costs of collection, treatment and environmentally sound disposal shall not be shown separately to purchasers at the time of sale of new products.

3.   The responsibility for the financing of the costs of the management of WEEE from products put on the market before the date referred to in paragraph 1 (historical waste) shall be provided by one or more systems to which all producers, existing on the market when the respective costs occur, contribute proportionately, e.g. in proportion to their respective share of the market by type of equipment.

Member States shall ensure that for a transitional period of eight years (10 years for category 1 of Annex IA) after entry into force of this Directive, producers are allowed to show purchasers, at the time of sale of new products, the costs of collection, treatment and disposal in an environmentally sound way. The costs mentioned shall not exceed the actual costs incurred.

4.   Member States shall ensure that producers supplying electrical or electronic equipment by means of distance communication also comply with the requirements set out in this Article for the equipment supplied in the Member State where the purchaser of that equipment resides.

Article 9

Financing in respect of WEEE from users other than private households

Member States shall ensure that, by 13 August 2005, the financing of the costs for the collection, treatment, recovery and environmentally sound disposal of WEEE from users other than private households from products put on the market after 13 August 2005 is to be provided for by producers.

For WEEE from products put on the market before 13 August 2005 (historical waste), the financing of the costs of management shall be provided for by producers. Member States may, as an alternative, provide that users other than private households also be made, partly or totally, responsible for this financing.

Producers and users other than private households may, without prejudice to this Directive, conclude agreements stipulating other financing methods.

Article 10

Information for users

1.   Member States shall ensure that users of electrical and electronic equipment in private households are given the necessary information about:

(a) the requirement not to dispose of WEEE as unsorted municipal waste and to collect such WEEE separately;

(b) the return and collection systems available to them;

(c) their role in contributing to reuse, recycling and other forms of recovery of WEEE;

(d) the potential effects on the environment and human health as a result of the presence of hazardous substances in electrical and electronic equipment;

(e) the meaning of the symbol shown in Annex IV.

2.   Member States shall adopt appropriate measures so that consumers participate in the collection of WEEE and to encourage them to facilitate the process of reuse, treatment and recovery.

3.   With a view to minimising the disposal of WEEE as unsorted municipal waste and to facilitating its separate collection, Member States shall ensure that producers appropriately mark electrical and electronic equipment put on the market after 13 August 2005 with the symbol shown in Annex IV. In exceptional cases, where this is necessary because of the size or the function of the product, the symbol shall be printed on the packaging, on the instructions for use and on the warranty of the electrical and electronic equipment.

4.   Member States may require that some or all of the information referred to in paragraphs 1 to 3 shall be provided by producers and/or distributors, e.g. in the instructions for use or at the point of sale.

Article 11

Information for treatment facilities

1. In order to facilitate the reuse and the correct and environmentally sound treatment of WEEE, including maintenance, upgrade, refurbishment and recycling, Member States shall take the necessary measures to ensure that producers provide reuse and treatment information for each type of new EEE put on the market within one year after the equipment is put on the market. This information shall identify, as far as it is needed by reuse centres, treatment and recycling facilities in order to comply with the provisions of this Directive, the different EEE components and materials, as well as the location of dangerous substances and preparations in EEE. It shall be made available to reuse centres, treatment and recycling facilities by producers of EEE in the form of manuals or by means of electronic media (e.g. CD-ROM, online services).

2. Member States shall ensure that any producer of an electrical or electronic appliance put on the market after 13 August 2005 is clearly identifiable by a mark on the appliance. Furthermore, in order to enable the date upon which the appliance was put on the market to be determined unequivocally, a mark on the appliance shall specify that the latter was put on the market after 13 August 2005 The Commission shall promote the preparation of European standards for this purpose.

Article 12

Information and reporting

1. Member States shall draw up a register of producers and collect information, including substantiated estimates, on an annual basis on the quantities and categories of electrical and electronic equipment put on their market, collected through all routes, reused, recycled and recovered within the Member States, and on collected waste exported, by weight or, if this is not possible, by numbers.

Member States shall ensure that producers supplying electrical and electronic equipment by means of distance communication provide information on the compliance with the requirements of Article 8(4) and on the quantities and categories of electrical and electronic equipment put on the market of the Member State where the purchaser of that equipment resides.

Member States shall ensure that the information required is transmitted to the Commission on a two-yearly basis within 18 months after the end of the period covered. The first set of information shall cover the years 2005 and 2006. The information shall be provided in a format which shall be established within one year after the entry into force of this Directive in accordance with the procedure referred to in Article 14(2) with a view to establishing databases on WEEE and its treatment.

Member States shall provide for adequate information exchange in order to comply with this paragraph, in particular for treatment operations as referred to in Article 6(5).

2. Without prejudice to the requirements of paragraph 1, Member States shall send a report to the Commission on the implementation of this Directive at three-year intervals. The report shall be drawn up on the basis of a questionnaire or outline drafted by the Commission in accordance with the procedure laid down in Article 6 of Council Directive 91/692/EEC of 23 December 1991 standardising and rationalising reports on the implementation of certain Directives relating to the environment ([1]). The questionnaire or outline shall be sent to the Member States six months before the start of the period covered by the report. The report shall be made available to the Commission within nine months of the end of the three-year period covered by it.

The first three-year report shall cover the period from 2004 to 2006.

The Commission shall publish a report on the implementation of this Directive within nine months after receiving the reports from the Member States.

Article 13

Adaptation to scientific and technical progress

Any amendments which are necessary in order to adapt Article 7(3), Annex IB, (in particular with a view to possibly adding luminaires in households, filament bulbs and photovoltaic products, i.e. solar panels), Annex II (in particular taking into account new technical developments for the treatment of WEEE), and Annexes III and IV to scientific and technical progress shall be adopted in accordance with the procedure referred to in Article 14(2).

Before the Annexes are amended the Commission shall *inter alia* consult producers of electrical and electronic equipment, recyclers, treatment operators and environmental organisations and employees' and consumer associations.

Article 14

Committee

1. The Commission shall be assisted by the Committee set up by Article 18 of Directive 75/442/EEC.

2. Where reference is made to this paragraph, Articles 5 and 7 of Decision 1999/468/EC shall apply, having regard to Article 8 thereof.

The period laid down in Article 5(6) of Decision 1999/468/EC shall be set at three months.

3. The Committee shall adopt its rules of procedure.

([1]) OJ L 377, 31.12.1991, p. 48.

Article 15

Penalties

Member States shall determine penalties applicable to breaches of the national provisions adopted pursuant to this Directive. The penalties thus provided for shall be effective, proportionate and dissuasive.

Article 16

Inspection and monitoring

Member States shall ensure that inspection and monitoring enable the proper implementation of this Directive to be verified.

Article 17

Transposition

1. Member States shall bring into force the laws, regulations and administrative provisions necessary to comply with this Directive by 13 August 2004. They shall immediately inform the Commission thereof.

When Member States adopt these measures, they shall contain a reference to this Directive or be accompanied by such reference on the occasion of their official publication. The methods of making such a reference shall be laid down by the Member States.

2. Member States shall communicate to the Commission the text of all laws, regulations and administrative provisions adopted in the field covered by this Directive.

3. Provided that the objectives set out in this Directive are achieved, Member States may transpose the provisions set out in Articles 6(6), 10(1) and 11 by means of agreements between the competent authorities and the economic sectors concerned. Such agreements shall meet the following requirements:

(a) agreements shall be enforceable;

(b) agreements shall specify objectives with the corresponding deadlines;

(c) agreements shall be published in the national official journal or an official document equally accessible to the public and transmitted to the Commission;

(d) the results achieved shall be monitored regularly, reported to the competent authorities and the Commission and made available to the public under the conditions set out in the agreement;

(e) the competent authorities shall ensure that the progress reached under the agreement is examined;

(f) in case of non-compliance with the agreement Member States must implement the relevant provisions of this Directive by legislative, regulatory or administrative measures.

4. (a) Greece and Ireland which, because of their overall:
   — recycling infrastructure deficit,
   — geographical circumstances such as the large number of small islands and the presence of rural and mountain areas,
   — low population density, and
   — low level of EEE consumption,

   are unable to reach either the collection target mentioned in the first subparagraph of Article 5(5) or the recovery targets mentioned in Article 7(2) and which, under the third subparagraph of Article 5(2) of Council Directive 1999/31/EC of 26 April 1999 on the landfill of waste ([1]), may apply for an extension of the deadline mentioned in that Article,

   may extend the periods referred to in Articles 5(5) and 7(2) of this Directive by up to 24 months.

   These Member States shall inform the Commission of their Decisions at the latest at the time of transposition of this Directive.

   (b) The Commission shall inform other Member States and the European Parliament of these decisions.

5. Within five years after the entry into force of this Directive, the Commission shall submit a report to the European Parliament and the Council based on the experience of the application of this Directive, in particular as regards separate collection, treatment, recovery and financing systems. Furthermore the report shall be based on the development of the state of technology, experience gained, environmental requirements and the functioning of the internal market. The report shall, as appropriate, be accompanied by proposals for revision of the relevant provisions of this Directive.

Article 18

Entry into force

This Directive shall enter into force on the day of its publication in the *Official Journal of the European Union*.

Article 19

Addressees

This Directive is addressed to the Member States.

Done at Brussels, 27 January 2003.

For the European Parliament	*For the Council*
The President	*The President*
P. COX	G. DRYS

([1]) OJ L 182, 16.7.1999, p. 1.

ANNEX IA

Categories of electrical and electronic equipment covered by this Directive

1. Large household appliances
2. Small household appliances
3. IT and telecommunications equipment
4. Consumer equipment
5. Lighting equipment
6. Electrical and electronic tools (with the exception of large-scale stationary industrial tools)
7. Toys, leisure and sports equipment
8. Medical devices (with the exception of all implanted and infected products)
9. Monitoring and control instruments
10. Automatic dispensers

ANNEX IB

List of products which shall be taken into account for the purpose of this Directive and which fall under the categories of Annex IA

1. Large household appliances

   Large cooling appliances

   Refrigerators

   Freezers

   Other large appliances used for refrigeration, conservation and storage of food

   Washing machines

   Clothes dryers

   Dish washing machines

   Cooking

   Electric stoves

   Electric hot plates

   Microwaves

   Other large appliances used for cooking and other processing of food

   Electric heating appliances

   Electric radiators

   Other large appliances for heating rooms, beds, seating furniture

   Electric fans

   Air conditioner appliances

   Other fanning, exhaust ventilation and conditioning equipment

2. Small household appliances

   Vacuum cleaners

   Carpet sweepers

   Other appliances for cleaning

   Appliances used for sewing, knitting, weaving and other processing for textiles

   Irons and other appliances for ironing, mangling and other care of clothing

   Toasters

   Fryers

   Grinders, coffee machines and equipment for opening or sealing containers or packages

   Electric knives

   Appliances for hair-cutting, hair drying, tooth brushing, shaving, massage and other body care appliances

   Clocks, watches and equipment for the purpose of measuring, indicating or registering time

   Scales

3. IT and telecommunications equipment

   Centralised data processing:

   Mainframes

   Minicomputers

   Printer units

   Personal computing:

   Personal computers (CPU, mouse, screen and keyboard included)

   Laptop computers (CPU, mouse, screen and keyboard included)

Notebook computers

Notepad computers

Printers

Copying equipment

Electrical and electronic typewriters

Pocket and desk calculators

and other products and equipment for the collection, storage, processing, presentation or communication of information by electronic means

User terminals and systems

Facsimile

Telex

Telephones

Pay telephones

Cordless telephones

Cellular telephones

Answering systems

and other products or equipment of transmitting sound, images or other information by telecommunications

4. Consumer equipment

Radio sets

Television sets

Videocameras

Video recorders

Hi-fi recorders

Audio amplifiers

Musical instruments

And other products or equipment for the purpose of recording or reproducing sound or images, including signals or other technologies for the distribution of sound and image than by telecommunications

5. Lighting equipment

Luminaires for fluorescent lamps with the exception of luminaires in households

Straight fluorescent lamps

Compact fluorescent lamps

High intensity discharge lamps, including pressure sodium lamps and metal halide lamps

Low pressure sodium lamps

Other lighting or equipment for the purpose of spreading or controlling light with the exception of filament bulbs

6. Electrical and electronic tools (with the exception of large-scale stationary industrial tools)

Drills

Saws

Sewing machines

Equipment for turning, milling, sanding, grinding, sawing, cutting, shearing, drilling, making holes, punching, folding, bending or similar processing of wood, metal and other materials

Tools for riveting, nailing or screwing or removing rivets, nails, screws or similar uses

Tools for welding, soldering or similar use

Equipment for spraying, spreading, dispersing or other treatment of liquid or gaseous substances by other means

Tools for mowing or other gardening activities

7. Toys, leisure and sports equipment

Electric trains or car racing sets
Hand-held video game consoles
Video games
Computers for biking, diving, running, rowing, etc.
Sports equipment with electric or electronic components
Coin slot machines

8. Medical devices (with the exception of all implanted and infected products)

Radiotherapy equipment
Cardiology
Dialysis
Pulmonary ventilators
Nuclear medicine
Laboratory equipment for *in-vitro* diagnosis
Analysers
Freezers
Fertilization tests
Other appliances for detecting, preventing, monitoring, treating, alleviating illness, injury or disability

9. Monitoring and control instruments

Smoke detector
Heating regulators
Thermostats
Measuring, weighing or adjusting appliances for household or as laboratory equipment
Other monitoring and control instruments used in industrial installations (e.g. in control panels)

10. Automatic dispensers

Automatic dispensers for hot drinks
Automatic dispensers for hot or cold bottles or cans
Automatic dispensers for solid products
Automatic dispensers for money
All appliances which deliver automatically all kind of products

ANNEX II

Selective treatment for materials and components of waste electrical and electronic equipment in accordance with Article 6(1)

1. As a minimum the following substances, preparations and components have to be removed from any separately collected WEEE:
   — polychlorinated biphenyls (PCB) containing capacitors in accordance with Council Directive 96/59/EC of 16 September 1996 on the disposal of polychlorinated biphenyls and polychlorinated terphenyls (PCB/PCT) (¹),
   — mercury containing components, such as switches or backlighting lamps,
   — batteries,
   — printed circuit boards of mobile phones generally, and of other devices if the surface of the printed circuit board is greater than 10 square centimetres,
   — toner cartridges, liquid and pasty, as well as colour toner,
   — plastic containing brominated flame retardants,
   — asbestos waste and components which contain asbestos,
   — cathode ray tubes,
   — chlorofluorocarbons (CFC), hydrochlorofluorocarbons (HCFC) or hydrofluorocarbons (HFC), hydrocarbons (HC),
   — gas discharge lamps,
   — liquid crystal displays (together with their casing where appropriate) of a surface greater than 100 square centimetres and all those back-lighted with gas discharge lamps,
   — external electric cables,
   — components containing refractory ceramic fibres as described in Commission Directive 97/69/EC of 5 December 1997 adapting to technical progress Council Directive 67/548/EEC relating to the classification, packaging and labelling of dangerous substances (²),
   — components containing radioactive substances with the exception of components that are below the exemption thresholds set in Article 3 of and Annex I to Council Directive 96/29/Euratom of 13 May 1996 laying down basic safety standards for the protection of the health of workers and the general public against the dangers arising from ionising radiation (³),
   — electrolyte capacitors containing substances of concern (height > 25 mm, diameter > 25 mm or proportionately similar volume)

   These substances, preparations and components shall be disposed of or recovered in compliance with Article 4 of Council Directive 75/442/EEC.

2. The following components of WEEE that is separately collected have to be treated as indicated:
   — cathode ray tubes: The fluorescent coating has to be removed,
   — equipment containing gases that are ozone depleting or have a global warming potential (GWP) above 15, such as those contained in foams and refrigeration circuits: the gases must be properly extracted and properly treated. Ozone-depleting gases must be treated in accordance with Regulation (EC) No 2037/2000 of the European Parliament and of the Council of 29 June 2000 on substances that deplete the ozone layer (⁴).
   — gas discharge lamps: The mercury shall be removed.

3. Taking into account environmental considerations and the desirability of reuse and recycling, paragraphs 1 and 2 shall be applied in such a way that environmentally-sound reuse and recycling of components or whole appliances is not hindered.

4. Within the procedure referred to in Article 14(2), the Commission shall evaluate as a matter of priority whether the entries regarding:
   — printed circuit boards for mobile phones, and
   — liquid crystal displays
   are to be amended.

(¹) OJ L 243, 24.9.1996, p. 31.
(²) OJ L 343, 13.12.1997, p. 19.
(³) OJ L 159, 29.6.1996, p. 1.
(⁴) OJ L 244, 29.9.2000, p. 1. Regulation as last amended by Regulation (EC) No 2039/2000 (OJ L 244, 29.9.2000, p. 26).

ANNEX III

Technical requirements in accordance with Article 6(3)

1. Sites for storage (including temporary storage) of WEEE prior to their treatment (without prejudice to the requirements of Council Directive 1999/31/EC):
   — impermeable surfaces for appropriate areas with the provision of spillage collection facilities and, where appropriate, decanters and cleanser-degreasers,
   — weatherproof covering for appropriate areas.
2. Sites for treatment of WEEE:
   — balances to measure the weight of the treated waste,
   — impermeable surfaces and waterproof covering for appropriate areas with the provision of spillage collection facilities and, where appropriate, decanters and cleanser-degreasers,
   — appropriate storage for disassembled spare parts,
   — appropriate containers for storage of batteries, PCBs/PCTs containing capacitors and other hazardous waste such as radioactive waste,
   — equipment for the treatment of water in compliance with health and environmental regulations.

———

ANNEX IV

Symbol for the marking of electrical and electronic equipment

The symbol indicating separate collection for electrical and electronic equipment consists of the crossed-out wheeled bin, as shown below. The symbol must be printed visibly, legibly and indelibly.

INDEX

A

Accounting, computerized systems for, 175, 179–180, 182
Advanced systems and technology
  bar coding, 183–184
  configuration control applications, 185–186
  for consumer goods, 176–178
  examples, 28, 54, 58, 176–178, 198–199
  functional specifications, 180–183
  for high tech products, 177, 179–180
  impact and value, 176, 180, 187, 192
  key functions, 175–177, 179–180
  life cycle costs, 3–4
  for logistics support, 175–192
  radio frequency identification system, 184–185
  selected vendor list, 187–191
  service-oriented
    business strategies, 19–20, 195
    importance, 5, 7, 29, 56, 199–200
  state-of-the-art, 180, 186–187
  warranty claim processing, 164–166
Aerospace, depot repair market, 51, 53
Analytical instruments, outsourcing reverse logistics, 31
Apparel
  life cycle, 115–116
  reverse logistics market, 48, 151, 177
Appliances, see White goods
Application service provider (ASP), 176, 200–201
Assembling, as manufacturing, 118

ATE softwar/fixturing, depot repair market, 52–53, 144
Automation
  benchmarking logistics support, 88–90, 93–94
  depot repair market, 51, 53, 143
  sales, see Point-of-sale (POS) automation
Automotive products, reverse logistics market, 49, 168

B

Baldrige Award, 87
Bar coding, 183–184
  for closed loop supply chain, 83–84
  for repair depot systems, 185
Bayesian inference, for high tech demand forecasting, 78–79, 81–82
Benchmarking
  depot repair models, 144, 146–148
  high tech product management, 87–102
    CLSC vs. simple RL process impact, 92–93, 95–96
    data sources, 88–89
    forecasting impact, 92, 97–98, 100
    objectives, 87–88
    product and technology impact, 92–94
    return velocity rates impact, 98, 101–102
    support organizations researched, 88–91
  targets, 5, 195
  warranty claim processing, 162–164

improved performance from, 165
    by independent firms, 165–166
Billing, computerized systems for, 175, 179,
    182
Brand choice, modeling of, 123
Branding, impact on returns
    of consumer goods, 122–124
    of technology, 122
Brand loyalty, influencing factors, 123–124
Broken calls, 69–70
Brown goods (electronics)
    commerical and industrial products vs.,
        204–205
    depot repair market, 51–53
    life cycle, 115–116
        costs, 3, 26–27
        returns and, 117–118, 120–122, 125
        support responsibility, 25, 118
    managing systems and technology for,
        118, 177
    product returns, 117–118
        actual rates, 127, 129–130, 132
        defective, 125, 127–130
    repair processes, 23–24
    reverse logistics
        benchmarking, 88–89, 91, 93–94
        key components, 34–35
        market, 47–48
        organization and structure, 117–120
        outsourcing potential, 31
    secondary markets, 169–170
Building equipment/systems
    depot repair market, 143
    reverse logistics
        benchmarking, 88–90, 93–94
        market, 46, 49
Business models, 12–18
    closed loop supply chain
        alternative for high tech products,
            13–15, 17
        consumer-oriented, 14–18
        full, 16–17
        for high tech products, 13–15
        for low tech products, 13–14, 17
    development stages, 194–195
    reverse logistics
        basic, 12–13, 37, 39
        embedded, 20
Business plan, 194–195
Business strategy(ies)
    for e-commerce, 172–174

    service-oriented, 19–20, 24, 40–41
    steps in developing, 194–195
    vendor perspectives, 209
Buyer behavior
    consumables returns, 125–126
    shift from in-store to non-store, 28, 39
    use of outside providers, 56, 59–60
    warranty perceptions, 153, 158–159

C

Call avoidance, 27, 59, 67–69, 85
Call management process
    benchmarking high tech products,
        88–91, 95–100
    for service requests, 67–70, 85
Capital investment, 28, 30, 39
Cash registers, see Point-of-sale (POS)
    automation
Chemical products, reverse logistics market,
    49
Circuit boards, 23
Closed loop supply chain (CLSC)
    business models, 12–18, 194–195
    business strategies, 19, 24, 40, 194–195,
        209
    consumer goods management, 107–137
    consumer-oriented, 14–18, 28
    depot repair and, 139–151
    framework for analysis, 5–6, 9–11,
        21–22, 193
    general market applications, 4–5, 12
    green laws impact, 28, 205–207
    high tech product management, 65–106
    increased interest in, 1–3, 23–24, 28
    management model, 193–210
    markets, 37–63
    quantitative forecast models, 2, 4–5, 199
    service-oriented, 19–20, 24, 40–41
    software for, 198–199
    strategic issues, 19–20, 194
Clothing, see Apparel
Commercial off-the-shelf (COTS) market,
        life cycle support patterns,
        28–29
Commercial product management, 4
    brown and white goods vs., 204–205
    life cycle support, 24, 27–29
    offshore secondary markets, 168–171
    returned products and, 8–9
Communications products/network

depot repair market, 51, 53, 143
for field service persons, 98–99
reverse logistics
key components, 34–35
market, 41, 46
outsourcing potential, 31
Compensation payment, as warranty
mechanism, 153–155
Competitive evaluation, of market
segments, 57–63
Computer-aided logistics support (CALS),
180
Computer technology; see also Software
for accounting, 175, 179–180, 182
for billing, 175, 179, 182
branding impact, 122
for customer relations management, 198
depot repair market, 51, 53, 143,
198–199
life cycle support, 3–4, 25–27
for logistics support, see Advanced
systems and technology
personal, 115–116, 118, 121
for procurement source management,
86–87, 172–173
reverse logistics
key components, 34–35
market, 46
outsourcing potential, 31
Confidentiality, of data, 30
Configuration control systems
advantages, 185
computerized, 175, 179–180
new developments, 186
protocols, 185–186
Consolidation centers, reduction of
returned goods, 134, 136–137
Consumer awareness, influence of, 28, 39
Consumer goods
anecdotal examples, 10
life cycle, 4, 25
as market segment, 1–2, 37–38, 50
offshore secondary markets, 168–171
recovery from end users, 7–8, 145,
149–151
return dynamics, 7–9, 18–19, 133
averages and metrics, 124–131
factors influencing, 112–137
reverse logistics management, 107–137
benchmarking, 88–89, 91, 93–94
branding impact, 122–124

competitive evaluation, 62–63
data collection for, 194, 196–197
key components, 34–35
life cycle impact, 115–118, 120–122,
125
manufacturer structure, 107–110
organization and structure, 117–120
outsourcing potential, 31–32
overview, 107, 137
practices to date, 132–137
process, 14–18
recommendations, 5, 207–210
retail distribution factor, 118–119
retailer/distributer structure, 108–115
retail policies and processes impact,
112–115, 118
returned products centralization, 133
returned products impact, 112–137
returned products issues, 114, 117,
127, 132–133
returned products statistics, 124–131
subsegments, 48–49
systems and technology for, 176–177
Consumer-oriented closed loop supply
chain, 14–18, 28
Containers; see also Packing, pallets, and
containers
reuseable, 28, 40
outsourcing reverse logistics, 31–32
Contract life cycle management (CLCM),
computerized systems for, 175,
181
Contract manufacturing, 54, 58, 142
Contracts, as consumables return factor, 127
Corporations, consumer goods reverse
logistics for, 107–109, 113
Cosmetics
life cycle, 115–116
reverse logistics market, 49
Cost center, field service as, 65–67
Cost competitiveness
in life cycle management, 3–4, 15,
25–27
for reverse logistics, 62, 171–172
sellers' desire for, 28, 39, 160
service process designs, 65–67, 73
in warranty process, 157–158, 160, 163,
165
Courier/van delivery
alliances with, 69, 85–86, 171, 178, 208
real-time control, 199, 201

Customer asset management strategy, 19, 28, 39–40
    data on existing processes, 194, 196–197
Customer complaints, in warranty management, 159, 162–164
Customer relationship management (CRM), software systems for, 176, 186–187
    vendors, 198–199
Customer satisfaction
    brand loyalty and, 123–124
    as consumables returns factor, 125–129, 132
    as field service goal, 65–66, 73
    retail chain strategy for, 113
    in warranty management, 159
Customer service, consumer goods reverse logistics for, 108, 110, 113
Customer site stocks, 175

D

Damaged products, as consumables return factor, 125, 127–130
Data
    confidentiality of, 30
    configuration, see Configuration control systems
    for consumer goods reverse logistics, 194, 196–197
    on high tech products
        for demand forecasting, 77–78, 80
        for service benchmarking, 88–89
Database management and reporting (DBMR), computerized systems for logistical, 175, 179–180, 182
Data processing technology, life cycle costs, 3–4
Dealers; see also Vendors
    warranty management and, 159–162
Decomposition, as depot repair practice, 145, 149–151
Defective products, as consumables return factor, 125, 127–130, 135
Delivery
    end-to-end for high tech products, 73, 86–87
    included in product sale, 65–66
    of parts or subassembly service
        in closed loop supply chain, 71–74, 86

    delayed, 69–70
    real-time control, 81, 199, 201
    return cost as issue, 205
Demand forecasting, for high tech products, 74, 77–82, 84
Demanufacturing, as depot repair practice, 145, 149–151
Department of Defense (DOD), see Military systems support
Department stores, reverse logistics market, 49, 135–137
Depot repair providers/systems
    computerized systems for, 175, 179, 183
    increased interest of, 2, 11, 28
    job shop approach, 144–145
    just in time approach, 74, 84, 144–145
    markets
        2001-2003 major segments, 43, 53, 118
        captive vs. outsourced, 55–58
        competitive evaluation, 57, 61–62
        demand per segments, 43, 51–52
        growth phases, 139–140
        North America, 42–43
        supply availability, 43, 45
        value-added services, 43, 54–57
    partnering with suppliers, 29, 201–202, 208
    reasons for using, 40, 118
    role of, 139–151
        benchmarking, 144, 146–148
        business models, 13–17
        in CLSC vs. simple RL, 145, 149–151
        external design, 144–148
        high tech products, 71–74, 76
        internal design, 144–148
        introduction, 139–141
        market structure, 12, 62, 141–144
        operating models, 144–145
        practices supporting, 145, 149
        reduction process, 145, 149–151
    software for, 52–53, 144, 198–199
Depot reworking/refurbishment operations control (DRROC), computerized systems for, 175, 179, 182
Device relationship management (DRM), 186
Diagnostic services
    in closed loop supply chain, 12
    remote, 27, 67–70, 85
Direct supply chain management

in closed loop supply chain, 12, 15–16
reverse logistics vs., 28–29, 208
revolutionary, 1–2, 6–8
traditional, 6
Disassembling, as depot repair practice,
145, 149–151
Discount merchandisers, of consumer
goods, 111
Disposal and disposal services
advanced technology development, 28
in closed loop supply chain, 12
business models, 12–16
original equipment manufacturer
responsibility, 118, 206
repair vs., 7–8, 118
typical historical, 66
Distribution channels
end-to-end for high tech products, 73,
86–87
indirect, warranty management and,
159–162
physical, computerized systems for, 175,
179, 182
reduction of returned goods, 132–137
retail types, 111–112
impact on returns, 118–119, 124–125
reverse logistics
as competitors, 59, 61–62
consumer goods management,
108–115, 132–137
depot repair, 141–143
in-house, 28, 30
service outside providers, 59
value complexity driven by, 4, 6, 20, 28
Document control, computerized systems
for, 175, 179–180, 182
Document storage and retrieval,
computerized systems for, 175,
179, 182
Drawing control, computerized systems for,
175, 179–180
Durable goods
managing systems and technology for,
177
product return issues, 205
reverse logistics market, 48, 115

E

E-commerce
as advanced management tool, 176–178,
200

challenges facing, 173–174
returned products, 136–137
as secondary market, 172–174
Economic issues
environmental concerns vs., 203–205
quantification of, 4–5
of reverse logistics, 7–8, 15–16
Economic value
of end products, 1–3, 168
of returned products, 23–24, 171
of service and support, 25–26
Efficiency impact
of advanced systems and technology,
176, 180, 187, 192
of closed loop supply chain, for high
tech products, 74–77, 87–88,
105–106
Electrical equipment, reverse logistics
market, 47
Electronic goods
consumer, see Brown goods
medial, see Medical equipment/supplies
Electronic manufacturing service (EMS)
providers, 142
E-marketplaces, see E-commerce
End-of-life management, 54, 58, 60
secondary markets, 168, 171
End-to-end approach, to closed loop
supply chain, 73, 86–87
End user
advanced support resources for,
198–202
control by, 6, 17
demand forecasting for high tech
products, 77, 79
life cycle support responsibility, 24–25
orientation to product, 66
product reclamation from, 32, 40
product return behavior, 7–9, 16–17, 39,
205
Engineering changes, derived from
warranty data, 156–158
Entitlement, 59
Entrepreneurs, in secondary markets,
172–173
Environmental concerns
economic issues vs., 203–205
increased interest in, 1–3, 7, 33, 206
Equipment configuration maintenance
(ECM), computerized systems
for, 175, 179, 181
European Union (EU), green laws, 2, 7, 204

long-term impact, 205–207
Exchanges, secondary markets for, 168, 170
Exponential smoothing, in high tech
    demand forecasting, 81–82
External depot repair operations, 144–148

F

Failure rate
    product, tracking through warranties,
      156–157
    product life cycle vs., 26–27, 118
Field service
    call management process, 67–69
      timeline, 69–70
    for consumer goods reverse logistics,
      108, 110
    cost center approach, 65–67
    full closed loop control for, 16–17
    for high tech products modular repair,
      2, 5, 7, 23, 70–73, 118, 120
    as important focus, 5, 7
    life cycle support, 28–29
    profitability strategies, 71, 74–75, 87
    returned products impact, 7–8, 118
    warranties and, 16, 156–157
Field service management systems (FSMS)
    communication devices, 98–99
    as integrated, 27, 72–73, 85, 141, 176,
      186–187
Financial automation, retail, benchmarking
    logistics support, 88–90, 93–94
Financial control and accounting (FCA)
    computerized systems for, 175, 179–180,
      182
    for consumer goods reverse logistics,
      107–109
Flexibility, in reverse logistics process, 41
Food products
    centralization of returns, 132–133, 135
    life cycle, 115–116
    reverse logistics market, 48–49, 132
Forecast models
    for closed loop supply chain
      management, 77–82, 84
      benchmarking high tech products,
        92, 97–98, 100
    for inventory, 175, 179, 181
      key operating parameters, 98, 100
    for materials and manufacturing
      scheduling, 74

quantitative market, 2, 4–5, 199
Forward logistics
    in closed loop supply chain, 12
    markets, 44–45
Fourth party service providers, see Depot
      repair providers/systems
Full closed loop control, 16–17, 28, 92
Full repair and return logistics, as
      competitors, 57, 61–62
Full swap out, see Pull-and-replace
      products
Furniture, secondary markets, 170

G

General merchandise, reverse logistics
      market, 49, 135–137
Geographic focus, of business strategy, 209
Global markets
    for reverse logistics and repair services,
      42
    as secondary markets, 171–172
      demand forecasting, 77, 79
Goods, see Consumer goods
Government; see also Green laws
    business model, 15–16
    increased interest of, 3, 29, 115
Green laws
    as driving force, 3, 39, 171
    European Union, 2, 7, 204
    long-term impact, 28, 205–207
Green products
    claim validation, 31
    control perspectives, 11, 204
    as market segment, 37–38, 50
    regulations, 2, 7, 15, 204
    reverse logistics
      key components, 34–35
      outsourcing potential, 31
Groceries, see Food products

H

Hazardous waste
    containerized categories, 33
    green law regulations, 15, 204
    ncreased interest in, 1–2, 7
    reverse logistics
      key components, 34–35
      market, 47, 49–50
      outsourcing potential, 33

High tech products/services
    anecdotal example, 9–10
    closed loop supply chain management,
        65–106
        advanced forecasting mechanisms,
            74, 77–82, 84
        alternative business model, 13–15, 17
        computerized systems for, 86–87
        control mechanisms within logistics
            pipeline, 83–86
        efficiency and productivity
            influences, 74–77, 105–106
        integrated business model, 13–14,
            72–73, 85, 174, 176
        introduction, 65–71
        metrics and parameters, 87–102
        process, 8, 11, 195
        recommendations, 5, 207–210
        returned products impact, 98,
            101–104
        strategy, 71–74
    field service benchmarking, 87–102
        CLSC vs. simple RL process impact,
            92–93, 95–96
        data sources, 88–89
        forecasting impact, 92, 97–98, 100
        objectives, 87–88
        product and technology impact,
            92–94
        return velocity rates impact, 98,
            101–102
        support organizations researched,
            88–91
    field service for
        advanced management systems for,
            177, 179–180
        benchmarking, 87–102
        importance, 5, 7
        modular repair of units, 2, 5, 7, 23,
            70–73, 118, 120
    life cycle costs, 3–4
    as market segment, 37–38, 50
        competitive evaluation, 62–63
        subsegments, 31, 46–47
Holt's method, for high tech demand
        forecasting, 81–82

I

Impulsive buying, 8, 205
Independent logistics support providers,
    199
Independent reverse logistics process,
    12–13, 15
Independent service organizations (ISO), 9,
    15, 35, 118
    benchmarking high tech products,
        88–91, 95–96
    for warranty processing, 165–166
Industrial product management, 4
    brown and white goods vs., 204–205
    life cycle support, 24, 27–29
    offshore secondary markets, 169–171
    returned products and, 8–9
    reverse logistics
        key components, 34–35
        market, 46
        outsourcing potential, 31
Industrial waste, 7
    reverse logistics
        key components, 34–35
        outsourcing potential, 33
Information systems, integrated for e-
        commerce, 172, 174
Information technology (IT), benchmarking
        logistics support, 88–90, 93–94,
        118
Innovative thinking, for e-markets, 173–174
Installation, service designs for, 65–66, 71
Installed base, value relationship
    to density, 71, 74–75
    to returned high tech products, 98, 104
    to service costs, 25–27, 77, 180
Instruments
    depot repair market, 144
    reverse logistics
        market, 46, 49
        outsourcing potential, 31
Integrated model
    depot repair market, 141–144
    e-commerce, 172, 174
    field service management, 27, 72–73, 85,
        176, 186–187
    high tech products/services recycling,
        13–14, 72–73, 85, 174
    waste management, 33
Internal depot repair operations, 144–148
Internet
    delivery control resources, 199
    returned product resources, 136–137
    as service logistics resource
        advanced systems and technology,
            176–178, 187
        for customer, 56, 200

trading hubs, 168–170, 172–173, 176, 200–201
Inventory(ies)
cost of, 8, 17–18
Internet trading hubs, 200
liquidation of liability, 136–137
Inventory forecasting and planning (IFP)
advanced systems for
closed loop supply chain management, 77–82, 84
computerized, 175, 179, 181
in manufacturing process, 74
benchmarking high tech products, 92, 97–100
key operating parameters, 98, 100
Inventory replenishment (IR), 56, 59
computerized systems for, 175, 179, 182
Inventory tracking and control (ITC)
for consumer goods, 134–137
market dynamics, 42, 54, 58
strategies maximizing, 20
systems and technology for, 176–177
closed loop, 71–74, 83–84
computerized, 175, 179–181
for high tech logistics, 71, 75, 177, 179–180
impact on profitability, 71, 75–76, 87
total support components, 181–182
Invoicing, computerized systems for, 175, 179, 182
ISO 900x process, for quality control, 87

J

Jobbers, 115, 176
Job shop approach, to depot repair operations, 144–145
Junk, management costs of, 3, 8, 11
Just in time approach, to depot repair operations, 74, 84, 144–145

K

Kits, parts vs., for service delivery, 75–76

L

Labels, embedded, 184
Laboratory equipment
depot repair market, 52–53
reverse logistics

key components, 34–35
outsourcing potential, 31
Leased products, 1, 8, 205
market dynamics, 54, 58
Legislation, environmental, 2–3
Liability inventory, liquidation of, 136–137
Life cycle management
consumer goods, 115–117, 120–122, 125
costs for products, 3–4, 15
installed base unit value vs., 25–27
defined service categories, 24–25
demand forecast for high tech products, 77–82, 84
end user responsibility, 24–25
field service importance, 5, 7
introduction, 24–28
market comparisons, 28–29
trends and opportunities, 28, 30–35, 74
Liquidation, of liability inventory, 136–137
Local retailers, of consumer goods, 111–112
return rate impact, 118–119, 124–125
Logistics database management and reporting (DBMR),
computerized systems for, 175, 179–180, 182
Logistics management and control (LMC),
computerized systems for, 175, 179–180
total inventory support, 181–182
Logistics planning and forecasting,
computerized systems for, 175, 179, 183
Logistics support; see also Service management
advanced systems and technology for, 175–192
bar coding, 183–184
configuration control applications, 185–186
for consumer goods, 176–178
examples, 28, 54, 58, 176–178, 198–199
functional specifications, 180–183
for high tech products, 177, 179–180
impact and value, 176, 180, 187, 192
key functions, 175–177, 179–180
radio frequency identification system, 184–185
selected vendor list, 187–191
state-of-the-art, 186–187
warranty claim processing, 164–166

benchmarking high tech products,
        88–91, 95–100
economic value, 25–26
increased interest in, 3, 11, 40
key operating parameters, 98, 100
markets
        captive vs. outsourced, 43, 55–56,
                59–60
        comparisons, 28–29
        competitive evaluation, 57, 61–63
        partnering with suppliers, 201–202,
                208–210
product design for reduced, 28
responsibility for, 24–25
reverse, see Reverse logistics (RL)
Low-tech products/services, closed loop
        supply chain business model,
        13–14, 17

M

Maintenance
        preventative, warranties and, 156–157,
                159
        service designs for, 65–66, 71
Management model, 193–202
        advanced systems, 175–192, 198–199
        application service providers, 200–201
        development stages, 194–197
        directions and trends, 2–4, 203–210
        economic vs. environmental issues,
                203–205
        for high tech products/services, 65–106
                advanced forecasting mechanisms,
                        74, 77–82, 84
                alternative business model, 13–15, 17
                computerized systems for, 86–87
                control mechanisms within logistics
                        pipeline, 83–86
                efficiency and productivity
                        influences, 74–77, 105–106
                integrated business model, 13–14,
                        72–73, 85, 174, 176
                introduction, 65–71
                metrics and parameters, 87–102
                process, 8, 11, 195
                recommendations, 5, 207–210
                returned products impact, 98,
                        101–104
                strategy, 71–74
        Internet and e-commerce, 176–178, 200

introduction, 193–194
outsourcing
        debate, 199, 201–202
        market segment potential, 30–33
        partnering with suppliers, 46–47,
                201–202, 208–210
        real-time control, 59, 81, 176, 199, 201
                communication devices for, 98–99
        recommendations, 5, 207–210
        software technology, 175–192, 198–199
        third party service providers, 198–202,
                208
Management organization, stages for
        developing, 194–197
Managers, increased interest of, 2, 4
Manufacturers
        of consumer goods
                reduction of returns, 132–137
                reverse logistics for, 107–110
        of equipment, see Original equipment
                manufacturers (OEM)
Market design, for consumer goods reverse
        logistics, 107–109, 113
Market segments and segmentation
        benchmarking analysis, 88–91
        as business strategy, 208–209
        competitive evaluation, 57–63
        depot repair and
                growth phases, 139–141
                as multidimensional, 141–144
        forecasts
                competition data, 57–63
                quantitative models, 2–4, 199
                research results, 42–55
                surveys, 41–43
        framework for focus, 9–11, 39–40,
                193–194
        introduction, 37–39
        key factors, 39–41
        North America, 43–44
        operating dynamics, 55–56, 58–60
        outsourcing potential, 30–33, 46–49, 51
        similarities and differences, 204–205
        structure, size, and dimensions, 41–43
        value-added services, 43, 55–57
Mass merchandisers, of consumer goods,
        111–112
        return rate impact, 118–119, 124–125
Material resource planning (MRP), 74
Materials
        anecdotal examples, 10

manufacturing demand patterns, 74
new array of, 1–2
recovery from end users, 7–8, 13, 40,
    145, 149–151
returns of vs. of products, 18–19
reverse logistics
    key components, 34–35, 40–41
    outsourcing potential, 31
    process, 14–18
Mean time between failures (MTBF), 157,
    159, 161, 180
demand forecasts based on, 80
Mean time to repair (MTTR), 161, 180
Measurement equipment, depot repair
    market, 52–53, 144
Medical equipment/supplies
    depot repair market, 51, 53, 144
    reverse logistics
        benchmarking, 88–89, 91,
            93–94
        key components, 34–35
        market, 46
        outsourcing potential, 31
Military systems support
    depot repair market, 51, 53, 143
    field service importance, 5
    life cycle
        costs, 3–4
        management, 24, 27, 29
    real-time control, 199
    secondary markets, 169
Milspec, life cycle support, 28–29
Modular repair of units, see Pull-and-
    replace products
"Mom and pop" retailers, of consumer
    goods, 111–112
Moving average, in high tech demand
    forecasting, 80, 82
Multiparty coordination, in reverse logistics
    process, 41
Multivendor equipment service
    organizations (MVEs)
    depot repair market, 141–143
    for high tech products, 87–89

N

Next flight out (NFO), in delivery control,
    199
North America market
    for closed loop supply chain, 43–44
    for reverse logistics and repair services,
        42–43
No trouble found (NTF) inventory, 144

O

Obsolete products, 8, 18, 28
    anecdotal example, 10–11
    return dynamics, 40, 120, 169
Office automation
    benchmarking logistics support, 88–90,
        93–94
    depot repair market, 51, 53, 143
Office equipment/products
    benchmarking logistics support, 88–90,
        93–94
    depot repair market, 51, 53, 143
    secondary markets, 169–170
Offshore secondary markets, 168, 171
On-site service calls, 67–70
Operating structure
    for consumer goods manufacturers,
        107–110
    for depot repair systems, 144–145
    stages for developing, 194–197
Order entry and processing (OEP),
        computerized systems for, 175,
        179, 181
Organizations
    closed loop supply chain process, 8
    increased interest of, 3–4
Orientation to product, included in sale, 66
Original equipment manufacturers (OEM)
    benchmarking high tech products,
        88–91, 95–96
    business model, 13–14, 16–17
    green laws affecting, 206
    life cycle support, 29, 35, 74, 118
    partnering with suppliers, 46–47, 201
    reverse logistics
        depot repair association, 141–143
        key components, 34–35, 118
        outsourcing potential, 32
    service arms as competitors, 57, 61–62
    warranty management and, 160–161
Outsourcing
    advantages, 30, 174
    competitive options, 34–35, 55
    debate, 199, 201–202
    market segment potential, 30–33
    service organizations, 67

value-added services in-house vs., 43,
55–60
depot repair, 55–58
logistics support, 55–56, 59–60
Overstock, see Surplus goods

P

Packing, pallets, and containers
as market segment, 37–38, 50
reuseable, 28, 31–32, 40
reverse logistics
hazardous waste, 33
key components, 34–35
outsourcing potential, 31–32
Partnering, with suppliers, 46–47, 201–202,
208–210
Parts
anecdotal examples, 9–10, 17
closed loop supply chain management,
65–106
advanced forecasting mechanisms,
77–82, 84
alternative business model, 13–15, 17
computerized systems for, 86–87
control mechanisms within logistics
pipeline, 83–86
efficiency and productivity
influences, 74–77, 105–106
integrated business model, 13–14,
72–73, 85, 174, 176
introduction, 65–71
metrics and parameters, 87–102
process, 8, 11, 195
product return experience, 98,
103–104, 117
recommendations, 5, 207–210
strategy, 71–74
demand forecast for high tech, 74,
77–82, 84
failure rate
life cycle and, 26–27, 118
tracking through warranties, 156–158
as free, 66
life cycle, 115–116
returns and, 26, 118, 120–122
recovery from end users, 7–8, 13, 40,
145, 149–151
returns of vs. of products, 18–19
reverse logistics
captive vs. outsourced, 58–60

value-added services, 42, 54
secondary markets, 168–169, 171
e-commerce as, 172–173
service management
call processing, 67–70
typical historical, 65–66
Parts management agreements (PMA),
computerized systems for, 175,
179, 181
Payment of compensation, as warranty
mechanism, 153–155
Personal computers, life cycle, 115–116
returns and, 118, 121
Pharmaceuticals
life cycle, 115–116
reverse logistics market, 49, 115
Photographic equipment/supplies, reverse
logistics, 31, 47
Physical distribution (PD), computerized
systems for, 175, 179, 182
Physical factors, of consumables return,
125–126
Planning technology, see Value-added
services; specific product or
service
Plant automation
benchmarking logistics support, 88–90,
93–94
depot repair market, 51, 53, 143
Plant building, depot repair market, 51, 53
Plug and play technology, 25–26
Point-of-sale (POS) automation, 177
consumer goods returns, 113–115, 135
logistics support, benchmarking, 88–90,
93–94
Postwarranty support, 158
in dealer environment, 159–162
Power generating systems, secondary
markets, 169
Preventative maintenance, warranties and,
156–157, 159
Pricing
as consumables return factor, 125–127
of warranties, 157–158, 160
Printing equipment/supplies, reverse
logistics, 31, 47
Processing services
in closed loop supply chain, 12
business models, 12–18
depot repair market, 51, 53, 143
Procurement source management

computerized, 86–87
e-commerce for, 172–173
Product design
    for consumer goods reverse logistics,
        107–109, 113
    for reduced support costs, 28
Productivity impact
    of advanced systems and technology,
        176, 180, 187, 192
    of closed loop supply chain, for high
        tech products, 74–77, 87–88,
        105–106
Product life cycle
    failure rate of product vs., 26–27, 118
    management strategies, see Life cycle
        management
    returns related to, 118, 120–122
Product management
    growing complexity of, 6–7, 74
    life cycle support costs, 3–4
    recycling focus, 7–8
Product quality
    advance monitoring systems, 180
    in warranty management, 157, 159
Product reliability, as consumables return
    factor, 125–126
Product reputation, brand loyalty and,
    123–124
Product research, for consumer goods
    reverse logistics, 107–109, 113
Product returns, see Returned products
Product roll-in, demand forecasting for,
    77–78
Product roll-out
    for consumer goods reverse logistics,
        108–109
    demand forecasting for, 77–78, 84
Products
    new array of, 1–2
    recovery from end users, 7–8, 13, 40,
        145, 149–151
Profitability
    field service strategies, 71, 74–75, 87
    of returned consumer goods, 114, 133,
        135–137
    strategy to increase, 19
    of warranty offers, 156–157, 161
        in dealer environment, 159–162
Pull-and-replace products, 2, 5, 7, 23
    high tech, 70–73, 118, 120
Purchasers, see Buyer behavior

Q

Quality control, 87; see also Benchmarking
    brand loyalty and, 123–124

R

Radio frequency identification system
    (RFID), 184–185
    for closed loop supply chain, 83–84
    for repair depot systems, 185
Real-time control, 59, 81, 176, 199
    communication devices for, 98–99
Recalled products, 8, 15
    anecdotal example, 10–11
Recommendations
    for consumer goods reverse logistics,
        207–210
    proprietary vs. nonproprietary, 5
Recovery centers
    depot repair providers as, 7–8, 13, 40,
        145, 149–151
    for returned goods, 134, 136–137
Recycling
    business models, 12–18
    field value of, 7–8
    increased interest in, 1–2
Refurbishment; see also Depot repair
        providers/systems
    of high tech products, 71–74, 76
Rehabilitation; see also Depot repair
        providers/systems
    of high tech products, 71–74, 76
Relevant performance metrics, for warranty
    claim analysis, 162–163
Remedial service, as warranty mechanism,
    154–155
Remote diagnostics, 27, 67–70, 85
Rental products, see Leased products
Repair processing
    call management vs. on-site requests,
        67–77
    fourth party providers, see Depot repair
        providers/systems
    full, and return logistics as competitors,
        57, 61–62
    market segments similarities and
        differences, 204–205
    North America market, 44
    recovery of goods through, 7–8, 13, 40,
        145, 149–151

software for managing, 198
as warranty mechanism, 154–155
Research and development
for consumer goods reverse logistics,
107–109, 113
proprietary vs. nonproprietary, 3, 5
for quantifying impacts, 4–5
Reselling; see also Secondary markets
recovered parts and materials, 8, 141,
149, 151
whole unit equipment, 19, 145, 168
Restocking fee, 118
Retail chains, of consumer goods
reduction of returns, 132–137
return rate impact, 118–119, 124–125
reverse logistics relationships, 112–113
with service capabilities, 111
Retail distribution
major types, 111–112
impact on returns, 118–119, 124–125
reverse logistics
consumer goods management, 108,
110–115, 132–137
outsourcing potential, 32
value complexity driven by, 4, 28
Retail financial automation, benchmarking
logistics support, 88–90, 93–94
Returned products
in consumer goods management
averages and metrics, 124–131
branding impact, 122–124
centralization, 133
issues, 127, 132
life cycle impact, 115–117, 120–122,
125
retail distribution factor, 118–119
retail policies and processes,
112–115, 118
seasonal, 114
warranty impact, 117
context importance, 9, 14, 204–205
costs of, 19, 133, 205
dynamics of, 7–8, 17–18, 59
economic value, 23–24
in high tech product management
experience estimates, 98, 103
impact on benchmarking, 98,
101–102
value estimates, 98, 104
managing systems and technology for,
177–178

processing options, 167–168
competitor evaluation, 57, 61–62
new, 28, 39
old, 65–66
reasons for, 8–9, 16–17, 127, 167, 205
secondary markets for, 168–174
warranty management with, 153–166
whole unit vs. parts, 18–19
Reuseable containers, 28, 40
outsourcing reverse logistics, 31–32
Revenue, see Profitability
Reverse logistics (RL)
broad application of, 4–5
business models, 12–18, 20, 37, 39,
194–195
business strategies, 19–20, 24, 40–41,
194–195, 209
in closed loop supply chain, 12
consumer goods management, 107–137
data collection for, 194, 196–197
cost competitiveness, 62, 171–172
depot repair and, 139–151
direct supply chain vs., 28–29, 208
framework for analysis, 5–6, 9–11,
21–22, 193
green laws impact, 28, 205–207
high tech product management, 65–106
increased interest in, 1–3, 7, 23–24, 28
management model, 193–210
markets, 37–63
captive vs. outsourcing, 43, 45,
55–56, 59–60
quantitative forecast models, 2, 4–5, 199
reasons for using, 40
software for, 198–199
Revlog, 206
RMA coordination, 59
Roving van, for field service, 85–86

S

Sales logistics, for consumer goods
retail/distributor management structure,
108, 111–115
reverse logistics for, 107–109, 113
Sales receipts, technological advances, 177
Scanning technology
bar coding, 183–185
radio frequency identification system,
184–185
repair depot applications, 185

Scheduling technology, see Value-added
    services
Seasonal returns, of consumer goods, 114
Secondary markets
    demand forecasting for high tech
        products, 77, 79
    economic value, 168, 171
    increasing for returned products, 118,
        167–168
    offshore, 168, 171
    third party service providers, 171–174
        e-commerce, 172–174
        established organizations, 168–170
Sellers, see Suppliers
Service commitment, as consumables return
        factor, 125–126
Service engineers, field
    alternative travel options, 85–86
    communication devices for, 98–99
    on-site calls, 67–70
    trunk stock of, 70–71, 73, 85
Service management; see also Logistics
        support
    call management process, 67–70
    for consumer goods, 108, 110, 113
    cost relationship to installed base value,
        25–27
    defined categories, 24–25
    fourth party providers, 2, 11–17
    market comparisons, 28–29
    North America market, 42–44
    third party providers, 198–202, 208
    typical historical, 65–66
    for warranties, see Warranty
        management
Service market, 28–29
    business strategies for, 19–20
    growing complexity of, 6–7, 40, 74
    life cycle support costs, 3–4
Shipping
    outside providers, 56, 59–60
    reverse logistics, 41, 44
Shipping errors, as consumables return
        factor, 128, 131–132
Simple average, in high tech demand
        forecasting, 80, 82
Small retailers, see Local retailers
Software; see also Advanced systems and
        technology
    depot repair market, 52–53, 144,
        198–199

for logistics support, 175–192, 198–199
    state-of-the-art, 180, 186–187
Software vendors
    partnering with, 187, 201–202, 209
    selected list of, 187–191
Spare parts procurement, e-commerce as
        secondary market, 172–173
Stickers, embedded, 184
Stock fill rate
    equation for, 73
    field engineers influence, 70–71, 73, 85
        methods for determining, 92, 97–99
    high tech product demand and, 74,
        77–82
Stocking companies, 115
Stocking locations, strategic, 59
Stock inventory, see Inventory(ies)
Stock-keeping unit (SKU)
    failure rate tracking through warranties,
        156–157
    management strategy, 71–73
        demand forecasting mechanisms,
            77–82, 84
        impact on profitability, 71, 75–76, 87
        stock control of key, 83–84
        systems and technology for, 176–177
Stockpiling, 85
Strategy, see Business strategy(ies)
Study(ies), see Research and development
Subassemblies
    anecdotal examples, 9–10
    failure rate tracking through warranties,
        156–158
    life cycle, 115–116
        returns and, 118, 120
    recovery from end users, 7–8, 13, 145,
        149–151
    returns of vs. of products, 18, 117
    secondary markets, 168–169
    service management
        call processing, 67–70
        typical historical, 65–66
Subcontractors, life cycle support, 29
Suppliers
    cost competition, 28, 39, 160
    partnering with, 46–47, 62, 201–202,
        208–210
    warranty perceptions, 153, 158–162
Supply chain management, see Closed loop
        supply chain (CLSC); Direct
        supply chain management

Surplus goods, secondary markets, 169–170
Survey(s), market forecasting, 41–43
  for quantifying impacts, 4–5
  results, 42–55
  segment competition, 57–63
Systems technology, see Advanced systems and technology

T

Technical assistance, 29, 54, 58–59
Technology innovations
  branding impact, 122
  in consumer goods, see Brown goods; Computer technology
  depot repair associaton, 143–144
  impact on benchmarking, 88–89, 91–94
  in managment systems, see Advanced systems and technology
Telecommunications
  depot repair market, 51, 53, 143
  reverse logistics
    benchmarking, 88–89, 91, 93–94
    market, 41
  secondary markets, 170
Terminal automation, see Point-of-sale (POS) automation
Testing and test equipment
  depot repair market, 52–53, 144
  outside providers, 60
Textiles, reverse logistics market, 48
Third party service providers, 198–202; see also Outsourcing
  application service providers, 200–201
  benchmarking high tech products, 88–91, 95–96
  consumer goods distribution, 115, 127, 136
  fourth party vs., see Depot repair providers/systems
  Internet and e-commerce, 136, 200
  partnering with suppliers, 46–47, 201–202
  real-time control, 199
  in secondary markets, 171–174
    e-commerce, 172–174
    established organizations, 168–170
  software vendors
    advanced tools, 199
    improved service logistics, 198
  use of, 40, 136, 142, 198, 208, 210

Time and timing focus, of business strategy, 40, 62, 209
Toxic products, see Hazardous waste
Tracking
  challenges with, 12, 17
  inventory, see Inventory tracking and control (ITC)
Trade-ins, 66
Trading hubs
  Internet, 168–170, 172–173, 200–201
  value-added differentiation, 173, 176
Transportation products, reverse logistics market, 49
Transportation services
  logistics service outside providers, 59, 62
  reverse logistics, 41, 44
Trash disposal, see Waste management
Truck/trunk stock
  of field engineers, 70–71, 73, 85
  methods for determining, 92, 97–99

U

Unsold, unused, unwanted goods, value in returning, 1, 9–11

V

Value(s)
  quantification of, 4–5
  of reselling, 8, 19, 141, 145, 149–151, 168
  resulting increase in, 4, 41, 171
  of returned products
    consumer goods, 132–137
    high tech, 98, 104
  in warranty management, 154, 156–159, 161
Value-added services
  with closed loop supply chain, 4
  depot repair association, 43, 54–55, 141, 150
  market
    allocation including expenditure, 55
    captive vs. outsourced, 55–60
    North America, 44
    projections, 43, 55
  resellers, 141
  with reverse logistics, 7–8
  trading hubs, 172–173, 176
Van stock
  of field engineers, 70–71, 73, 85

methods for determining, 92, 97–99
Vendors
  in e-commerce, 171–174
  increased interest of, 3, 11
  management recommendations, 5,
    208–209
  partnering with, 62, 201–202, 208–209
  reverse logistics
    consumer goods, 135–137
    depot repair association, 141–144
    key components, 34–35
    outsourcing potential, 32–33
Vertical integration, see Integrated model

W

Warehouse(s)
  in closed loop supply chain strategy,
    71–72
  in-house reverse logistics preference,
    28, 30
  markets
    competitive evaluaton, 57, 61–62
    North America, 44
Warranty claims processing
  benchmark anaylsis, 162–164
    of independent firms, 165–166
  e-commerce as secondary market,
    172–173
  management systems for, 164–165
    improved performance from, 165
  methods for routing, 162–164
  time and costs, 163, 165
Warranty exchanges, 173
Warranty management
  advanced systems for, 164–165
  benchmark analysis, 162–165
  cost competitiveness, 157–158, 160, 163,
    165
  in dealer environment, 141, 159–162
  depot repair market, 141–142
  failure rate component, 156–157, 159,
    161
  by independent firms, 141, 165–166
  market dynamics, 54, 59, 117
  perceptions importance, 153, 158–159
  price and design guidelines, 157–158
  requirements, 161–162

reverse logistics, 17, 117, 153–154
stategic types, 16–17, 153–155
stategic value, 154, 156–159, 161
underutilization by customers, 154, 156
Waste Electrical and Electronic Equipment
    (WEEE) directive, 2, 204, 206
Waste management; see also Hazardous
    waste; Industrial waste
  increased interest in, 1–2, 6–7
  as market segment, 37, 49–50
    competitive evaluation, 57, 61–62
  reverse logistics
    key components, 34–35
    outsourcing potential, 32–33
  secondary markets, 170
Weapon systems support, see Military
    systems support
Weighted moving average, in high tech
    demand forecasting, 80, 82
White goods (appliances)
  branding impact, 123
  commerical and industrial products vs.,
    204–205
  life cycle, 115–116
    returns and, 117, 120–122, 125, 205
    support responsibility, 25
  managing systems and technology for,
    118, 177
  product returns
    actual rates, 127, 129, 132
    defective, 125, 127–129
  reverse logistics
    benchmarking, 88–89, 91, 93–94
    market, 48, 118
    organization and structure,
      117–120
Wholesale distribution
  reverse logistics
    market, 47, 118
    outsourcing, 32
  value complexity driven by, 4
Whole unit equipment
  failure rate tracking through warranties,
    156–157
  life cycle, 115–116
    returns and, 120–122
  return and resale of, 19, 145, 168
  typical service processes, 19, 65–66, 168

Word of mouth reputation, brand loyalty
    and, 123–124
Working capital, requirement reduction, 28,
    39
Work in process (WIP) inventory, 76, 144
World wide web resources, see Internet

Z

Zero sum game
    in consumer goods returns,
       114–115
    in warranty process, 160–161